Basics of Music

Basics of Music

Opus 1

SECOND EDITION

MICHAEL ZINN

ROBERT HOGENSON

SCHIRMER BOOKS
An Imprint of Macmillan Publishing Company
New York

Maxwell Macmillan Canada
Toronto

Maxwell Macmillan International
New York Oxford Singapore Sydney

Schirmer Books
An Imprint of Macmillan Publishing Company
866 Third Avenue
New York, NY 10022

Maxwell Macmillan Canada, Inc.
1200 Eglinton Avenue East, Suite 200
Don Mills, Ontario M3C 3N1

Macmillan Publishing Company is part of the Maxwell Communication Group of Companies.

Library of Congress Catalog Card Number: 93–3591

Printed in the United States of America

printing number
2   3   4   5   6   7   8   9   10

Library of Congress Cataloging-in-Publication Data
Zinn, Michael.
    Basics of music : opus 1 / Michael Zinn, Robert Hogenson.—2nd
ed.
        p.   cm.
    Includes index.
    ISBN 0–02–873012–7 (alk. paper)
    1. Music—Theory, Elementary.   I. Hogenson, Robert.   II. Title.
MT7.Z75   1994
781—dc20   93–3591
                                                                   CIP
                                                                   MN

The paper used in this publication meets the minimum requirements of American National Standard for Information Sciences—Permanence of Paper for Printed Library Materials. ANSI Z39.48-1984. ∞ ™

Contents

Preface

DESIGN AND STRUCTURE

Basics of Music: Opus 1, second edition, is a textbook designed and structured for the beginning student with little or no background in music. This concise, self-contained text presents all the concepts necessary for a solid understanding of the basic fundamentals of music theory. It represents the authors' combined experience of over fifty years of teaching, composing, and presenting concepts to students of all ages. Written in a succinct, direct style, and richly illustrated with musical examples, many from the literature, this text systematically teaches the essential concepts of music theory, from basic notation to harmonization, cadence structures, motivic development, and simple phrase structure and part forms. Taking a conceptual approach representative of the most current theoretical ideas, the authors emphasize the broad concepts of music theory, minimizing memorization while facilitating conceptual understanding and abstraction. Numerous exercises and drills at the end of each chapter—plus six appendices, including three covering ear training, keyboard exercises and drills, and harmonic overtone series, and three more containing reference charts for scales, key signatures, triads, and guitar fingerings, a complete unit on modes and modal scale structures, and a collection of melodies—apply the concepts presented in the text and provide for ample practice opportunities.

ORGANIZATION AND APPROACH

This text provides a complete teaching package—one that requires no further handouts, manuscript paper, ear training, or keyboard supplements. Each chapter includes educational goals and objectives, which state the concepts to be covered in the chapter; concise, to-the-point explanations supported by clear musical examples, charts, and diagrams; numerous practice exercises and drill materials; and blank staff paper—perforated for easy removal—for in-class exercises and notes. The authors have presented the material in the order they have found produces optimal results. Since each chapter is self-contained, the instructor will be free to vary that order in accord with personal teaching preferences. Topics covered, in order, include:

- properties of sound
- basic notation
- rhythm duration
- pitch notation
- basic meters

- basic scale concepts: diatonic, major, minor, whole-tone, and chromatic scales
- parallel and relative scale structures

- intervals
- transposition: major and minor scales
- key signatures
- triads (basic and diatonic)
- cadence structures

- basic harmonization
- melodic motivic structures, phrase structures, and part form
- harmonic overtone series
- modal scales and transpositions

Concepts such as pitch notation, scales, and triads are covered at both the elementary and, in later chapters, the advanced levels, allowing a period of incubation (with regard to student comprehension) to take place. Finally, the text includes four chapters that discuss the function and use of triads, without dealing with the more technical concepts of part writing or voice leading.

Since music fundamentals is often the only formal music course a student may take, the broad coverage of this text is designed to provide the nonmajor with the necessary background to continue lifelong musical skills as well as independent music study. Among the features of this second edition are:

a complete, self-contained teaching package, including examples, exercises, drills, optional ear-training and keyboard applications, and blank staff paper; no additional materials are needed;

economical presentation; a terse, no-nonsense style featuring clear, concise definitions supported by numerous diagrams, charts, and musical examples;

broad scope, streamlined and concise for quick comprehension, including four chapters on the use and application of triads. This approach emphasizes application of theoretical concepts, thereby providing a solid foundation for the future study and enjoyment of music;

chapter goals, to highlight key concepts presented in each chapter and to facilitate review;

numerous exercises and drills, direct and to the point, many from the literature, and perforated for easy removal—to provide ample practice of text concepts;

ear-training and keyboard appendices, to provide the link between theoretical concepts and actual sound application and expression;

reference charts, providing quick access to all major and minor scales, key signatures, all triads, and guitar chord fingerings;

cross-cultural collection of well-known melodies, providing extensive drill opportunities in harmonization and analysis.

The authors are grateful to the many students who have used this book and for their comments and suggestions. The authors wish to express their appreciation to Dr. David Herman, Chairperson, Department of Music, University of Delaware, for his support and encouragement. Also the theory faculty, including Dr. Michael Arenson and Dr. Peter McCarthy, whose suggestions were invaluable. The authors also wish to express their gratitude to Maribeth Anderson Payne, Editor-in-Chief, Schirmer Books, for her interest in and dedication to this project and her unending patience; to theorists and colleagues, nationwide, who have contributed their comments and criticisms in order to help make this a better edition; and to the many theory and composition majors who have made valuable observations and comments with regard to pedagogical approaches and techniques.

To the Student

Basics of Music: Opus 1 is carefully structured to maximize comprehension and to minimize the time you must spend reading and memorizing. Designed to teach concepts and skills to beginners or persons with little or no background in music, each chapter presents a carefully prescribed amount of information.

Read each chapter carefully and then complete the drills and exercises that follow. In order to encourage student–instructor interaction, answers are not given. All pages are perforated so that exercises and drills can be removed and collected by your instructor for evaluation. Self-tests are presented at the conclusion of the drills and exercises in each chapter. These should provide you with instant feedback with regard to your understanding of the material contained in each chapter. In addition, a fold-out keyboard diagram is included in an envelope attached to the inside front cover.

Appendix A deals with ear-training exercises, which are optional to many courses in rudiments of music theory. Appendix B contains keyboard exercises that will enhance your comprehension of the material and form a vital link between the written word and the sound experience. Keyboard assignments provide an excellent opportunity for nonverbal responses and allow you to express your understanding of concepts through simple motor skills. These keyboard assignments require a minimal amount of technical proficiency, and all can be performed by the beginner with little or no previous keyboard experience.

Appendix C presents optional coverage of the harmonic overtone series. Appendix D contains reference charts for scales, key signatures, triad qualities, and guitar chord fingerings; you might find these charts especially useful. Appendix E presents optional coverage of modes and modal scale structures. Appendix F is a collection of melodies that can be used for additional practice in harmonization and motivic analysis (chapters 12 and 13). At the conclusion of each chapter you will find blank sheets of staff paper, also perforated for easy removal and provided so that you may take notes or practice specific examples without having to purchase blank staff paper.

To the Instructor

There are many theory fundamentals texts in the field today. *Basics of Music: Opus 1* was inspired by the shortcomings of most of these texts. The authors were dissatisfied not only with the content, scope, and depth of coverage of most texts but also with their presentation and format.

Texts written in a programmed instruction format can be useful to the student with regard to self-pacing and immediate feedback; however, they provide little reference material and almost no continuity with classroom instruction. The authors feel that nonprogrammed texts dealing with technical information should be succinct, straight to the point, and direct—encouraging student–teacher interaction and promoting classroom discussion.

Educational goals are clearly displayed at the beginning of each chapter, thereby affording easy access to the material in review. The book is intended to minimize the amount of material that other texts expect students to memorize. In place of blind memorization, a broader conceptualization is encouraged, an approach that not only provides for student comprehension but also allows for the abstraction of material essential to the understanding of music theory.

Each chapter is succinct in its text and richly illustrated with examples. Exercises and drills follow each chapter and may be used for in-class drill and discussion as well as for handed-in assignments; pages are perforated for easy removal. A wide variety of material has been provided in the appendices. By selecting from those drills, charts, and examples, you may shape the course material to the requirements of your particular class. Appendices A and B are optional, although many classes make use of ear-training skills (Appendix A) and keyboard applications (Appendix B). Keyboard drills enhance the musical experience for the student by providing the link between verbal abstraction and actual sounds. The keyboard assignments require a nonverbal, musical expression from the student and do not require any previous keyboard proficiency. Appendix C presents a full coverage of the harmonic overtone series, which you may find to be a useful enhancement to student comprehension of tonal materials. It can serve also as additional reinforcement of interval skills. Appendix C is treated as a full, isolated chapter, having its own written drills and exercises. Appendix D contains reference charts for all major and minor scales, key signatures, and all qualities of triads. In addition, a guitar chord fingering chart is included. Appendix E also presents a full coverage of modes, modal scales, and transpositions. Many instructors include this information along with the three chapters covering scale structures; many do not want this information to "cloud" the scale presentation and may cover modes separately or even omit this unit altogether. Appendix E is also treated as a full, isolated chapter, having its own written drills and exercises. Appendix F contains a collection of melodies that may be used for written, keyboard, and ear-training drills as well as for harmonization, motivic and phrase analysis, as well as exercises in cadence structures.

Answer sheets for exercises and drills have not been provided in order to stimulate class discussion and to avoid providing answers, which the authors feel would inhibit the conceptualization of the material. Answers are provided in the accompanying Instructors' Manual.

You may choose to present chapters out of their original order; feel free to do so, since each chapter is a complete unit. The authors have presented the material in its current order for the following reasons:

1. The presentation of pitch notation, followed by rhythm and duration, followed by a return to pitch notation, allows a period of incubation for student comprehension.

2. The concepts of intervals and of scale structures are best presented in the order prescribed here. The idea of presenting scales first, followed by intervals and related material, followed by a "scales revisited" chapter attempts to interrelate scale structures with intervallic relationships—a beneficial abstraction and conceptualization of the material.

3. Most theory texts deal with triads, and rightfully they should. This text contains four chapters beyond triads that demonstrate the use of triads without delving into technical aspects of part writing and voice leading. These aspects fall outside the scope of this book.

4. Since many students may never take advantage of further formal study in music theory, this text is structured to provide the necessary background for the layperson to continue studying music literature and history or a musical instrument.

Chapter 3 addresses the topic of meter. Many concepts with regard to meter have recently been developed and have gradually moved into the arena of common practice. The reason that the authors chose a more traditional route in this text should be obvious, as this text is intended for use in an introduction to music fundamentals. The spirit of contemporary thought, however, permeates its pages.

In summary, this book presents a complete package—one that requires no supplementary materials. It is intended as a rudiments edition, covering basic fundamentals of music theory. Some instructors may feel that the scope and content may be beyond that of their own individual courses. Such items as pentatonic scales, modal scales, the overtone series, and motivic melodic structures and phrases may be considered optional material and their inclusion left to the discretion of the instructor.

Properties of Sound–
Basic Notation

GOALS

Part A
• The understanding of the concepts of music and music theory

• The understanding of the basic properties of sound

• The ability to trace the development of music notation

Part B
• The ability to identify and define the basic elements of pitch notation

• The ability to identify and understand commonly used musical signs and symbols dealing with pitch

• The ability to write, in a clear and concise manner, basic musical signs and symbols

Part C
• The ability to identify and define the basic elements of duration notation

• The ability to identify and understand commonly used musical signs and symbols dealing with duration

• The understanding of note values and specific components of duration notation

PART A: MUSIC AND MUSIC THEORY

Music is one of the more abstract art forms because it is aural and therefore must exist within a specific time span. In this respect, it is similar to dance and dramatic arts (theater) because it requires what might be termed "durational memory." It is necessary to hold in your consciousness the events in the artform, the transition into and out of each of these events, and the interrelationships that exist between each of these events in order to fully appreciate the performance. The visual arts can be viewed and appreciated in their entirety, and at one time, and therefore do not require this unique element of time, although you can certainly isolate your attention and concentrate specifically on textures, brush strokes, blending of colors, composition, and so forth. As an artform, the live performance of music might also be analogous to sculpture: both arts are limited by the space in which they exist; and both are perceived by their respective audiences differently depending upon the physical location and position of those audiences. Music utilizes space by means of the actual, physical location of its sound source—that is, the location of the various instruments and groups of instruments within an ensemble.

Music theory is the study of the specific elements of music—melody, harmony, counterpoint, orchestration, form, and so on—which, when combined, can reflect performance practices according to historical periods and cultures. In this text, the fundamentals of music theory are presented in the form of rules of common practice pertaining to the functions of various musical components. A knowledge of theory will provide a solid background in the performance practice of your own instrument or voice. It also can provide some understanding with respect to why a melodic phrase or specific harmony is interesting or perhaps boring; what makes a musical phrase work or causes it to fall apart; what actually holds a piece of music together; or why a particular piece may sound disjointed or lacking in unity.

BASIC PROPERTIES OF SOUND

The four basic properties of sound are:
1. frequency   3. timbre
2. amplitude   4. duration

Frequency indicates how high or low the sound is perceived. The number of vibrations per second (**VPS**), hertz (**Hz**), or cycles per second (**CPS**) are additional terms used to define frequency. The actual frequency of a sound wave is referred to in musical terms as **pitch**.

Example 1.1a illustrates graphically a sound wave vibrating at one VPS; Example 1.1b represents a sound wave vibrating at two VPS.

Example 1.1

a.

One Cycle

point of rest | half cycle | half cycle

:1 second

b.

Two Cycles

point of rest

cycle 1   cycle 2

:1 second

Example 1.1b represents a 2:1 ratio when compared to Example 1.1a. This 2:1 frequency ratio results in Example 1.1b sounding one **octave** higher than Example 1.1a. The octave can be thought of acoustically as the most perfect interval (distance between two pitches) since the higher frequency gives the impression of merely duplicating the lower one. As a perfect consonant interval, it is common to all cultures; it is found in every scale and tuning system worldwide. The term **diapason** (from the Greek, meaning "all the tones") is also used to refer to the octave. Consonant and dissonant intervals are differentiated by the relative, subjective sense of either repose/relaxation (**consonance**) or stress/tension (**dissonance**).

Amplitude, or, in musical terminology, **intensity**, refers to how loud or soft a sound is perceived—that is, volume.

The amplitude of a pitch can be shown graphically as in Example 1.2.

Example 1.2

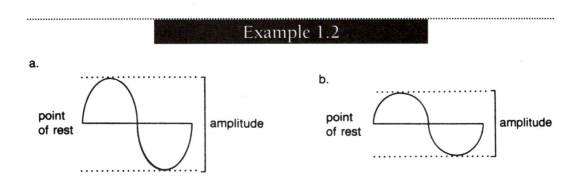

a.

point of rest   amplitude

b.

point of rest   amplitude

The amplitude in Example 1.2a would sound louder than that in Example 1.2b because of the greater distance the sound wave moves away from the point of rest.

MUSICAL DYNAMICS

Musical volume is expressed as sound intensity or amplitude. This sound energy is measured as **decibels** (**db**) levels. A decibel is a just-noticeable, or the smallest perceptible difference in volume or amplitude. We live our everyday lives working within a sound environment of various decibel levels. For example:

- the sound of a quiet room is ca. 24–28 db
- the sound of normal conversation is ca. 65 db
- the sound of an operating factory or an orchestra at full volume is ca. 100 db
- the sound of a jet plane taking off is ca. 140 db

Amplitude is expressed in musical terms as **dynamics**—a continuum of intensity values, from very soft to extremely loud and strong. The more commonly used terms are as follows:

Italian term	Definition	Symbol
Pianissimo	Very soft	*pp*
Piano	Soft	*p*
Mezzopiano	Medium soft	*mp*
Mezzoforte	Medium loud	*mf*
Forte	Loud	*f*
Fortissimo	Very loud	*ff*

Timbre refers to the tone quality of a sound and is the property enabling one to distinguish between different instruments or sound sources. The timbre or **tone color** is determined by several factors:

- the material of which the instrument creating the sound is constructed (wood, metal, string, vocal chords, etc.)
- the manner in which the sound is generated (plucked, bowed, struck, blown, etc.)
- the number and intensity of the overtones[1] present in the sound
- the acoustics of the environment in which the sound is produced

No acoustical musical instrument is capable of producing a pure sound or single solitary pitch. All produce a composite sound, which consists of a principal (fundamental) pitch along with a number of other pitches (overtones) of lesser intensity. For a complete discussion of this subject see Appendix C. Examples 1.3a and 1.3b compare graphically the same frequency or pitch as sounded by instruments with different timbres or tone qualities. Note that the wave lengths and intensities are the same. The contour differences illustrate different timbres caused by the presence of different overtones.

---

[1]See Appendix C, "Harmonic Overtone Series," for a complete discussion of overtones.

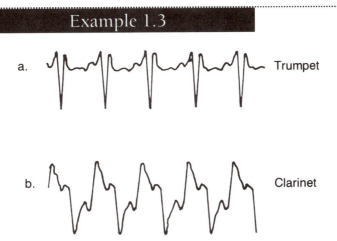

Example 1.3

a. Trumpet

b. Clarinet

Duration is the property of sound that deals with all of the temporal (mensural) aspects of music. The time element in music includes concepts such as how long a piece or musical phrase may last, the length of time a pitch may be sustained, or how much time elapses between sounds. It may also refer to rhythm or the patterns of sounds as they relate to a time frame. Durational aspects of music can also be used to measure the basic distance between pulses or beats within a musical phrase, thus determining the concept known as **tempo**, the rate of speed at which steady, recurring pulses of time may pass. Chapter 2 will examine the various aspects of duration in detail.

DEVELOPMENT OF MUSIC NOTATION

Musicians of other cultures have relied, and continue to rely, upon the oral (aural) transmission of their musical art. Western musicians, however, have constantly searched for notational techniques that would convey as precisely as possible the true pitch, duration, and intensity, along with other nuances, of their aural art forms. Inadequacies of earlier notational systems were and continue to be the prime motivation in the search for clearer graphic representation. Current standard **Western notation**—referring exclusively to musical cultures of Western Europe and their influence worldwide—is the cumulative result of our attempts to arrive at a more or less authentic score, one that is true to its actual sound.

Early attempts at musical notation witnessed the use of nonstaved scores, which used letters, dots and dashes, or other signs and configurations to express relative pitch. The durational aspect was excluded for the most part. The relative vertical position of the written symbols was meant to suggest the highness or lowness of the sounds. The durational aspects (mensuration) continued to be inadequately represented until measured (durational) notation came into use approximately 1250 A.D. This thirteenth-century durational notation remains subject to interpretation by music scholars. Prior to the eleventh century, a one-line (Ex. 1.4) or sometimes two-line staff appeared; a red line represented the note F, and a yellow (or sometimes green) line represented the note C. The use of the four-line staff, which

Example 1.4

One-Line Staff (facsimile) ca. 1000 A.D.

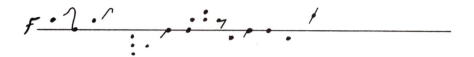

more than doubled the number of pitches that could be precisely notated, first appeared as early as 1000 A.D., and eventually became the standard for **plainsong**[2] notation (Ex. 1.5). As early as the thirteenth century the five-line staff was used for **polyphonic** music—music for several vocal or instrumental lines sounding simultaneously, each having a more or less individual character. It is speculated that this fifth line was added to the existing four in order to more accurately represent and accommodate, in notation, the human vocal range.

Example 1.5

Plainsong (Gregorian Chant): Four-Line Staff with Modern Interpretation

Ho - di - e   Chri   -   stus na - tus   est:

modern interpretation

Various types of tablature notation were used between the fifteenth and seventeenth centuries, **tablature** being a general term to define notational devices using systems other than the staff and notes to represent music. One of the more innovative was lute tablature, where horizontal lines represented the actual strings of the lute (Ex. 1.6). One of the major weaknesses of this notation was the fact that the tuning of the strings was not standardized and had to be qualified. The use of two staves for the notation of keyboard music came into use in the sixteenth century.

---

[2]Plainsong is commonly used to refer to Gregorian chant, a single-line music that is unaccompanied and nonmetric.

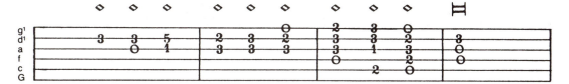

Example 1.6

Spanish Lute Tablature: Renaissance Tuning (facsimile)

PART B: MODERN STANDARD NOTATION

MODERN STAFF

Most Western music today is written on an arrangement of five equally spaced horizontal lines. The five lines and the four spaces that occur between the lines are called a staff (plural staffs or, preferably, staves). The lines and spaces are numbered upward from the bottom to the top (Ex. 1.7).

Example 1.7

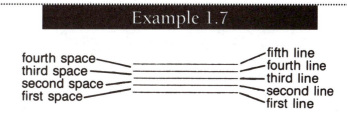

CLEFS

Letter names cannot be given to the lines and spaces of a staff until a clef is employed. When this occurs, a letter name can be assigned to each line and space. The most commonly used clefs are given in Example 1.8.

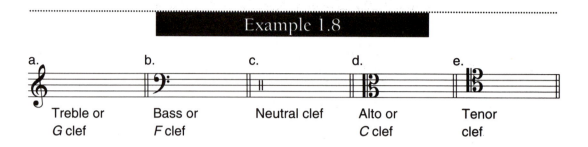

Example 1.8

a.   b.   c.   d.   e.

Treble or   Bass or   Neutral clef   Alto or   Tenor
G clef   F clef   C clef   clef

1. Example 1.8a shows the treble or *G* clef, in which the second line of the staff is always *G*.
2. Example 1.8b shows the bass or *F* clef, in which the fourth line of the staff is always *F*.
3. Example 1.8c shows the neutral clef, in which no exact letter name is assigned to any given line or space. This is frequently used for percussion notation.
4. Example 1.8d shows the alto or *C* clef, in which the third line of the staff is always *C*.[3] The line or space on which it is placed is always middle *C*.
5. Example 1.8e shows the tenor *C* clef, in which the fourth line of the staff is always middle *C*.

MUSICAL ALPHABET—PITCH READING

The **musical alphabet** contains seven letters: A, B, C, D, E, F, and G. Example 1.9 illustrates the placement of the letter-named pitches assigned to specific lines and spaces when various clefs are used.

Example 1.9

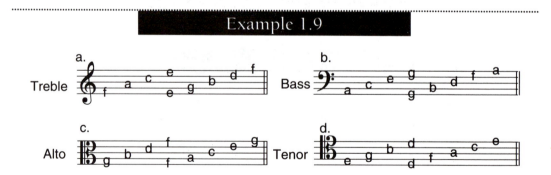

a.

Treble

b.

Bass

c.

Alto

d.

Tenor

Example 1.10a shows the musical alphabet as it appears on the keyboard and Example 1.10b as it appears on the combined treble and bass clef staves.

---

[3]The *C* clef is a moveable clef. It may appear in different positions, naming various lines of the staff as *C*. Its flexible positioning avoids the excessive use of leger lines and spaces as it best accommodates the range of various instruments or voices.

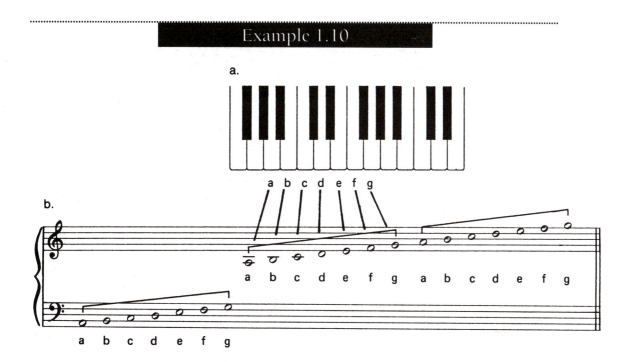

LEGER LINES AND SPACES

When notes extend beyond the range of the staff, **leger lines** and **leger spaces** are employed.[4] Leger lines and spaces are generally short-term extensions of the five-line staff system. They enable one to write specified notes beyond the range of the five-line staff (Exx. 1.11 and 1.12[4]).

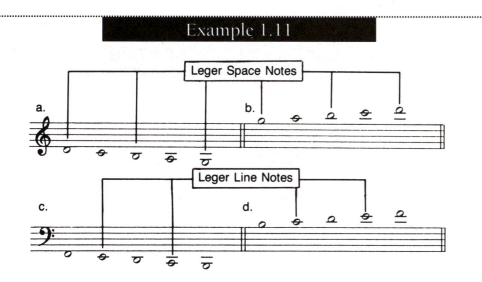

---

[4]Either "leger" or "ledger" are considered acceptable spellings.

Example 1.12

a. Second leger line above the treble clef.
b. Third leger space above the treble clef.
c. Second leger line below the treble clef.
d. First leger space above the bass clef.
e. Third leger line above the bass clef.
f. First leger line below the bass clef.

Example 1.13 illustrates how notes written below the treble clef would be notated at the same pitch in the bass clef.

Example 1.13

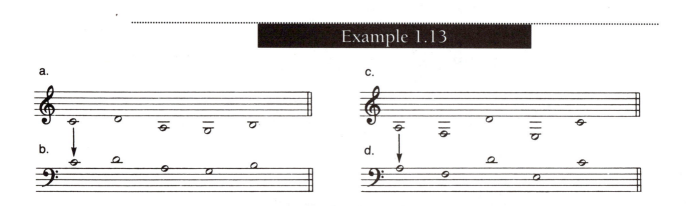

Example 1.14 shows how notes written above the bass clef would be written at the same pitch in the treble clef.

Example 1.14

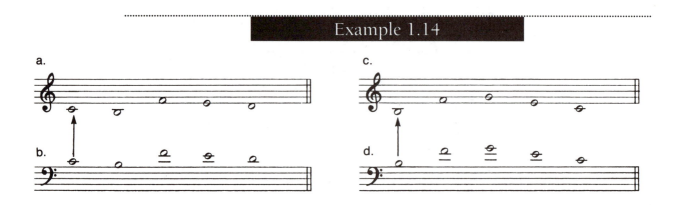

GRAND STAFF AND BRACE

When the treble and bass clefs are joined together with a **brace**, the two clefs are called the **grand staff**. The *C* between the bass and treble clefs is called "middle" *C*. It may also be notated as the first leger line above the bass clef. Note that only three notes separate the treble and bass clefs: *B*, *C*, and *D* (Ex. 1.15).

Example 1.15

SPECIAL USES FOR CLEFS

The *C* clef (Ex. 1.16a) is occasionally used for the tenor (high male) voice of a choral composition and is placed in the third space. This placement enables the singer to "think" in the treble clef because all of the lines and spaces have the same letter names as those in the treble clef. The actual pitch will sound an octave lower. Example 1.16b is also used for the tenor voice in some choral works. The notes sound an octave lower than written. Example 1.16c indicates that the notes sound an octave higher than written.

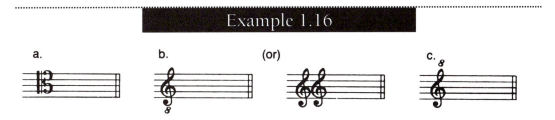

Example 1.16

In notating by hand the various clefs, try to duplicate each clef exactly as it appears in print. Careful notation is critical in order to facilitate the reading of music. You should apply this principle of clear music notation to all signs and symbols used to represent musical sound.

HALF STEPS AND WHOLE STEPS

On the keyboard, the interval of a **half step** is the difference in pitch between any key and the key immediately above or below it. **A whole step** is an interval that contains two half steps. Example 1.17 illustrates where half and whole steps appear between white keys on the keyboard.

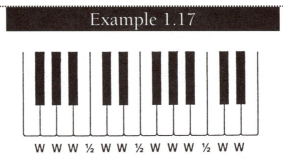

Example 1.17

W W W ½ W W ½ W W W ½ W W

CHROMATIC SIGNS

There are five common **chromatic signs** that are used to alter the pitch of a written note.[5] A chromatic sign affects only the pitch to which it is applied within a given measure and only in the particular octave in which it appears (Ex. 1.18).

Example 1.18

♭♭	♭	♮	♯	× or 𝄪
Double Flat	Flat	Natural	Sharp	Double Sharp

When placed before a note:

1. a double flat lowers a note two half steps;
2. a flat lowers a note one half step;[6]
3. a natural cancels a previously placed chromatic sign;
4. a sharp raises a note one half step;[6]
5. a double sharp raises a note two half steps;
6. an individual chromatic sign alters only the specific note to which it is applied and no other octave occurrence of that note;
7. a bar line cancels a chromatic sign alteration.[7]

---

[5]The term "accidental" is a frequently encountered synonym for chromatic sign.

[6]Chromatic signs are "relative" symbols. In a certain context, a flat can be used to raise a note (if preceded by a double flat) and a sharp to lower one (if preceded by a double sharp).

[7]Occasionally, a chromatic sign is inserted after a barline as a reminder to the performer, thus serving a redundant function.

ENHARMONIC EQUIVALENTS

Notes that are of the same pitch but that have a different spelling are called **enharmonic.** Example 1.19 illustrates the enharmonic equivalents for the black and white keys of the keyboard.

Example 1.19

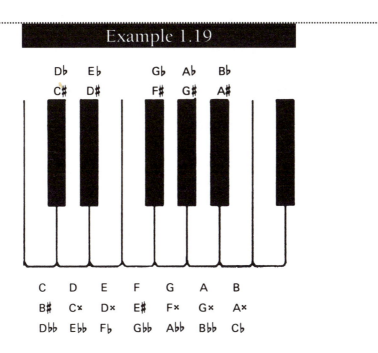

CHROMATIC AND DIATONIC MOTION

A half step is labeled **chromatic** if the same letter of the musical alphabet is used for both pitches. If adjacent letters are used, it is labeled a **diatonic** half step (Ex. 1.20).

Example 1.20

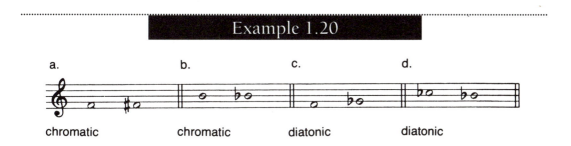

Most whole steps are diatonic and are written with adjacent letters of the musical alphabet (Exx. 1.21a, b, and c). Occasionally a chromatic whole step will appear (Ex. 1.21d).

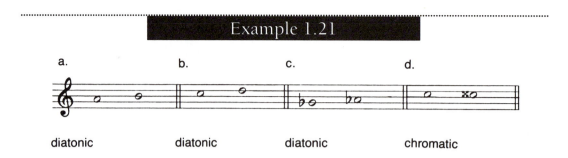

Example 1.21

a.   b.   c.   d.

diatonic   diatonic   diatonic   chromatic

On the staff or keyboard, when chromatic signs are not used, diatonic half steps naturally occur between *E* and *F* and between *B* and *C*. The rest of the adjacent letter relationships are diatonic whole steps. Throughout this text these "naturally occurring half steps" will be referred to as **NOHS**.

THE OCTAVE

An octave is an interval in which two notes are separated by the distance of twelve half steps or six whole steps. Each of the two notes will have the same number and kind of chromatic sign and will have the same letter name (Ex. 1.22).

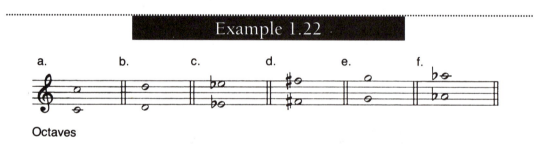

Example 1.22

a.   b.   c.   d.   e.   f.

Octaves

Example 1.23 illustrates octave intervals as they appear on the keyboard.

Example 1.23

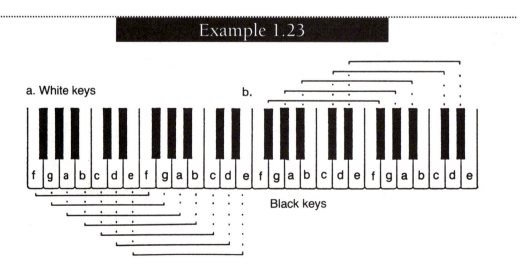

a. White keys   b.

f g a b c d e f g a b c d e f g a b c d e f g a b c d e

Black keys

OCTAVE SIGN

The **ottava** (octave) sign is represented by the symbol 8, or 8ᵛᵃ, and indicates that the notes are:

1. to be played an octave higher if the sign is placed *above* the notes (Ex. 1.24a)
2. to be played an octave lower if the sign is placed *below* the notes (Ex. 1.24b)

Example 1.24

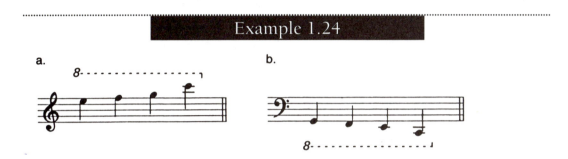

The **double octave sign** is represented by the symbol **15**, or **15ma** (abbreviation for **quindicesima**), and is used to indicate that the note or notes are to be played two octaves higher or lower than written, depending upon the placement of the sign (Ex. 1.25). Publishers and composers have occasionally used the erroneous symbol "16va" to indicate a double octave displacement.

Example 1.25

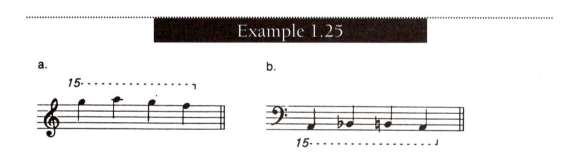

OCTAVE REGISTERS

It is possible to be quite specific when referring to any pitch on the staff or keyboard. Examples 1.26a and b show the letter designations as well as the **register** label. The distance encompassed by each register is one half step smaller than an octave; all *C*s initiate a change in register designation.

Example 1.26

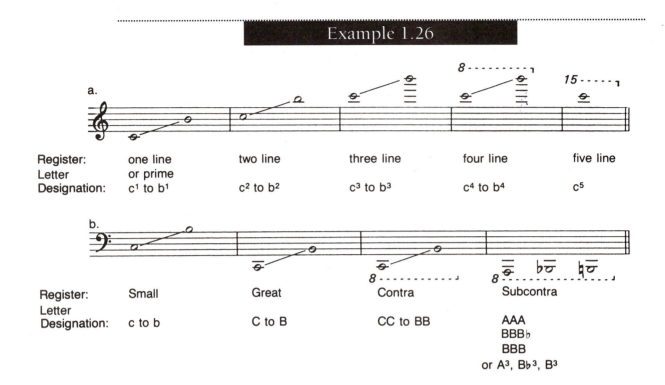

Register:	one line or prime	two line	three line	four line	five line
Letter Designation:	c^1 to b^1	c^2 to b^2	c^3 to b^3	c^4 to b^4	c^5

Register:	Small	Great	Contra	Subcontra
Letter Designation:	c to b	C to B	CC to BB	AAA BBB♭ BBB or A^3, $B♭^3$, B^3

Note that middle *C* has a superscript "1" and that the number increases by one with each subsequent higher register. All notes from small *c* and above are lower-case letters.

Note also that on the standard piano keyboard only three notes are found in the subcontra register, the lowest note being *AAA* or *A³*. Only one note, c^5, the highest key on the piano keyboard, is found in the five-line register. The type of letter designation, that is c^1, d^1, e^1, and so on, remains the same throughout each register.[8]

Example 1.27 shows octave registers from the subcontra to the five-line range as they appear on the grand staff and standard piano keyboard.

---

[8]An alternate system exists for the labeling of octave registers. It consists of naming the lowest C on the piano keyboard as C^1, the note one octave higher as C^2, the note an additional octave higher as C^3, and so on. In this system all letters are capitalized and the superscript number remains the same for all notes in the register. The highest sound on the piano keyboard would be C^8, and the three lowest notes would be A^0, B^0, and B^0. The problem with using this system is that it tends to be limited to the 8va ranges of the acoustical piano, in that it assumes that this instrument is the standard and the norm, not accounting for the extended range of electronic instruments (such as keyboards and synthesizers) of the twentieth century.

Example 1.27

Octave Registers

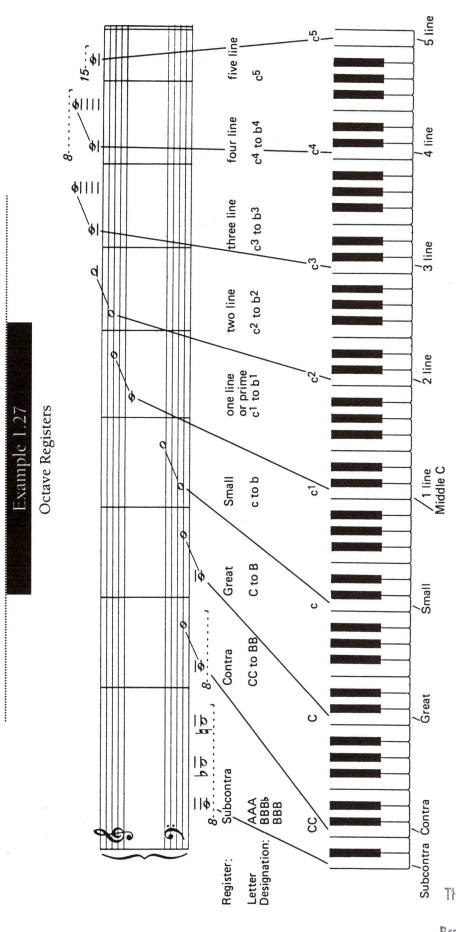

Example 1.28 displays notes from different registers along with their respective letter designations.

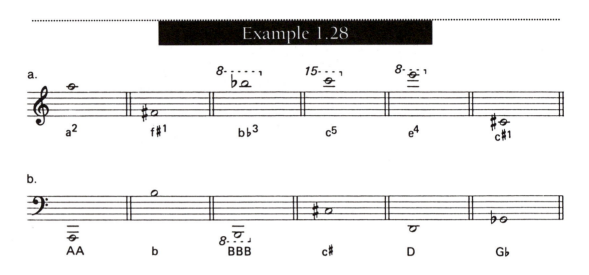

Example 1.28

PART C: ELEMENTS OF MUSICAL DURATION

MEASURE, BAR LINE, AND DOUBLE BAR LINE

A **measure** is the staff space that occurs between two bar lines, and it contains a measured amount of musical material (note and rest values). A **bar line** is represented by a single vertical line. It divides musical material into measures. A **double bar line** is represented by a double vertical line. The double bar appears, for the most part, at the end of a composition and may also appear at the end of a section of a piece (Ex. 1.29).

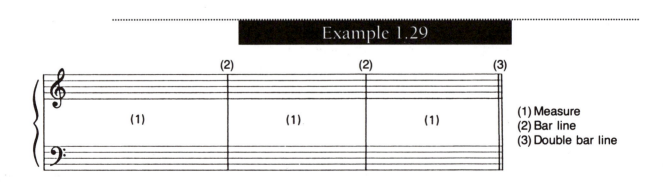

Example 1.29

(1) Measure
(2) Bar line
(3) Double bar line

NOTES, STEMS, FLAGS, AND BEAMS

The various parts of a note, as well as **flags** and **beams**, are illustrated in Example 1.30. Note that beams are frequently used instead of a series of flagged note values.

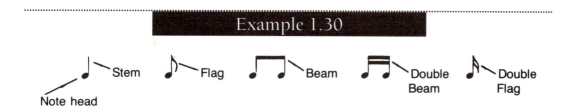

NOTES AND RESTS

The names given to notes and their corresponding rests are given in Example 1.31, which shows the range of notes and rest values, from the longest to the shortest. Each successive note or rest value equals one-half of the duration of the preceding note or rest.

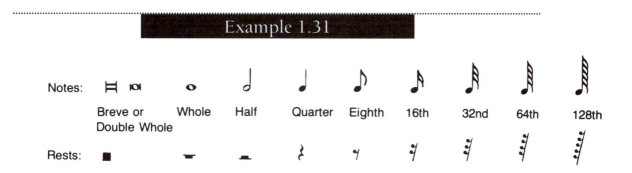

TIES, SLURS, AND PHRASE MARKS

Slurs and ties are identical markings in terms of notation. Their functions are the same regardless of which of the two terms you see. A **tie** is a curved line that connects two or more adjacent notes of the same pitch. It asks the performer to connect these notes, which, in this case, means to sustain the first pitch into the second without a break or release. A **slur** is a curved line that connects two or more different notes in a musical phrase. This time the same curved line means to perform these notes as connected as possible. This type of articulation in which the notes are connected in a smooth manner is called legato.

A **phrase mark** is a curved line that indicates a complete musical thought. Some musicians like to think of a phrase as being analogous to a written sentence (see Ex. 1.32).

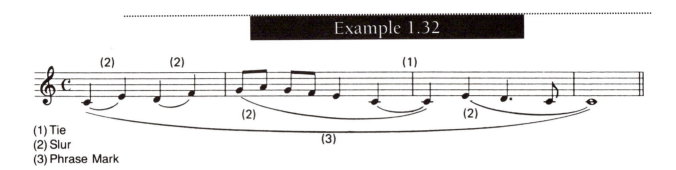

Example 1.32

(1) Tie
(2) Slur
(3) Phrase Mark

DURATION DOTS

Any note or rest may be followed by one or more dots (i.e., placed to the right of a note head or rest).[9] A single dot will increase the duration of a note or rest by half again its original value. Additional dots add one-half the duration of each previous dot. A dot placed *above* or *below* a note is not a durational dot but rather an articulation dot; it indicates a short or staccato articulation. Example 1.33 illustrates how dotted and doubly dotted notes would be represented if ties were employed in place of the dots.

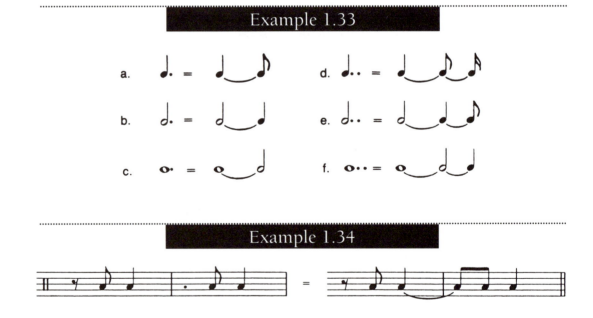

Example 1.33

Example 1.34

---

[9]Earlier musical scores sometimes followed the practice of placing a dot after the bar line in place of tying a note across the bar line (see Ex. 1.34); however, this system is no longer in practice.

STEM DIRECTION

The rules frequently followed for determining stem direction in a single-line melody are given below.

1. Notes that occur on the middle line of the staff may have the stem going upward or downward (Ex. 1.35a).
2. Notes below the middle line have stems that go upward (Ex. 1.35b).
3. Notes above the middle line have stems that go downward (Ex. 1.35c).
4. Stems generally extend to the next octave (a vertical distance encompassing eight lines and spaces) from any given pitch, whether placed above or below the note head.
5. Flags always appear on the right side of the note value, regardless of stem direction.

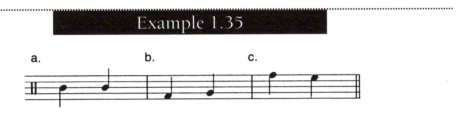

Note that when the stem comes downward from the note head it is attached to the left side of the head. When the stem goes upward it is attached to the right side of the note head. The stem direction of a group of notes to be beamed together is determined by the greater number of notes that lie either above or below the middle line as well as by their proximity to the middle line (Ex. 1.36).

It is sometimes acceptable to allow the stems of beamed notes to go in either direction (Ex. 1.37). Notice that when notes are beamed together, some stems may exceed an octave in length; however, the shortest stem must span the distance of an octave on the staff.

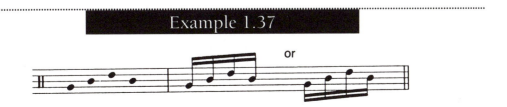

In four-part choral writing with two voices sharing the same staff, it is customary to have the stems of the soprano and tenor voices going upward and those of the alto and bass voices going downward (Ex. 1.38).

Example 1.38

STEM LENGTH

Note heads written two or more leger lines above or below the staff will generally have stems extending to the middle line of the staff. Exceptions are 32nd and 64th notes, which generally require slightly longer stems in order to accommodate the additional flags or beams.

FERMATA

A **fermata** (⌒) is a symbol that can indicate one of two things.

1. The notes or rests above or below the fermata will have a longer, indeterminate duration.
2. The conclusion of the phrase. In this case, the final chord or note does not necessarily receive a longer duration.

A type of fermata that indicates holding a given note, chord, or rest for a longer duration, but to a lesser degree than the standard fermata, is the "short fermata" (◻). Some contemporary composers use this "square" fermata to indicate a longer duration by notating actual duration in seconds over it (◻).

Complete the chapter 1 drill sheets on the following pages before continuing. See Appendix A and Appendix B for further applications of this material.

CHAPTER ONE DRILLS AND EXERCISES

PARTS A & B: BASIC PROPERTIES OF SOUND AND MUSICAL DYNAMICS

1. The four basic properties of sound are:

a.

b.

c.

d.

2. The property of sound that refers to a sound's tone color is _____.

3. The property of sound that refers to the highness or lowness of a pitch is _____.

4. The property of sound that refers to how loudly or softly a sound is perceived is called _____
    _____.

5. The property of sound that refers to how long the sound or silence is perceived is _____
    _____.

6. The dynamic symbol used to indicate "softly" is _____.

7. The dynamic symbol used to indicate "very loud" is _____.

8. The dynamic symbol used to indicate "moderately loud" is _____.

PART C: MUSIC NOTATION

1. Beam each group of notes as eighth notes.

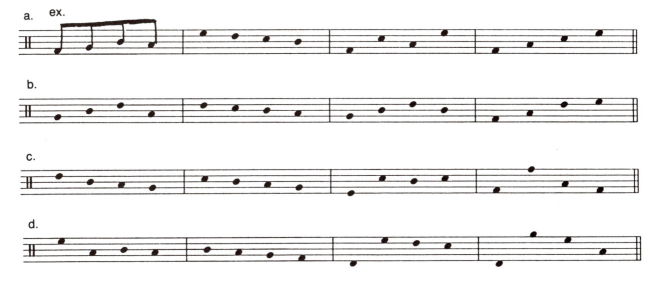

2.   Identify the pitches as notated below.

a.

ex. F   ___   ___   ___   ___   ___   ___

b.

c.

d.

e.

f.

g.

h.

i.

3. Identify the intervals given as: Enh. (enharmonic), CH (chromatic half step), DH (diatonic half step), DW (diatonic whole step), or CW (chromatic whole step).

4. Notate the requested type of motion (up ↑ or down ↓).

    D = diatonic   **C** = chromatic   **W** = whole step   **H** = half step   **Enh**. = enharmonic

5. In the following drill, pitches are notated in one of the two clefs of the grand staff. Renotate the pitches given in the other clef so that each will sound at the "unison" (same pitch), and identify each note with the appropriate register designation.

a.

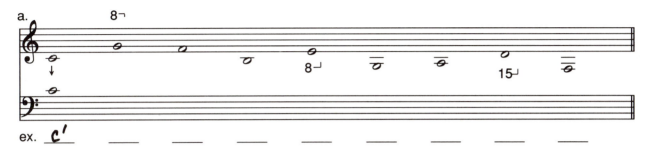

ex. *c'* ____ ____ ____ ____ ____ ____ ____ ____ ____

b.

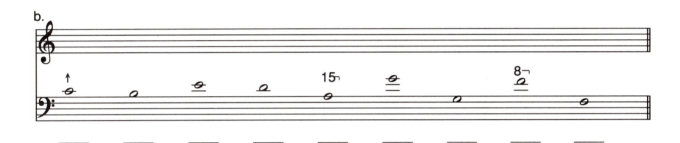

____ ____ ____ ____ ____ ____ ____ ____ ____

c.

____ ____ ____ ____ ____ ____ ____

d.

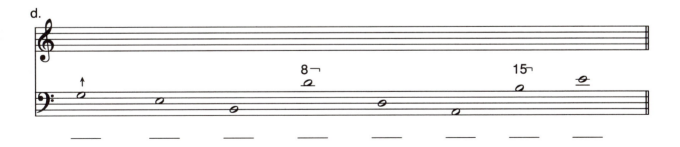

____ ____ ____ ____ ____ ____ ____

6.   Write the pitches indicated.

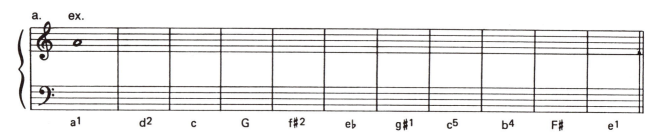

a.   ex.

a¹   d²   c   G   f♯2   e♭   g♯1   c⁵   b⁴   F♯   e¹

b.

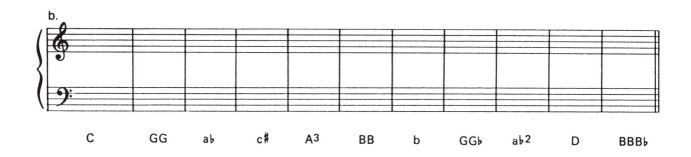

C   GG   a♭   c♯   A³   BB   b   GG♭   a♭2   D   BBB♭

7.   Identify each note with the proper register designation.

a.

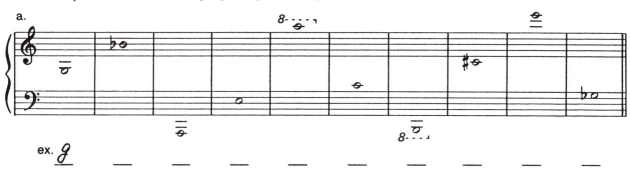

ex.

b.

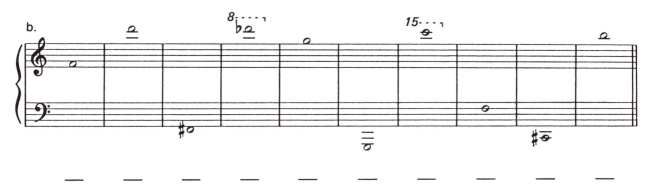

8. Identify each pitch in the example below according to its octave register designation.

NOTATION REVIEW (SELF-TEST: CHAPTER ONE)

1. The G clef is also known as the _____ clef.

2. When the two dots of the *F* clef surround the fourth line of the staff it is also called the _____ clef.

3. When the *C* clef appears on the third line of the staff it is also called the _____ clef.

4. When the range of the music extends above or below the staff, notes are written on _____ _____ lines or in _____ spaces.

5. Stems are normally an _____ (interval) in length.

6. An eighth note is written with _____ flag(s) or _____ beam(s).

7. A 16th note is written with _____ flag(s) or _____ beam(s).

8. A _____ is a curved line that connects two or more adjacent notes of the same pitch.

9. A single dot placed after a note or rest increases its value by _____.

10. A second dot increases the value of the note or rest by _____.

11. The musical alphabet contains _____ (number) letters.

12. NOHS occur on the staff and keyboard between _____ and _____ and _____ and _____.

13. Chromatic half steps are written with (check one) _____ adjacent/ _____ the same letters of the alphabet.

14. Diatonic half steps are written with (check one) _____ adjacent/ _____ the same letters of the alphabet.

15. The sign *8va* placed above notated pitches indicates _____.

16. The sign *15ma* placed below notated pitches indicates: _____.

Rhythm

GOALS

- An understanding of the terms used to define the temporal aspects of music

- An understanding of simple and compound beat units

- The ability to solve simple rhythmic problems

- The ability to tap simple and complex rhythmic patterns

- The ability to divide and subdivide beat units into regular, irregular, or borrowed divisions and subdivisions

TERMINOLOGY: BEAT, PULSE, TEMPO, RHYTHM

The terms **beat, pulse,** or **stress** refer to regularly recurring pulses within a given period of time. **Tempo** indicates the speed at which these pulses occur. **Rhythm** can be defined as a temporal pattern played against a background of beat units, at times corresponding to, and at times conflicting with, the beat, pulse, or stress. Any single note value may serve as the designated beat unit of a composition. Meter and tempo are two factors that help to determine this designation.

SIMPLE AND COMPOUND TIME

Simple and **compound** are terms that indicate how the beat unit divides (see Ex. 2.1).

1. If the beat unit is an undotted note value, the unit will divide equally into two parts and multiples of two (simple time).
2. If the beat unit is a dotted note value, the unit will divide equally into three parts and multiples of three (compound time).

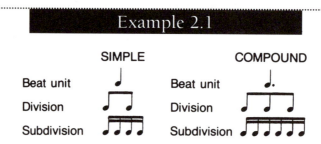

Example 2.1

BEAT DIVISIONS

Regular Divisions

The divisions and subdivisions of a beat may be **regular** (or normal), **irregular,** or **borrowed.** Example 2.2 illustrates how regular divisions and subdivisions would occur in simple and compound time if the quarter note and dotted quarter note were to serve as the beat unit.[1]

---

[1]The beat-unit values chosen in Examples 2.2 and 2.3, although commonly used, were arbitrarily selected; any note value can serve in this capacity.

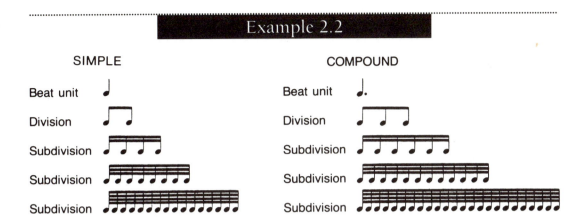

Example 2.3 illustrates the regular divisions and subdivisions of the half note and dotted half note.

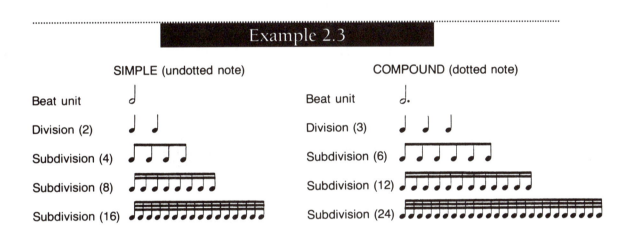

Note that an undotted note divides and subdivides into patterns of 2, 4, 8, 16, 32, and so forth. A dotted note divides and subdivides into patterns of 3, 6, 12, 24, and so on. All of the divisions and subdivisions in Examples 2.2 and 2.3 are regular patterns.

Borrowed Divisions: Duplets and Triplets

An irregular division is labeled **borrowed** when it appears as a division of a simple beat unit into three equal parts or as a division of a compound beat unit into two equal parts. Equal patterns of 6, 12, or 24 notes may be thought of as borrowed subdivisions of a simple beat, and equal patterns of 4, 8, 16, or 32 notes may be thought of as borrowed subdivisions of a compound beat. Generally, only irregular divisions of two or three equal parts (duplets and triplets) are termed borrowed.

Example 2.4 illustrates borrowed divisions (duplets and triplets) for various simple and compound beat units.

Example 2.4

The notation for the duplet is not standardized; it occurs in compound time with different note values, depending on the composer or publisher. A duplet appearing as a borrowed pattern with a beat unit of a dotted quarter note has been found in published compositions as illustrated in Example 2.5. Similar duplet notational discrepancies can be found based on other compound beat-unit values as well.

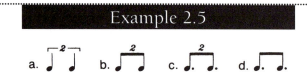

Example 2.5

Irregular Divisions and Subdivisions

It is possible to have a beat unit divide into any desired number of notes of equal duration. If the number of notes is not a regular division or subdivision, the pattern is called **irregular**. Example 2.6 shows regular and irregular divisions of a quarter note.

Example 2.6

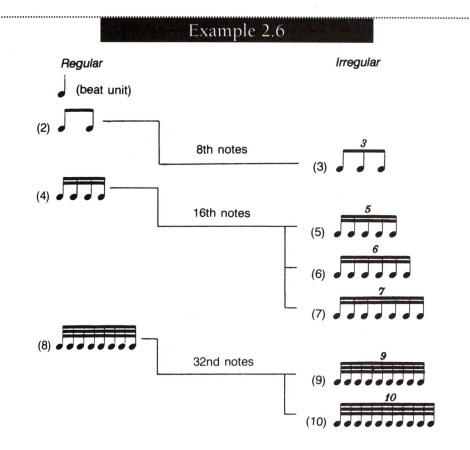

For determining the correct note values for irregular divisions and subdivisions, the guidelines listed below should be followed.

1. Keep in mind the note values of the regular divisions and subdivisions.
2. To determine the note values to be used, employ the note values of the regular division or subdivision that occur prior to the number of notes in the irregular pattern (Ex. 2.6). When considering note values for duplets, since there is no previously used division value, the assigned note value should be the same as it appears in the division.
3. For an irregular pattern, the number of notes in the pattern must be written above or below the unit, as an Arabic numeral (usually at stem or beam side).
4. If the group of notes in the irregular pattern are not beamed together (quarter notes or longer note values), they must be grouped within a bracket.

In Example 2.6, with the quarter note as the unit, irregular divisions of 5, 6, and 7 notes appear as 16th notes. Sixteenth notes are appropriate for these irregular divisions because the use of 32nd notes would not occur until at least 8 notes (regular subdivision) were to be used. In Example 2.7a no bracket is necessary because the notes are beamed together. In Example 2.7b a bracket is necessary.

Example 2.7

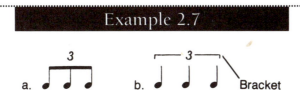

Example 2.8 illustrates irregular rhythmic patterns that require the use of a bracket.

Example 2.8

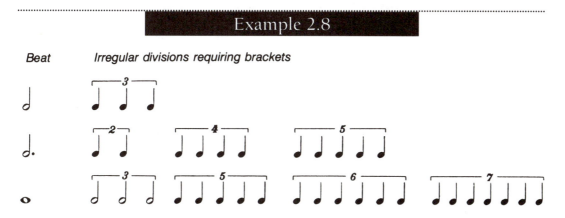

Regular divisions and subdivisions do not require the use of either the bracket or number.

Example 2.9 illustrates the regular, borrowed, and irregular subdivisions of a half note and a dotted quarter note.

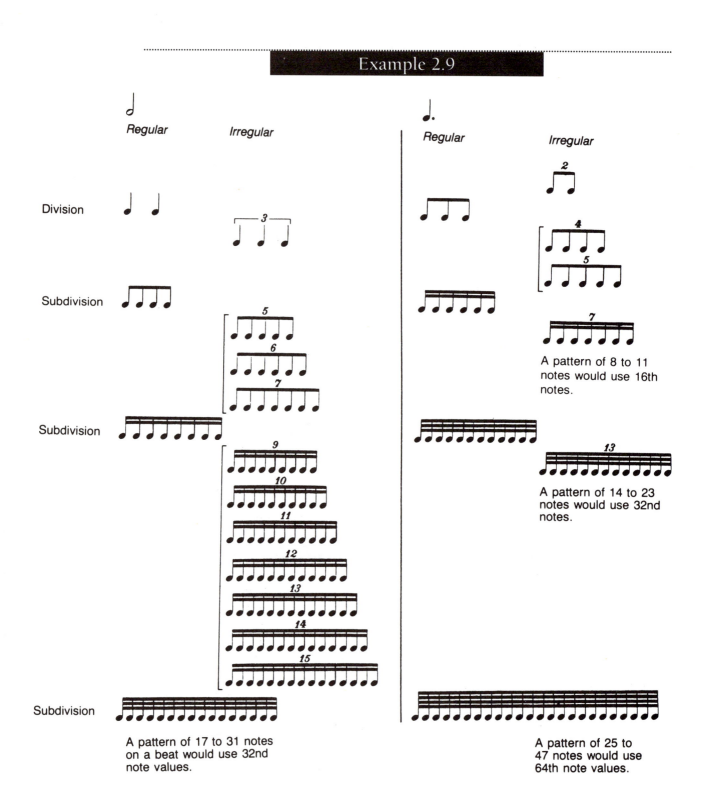

Example 2.9

A pattern of 8 to 11 notes would use 16th notes.

A pattern of 14 to 23 notes would use 32nd notes.

A pattern of 17 to 31 notes on a beat would use 32nd note values.

A pattern of 25 to 47 notes would use 64th note values.

METRONOME TEMPO INDICATIONS

The tempo of a composition is usually indicated by a metronome marking at the beginning of the piece; for example, M.M. (Mälzel's Metronome) ♩ = 60. This means that sixty quarter notes will occur within a minute's duration, at a rate of one per second.

COMMONLY USED TEMPO MARKINGS

Although somewhat subjective, the following Italian terms are frequently used to describe the general range of tempos, from extremely slow to very fast.

Tempo	Metronome Setting
Adagissimo (extremely slow)	40
Grave (slow, solemn)	
Largo (slow)	
Larghetto (slow, somewhat faster than largo)	
Lento (slow)	
Adagio (slow)	
Andante (moderately slow)	60
Andantino (somewhat quicker than andante)	
Moderato (a moderate tempo)	
Allegretto (moderately fast)	
Allegro (fast)	120
Presto (very fast)	
Prestissimo (as fast as possible)	208+

Because of the lack of universal agreement on the exact meanings and tempos of these terms, it is recommended that a metronome indication be included with the general tempo indication.

SUMMARY OF REGULAR, IRREGULAR,
AND BORROWED DIVISIONS

1. Given a simple beat unit, a pattern of 2 equal notes is a regular division, and patterns of 4, 8, 16, 32, and so forth equal notes are regular subdivisions.
2. Given a compound beat unit, a pattern of 3 equal notes is a regular division, and patterns of 6, 12, 24, 48, and so on equal notes are regular subdivisions.

3. Irregular patterns of 2 and 3 (duplet and triplet) are given the special designation of borrowed. Generally only duplets and triplets are labeled borrowed.

4. In simple time, equal note patterns of 6, 12, 24, and so on may be termed borrowed subdivisions. Generally, they are referred to as irregular.

5. In compound time, equal note patterns of 4, 8, 16, and so on may be termed borrowed subdivisions. Generally, they are referred to as irregular.

6. Equal note patterns other than 2, 3, 4, 6, 8, 12, 16, 24, 32, and similar multiples are always labeled as irregular, regardless of the value of the beat unit.

7. Borrowed divisions are "borrowed" only from divisions of a similar beat unit, the only difference being the addition or omission of the dot. Therefore, a beat unit of a quarter note borrows rhythmic patterns from a beat unit of a dotted quarter note and vice versa. This procedure applies to borrowed divisions for all beat-unit values.

Complete the chapter 2 drill sheets on the following pages before continuing. Also, see Appendix A for ear-training exercises.

CHAPTER TWO DRILLS AND EXERCISES

1. Divide each beat unit into regular divisions and subdivisions.

a. Beat unit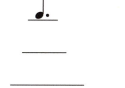

Division   _____ _____

Subdivision _____ _____

Subdivision _____ _____

b. Beat unit

Division _____ _____ _____

Subdivision _____ _____ _____

Subdivision _____ _____ _____

2. Notate the divisions and subdivisions indicated for each beat unit. The number of notes in each pattern is given in parentheses. Classify as regular, irregular or borrowed.

a. Beat unit		Division or subdivision	Classification
	ex. (3)		*Borrowed*
	(4)	_____	_____
	(7)	_____	_____
	(2)	_____	_____
	(9)	_____	_____
b.	(4)	_____	_____
	(2)	_____	_____
	(6)	_____	_____
	(8)	_____	_____
	(3)	_____	_____

c. ♩ (5) _____ _____

(3) _____ _____

(4) _____ _____

(8) _____ _____

(7) _____ _____

(2) _____ _____

d. ♩. (6) _____ _____

(3) _____ _____

(4) _____ _____

(2) _____ _____

(9) _____ _____

e. 𝅝 (10) _____ _____

(2) _____ _____

(3) _____ _____

(7) _____ _____

(4) _____ _____

f. 𝅝. (7) _____ _____

(2) _____ _____

(6) _____ _____

(3) _____ _____

(4) _____ _____

3. Classify the rhythmic patterns given as regular, irregular, or borrowed.

		Beat	Pattern	Classification
a.	ex.	♩	(four 16th notes)	_Reg._
b.		♩.	(5 — five eighth notes)	_____
c.		♪ (half)	(3 — three quarter notes)	_____
d.		♩. (dotted half)	(six eighth notes)	_____
e.		♩.	(4 — four eighth notes)	_____
f.		o	(3 — three half notes)	_____
g.		♩	(eight 32nd notes)	_____
h.		♪ (half)	(6 — six eighth notes)	_____

4. Complete the following:

ex. A ♩ = __4__ (number) 16th notes   A ♩. = _____ eighth notes

An ♪ = _____ 32nd notes   A o· = _____ 16th notes

A o· = _____ quarter notes   A ♪ (half) = _____ 16th notes

A ♪. = _____ 16th notes   An ♪ = _____ 16th notes

A ♩ = _____ 32th notes   A ♩. = _____ eighth notes

A ♪ (half) = _____ eighth notes   A o = _____ quarter notes

A ♩. = _____ 16th notes   A o· = _____ half notes

A ♪ (half) = _____ 32nd notes   A ♩. = _____ 32nd notes

A ♩ = _____ eighth notes   A ♪. (dotted half) = _____ quarter notes

5. Complete the following:

ex.	A	𝄽	=	*2*	𝄾	rests	A	𝄽.	=	____	𝄾 rests
	An	𝄾	=	____	𝄿	rests	A	𝄾.	=	____	𝄿 rests
	A	𝄼	=	____	𝄽	rests	A	♩ ♪	=	____	𝄾 rests
	A	𝄽	=	____	𝄿	rests	A	♩. ♪	=	____	𝄿 rests
	A	𝄼	=	____	𝄾	rests	A	♩.	=	____	𝄽 rests

6. Rewrite the examples given using dots.

ex.

♩ ♪ = *♩.*   ♪ 𝅘𝅥𝅰 = ____

♩ ♩ = ____   ♩ ♩ ♪ = ____

𝅝 ♩ = ____   ♪ ♪ 𝅘𝅥𝅰 = ____

♪ 𝅘𝅥𝅰 = ____   𝅝 ♩ ♩ = ____

7. Describe the tempos of the musical terms given.

Largo_____	Allegro _____
Lento_____	Presto_____
Andante_____	Adagio_____
Grave _____	Allegretto _____

8.   Fill in the blanks, giving the correct number of divisions and subdivisions.

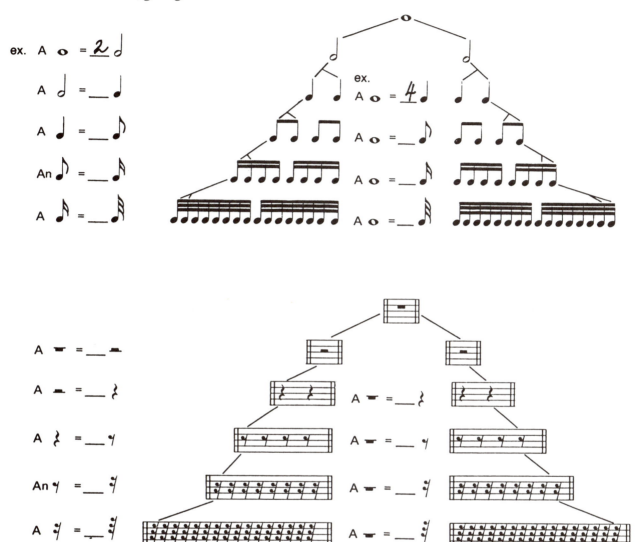

9. Classify the bracketed patterns in the musical examples given as regular (R), irregular (I) or borrowed (B). The beat unit is given with the metronome marking.

This Old Man, English Folk Song

Allegretto M.M. ♩ = 100
ex. R

a.

Old Joe Clark (variation), American Folk Song

Moderato M.M. ♩ = 144

b.

Invention No. 8, J. S. Bach

Vivace (lively) M.M. ♩ = 144

c.

Invention No. 13, J. S. Bach

Allegro M.M. ♩ = 104

d.

Prelude No. 1, Alexander Scriabin

Andante M.M. ♩ = 72

e.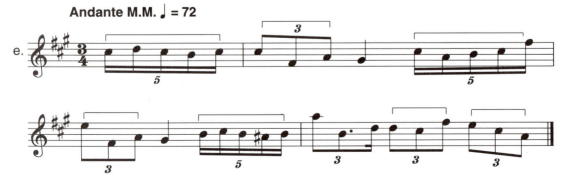

Variations and Fugue on a Theme by Handel (Var. 2), Brahms

To Spring, Edvard Grieg

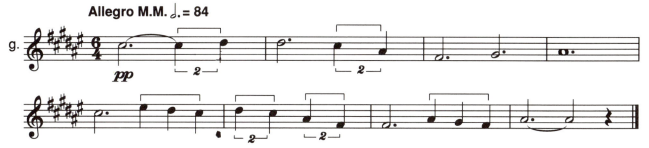

Fugue in G Minor (The Little), J. S. Bach

Carnaval, R. Schumann

10. To solve the following metronome problems, determine the ratio between the note value given and the note value requested. Multiply or divide as necessary, as in Exercise 10a below. In obtaining the answers to 10a, the following methods were employed.

1. The ratio of a quarter note to a half note is 2:1 (half as many). Divide 60 by 2. ♩ = 30.
2. The ratio of a quarter note to an eighth note is 1:2 (twice as many). Multiply by 2. ♪ = 120.
3. The ratio of a quarter note to a 16th note is 1:4 (four times as many). Multiply by 4. ♬ = 240.

a. Given M.M. ♩ = 60, what would be the tempos (metronome markings) of the following note values?

    ex.   1. ♩ = __30__   2. ♪ = __120__   3. ♬ = __240__

b. Given M.M. ♩. = 30, what would be the tempos of the following note values?

    1. ♩ = _____   2. ♪ = _____   3. 𝅝. = _____

c. Given M.M. ♩. = 120, what would be the tempos of the following note values?

    1. ♪ = _____   2. ♩. = _____   3. ♩ = _____

d. Given M.M. ♩. = 60, what would be the tempos of the following note values?

    1. ♩. = _____   2. ♩ = _____   3. 𝅝. = _____

e. Given M.M. ♩ = 120, what would be the tempos of the following note values?

    1. ♩ = _____   2. ♩ = _____   3. ♪ = _____

f. Given M.M. 𝅝 = 48, what would be the tempos of the following note values?

    1. ♪ = _____   2. ♩ = _____   3. ♩. = _____

g. Given M.M. ♩ = 108, what would be the tempos of the following note values?

    1. ♩. = _____   2. ♩ = _____   3. ♪ = _____

RHYTHM REVIEW (SELF-TEST: CHAPTER TWO)

1. Simple time means _____.

2. Compound time means _____.

3. In simple time, the beat unit divides and subdivides into regular patterns of _____, _____, _____ or _____ equal notes.

4. In compound time, the beat unit divides and subdivides into regular patterns of _____, _____, _____ or _____ equal notes.

5. A duplet is a borrowed pattern in _____.

6. A triplet is a borrowed pattern in _____.

7. Circle the subdivisions that are always labeled irregular.
   5   7   9   10   11   13   14   15   17

8. Additional terms used to identify the beat are _____ and _____.

9. M.M. ♩ = 60 means _____.
    M.M. ♩ = 120 means _____.
    M.M. ♪ = 144 means _____.

10. Brackets are used to enclose an irregular pattern if the note values are quarter notes or longer note values. True _____ False _____

11. The tempo of a composition refers to _____.

12. Borrowed divisions are "borrowed" from _____.

13. Only simple beat units can divide or subdivide into any number of equal notes. True _____ False _____

14. Note values for irregular patterns (except for the duplet) use the note values of the regular division or subdivision that occur prior to the number of notes in the irregular pattern. True _____ False _____

15. The assigned note value for a duplet is the same as it appears in the regular division. True _____ False _____

16. As a borrowed division, duplets are the only irregular pattern that requires an actual expansion of note values in time. True _____ False _____

Meter and Meter Signatures

GOALS

- The understanding of the concepts of meter

- The ability to classify compound and simple meters

- The ability to determine beat units in any given meter

- The ability to correctly notate according to meter

METER

Meter is the grouping of beats into units known as measures. This grouping is not a contrived phenomenon but rather a combination of the natural tendencies of beats to group themselves into measures according to musical elements (melodic, harmonic, rhythmic, etc.). Using the symbols below, meter can be determined by the perception of stressed or strong beats, which contrast with nonstressed or weak beats.

>   > = strong or stressed beat
>   ∪ = weak or nonstressed beat

Meters can be duple (two beats), triple (three beats), quadruple (four beats), quintuple (five beats), septuple (seven beats), and so forth (Ex. 3.1).

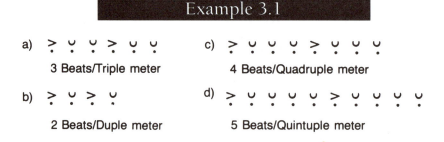

Meters containing four or more beats often contain a secondary stress within the measure (Ex. 3.2).

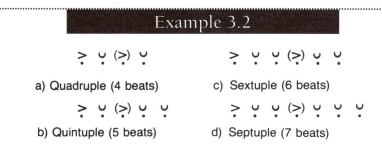

SIMPLE METER SIGNATURES

A meter signature appears as two numbers, one over the other, such as $\frac{3}{4}$. This does not represent a fraction and should not be thought of as such. No fraction line should appear between these numbers. This chapter will focus primarily on traditional practice while at the same time incorporating some contemporary thought and opinion.

In the meter signature of $\frac{3}{4}$, for example, it should be noted that these numbers tell you very little with regard to the number of beats in a given measure, type of note that receives a beat, or how quickly these beats will occur. It would be a mistake to think of $\frac{3}{4}$ as a measure always containing three beats with the quarter note always equaling the beat.

While this might be the case, it certainly does not account for the tempo, which may well be the determining factor with regard to what note value will receive the beat and how many beats will be perceived within a measure. In a slow-to-moderate tempo, for example, three beats will be evident, the quarter note receiving the beat. In a fast tempo, however, there might seem to be only one beat per measure, and the dotted half note might be perceived as the beat.

The entire concept of meter is very closely related to tempo, and it is difficult to think of meter outside of a temporal context. It would be far more accurate to think of $\frac{3}{4}$ as a meter signature indicating that each measure will contain the equivalent of three quarter notes—period. One should refrain from pinning down the concept of beat with regard to $\frac{3}{4}$ as a meter until one examines the tempo indication. In a slow-to-moderate context three distinct beats will be felt; in a moderately fast context one may feel only one beat in a measure.

In a simple meter signature, while the upper number usually represents the number of beats per measure, the lower number refers to a note value; 1 refers to a whole note, 2 refers to a half note, 4 a quarter note, 8 an eighth note, and so on. At first, these numbers seem to be almost interchangeable, but on closer examination certain note-value numbers are more appropriate to a given situation than others. Since the lower number sometimes refers to a beat unit, a musical example with complex levels of division would best be served by a number representing a longer duration, such as 2 (half note) or 4 (quarter note). A meter signature with a lower (bottom) number such as 8 or 16 would quickly become rather cumbersome when dealing with divisions resulting in 64th and 128th notes. On the other hand, a musical example exhibiting rather few and simple divisions of the beat might best be served by a lower number such as 4, 8, or 16. The meter signatures in Example 3.3 are representative of simple meter.

Example 3.3

a.	b.	c.	d.	e.
$\frac{2}{2}\ \frac{2}{4}\ \frac{2}{8}\ \frac{2}{16}$	$\frac{3}{2}\ \frac{3}{4}\ \frac{3}{8}\ \frac{3}{16}$	$\frac{4}{2}\ \frac{4}{4}\ \frac{4}{8}\ \frac{4}{16}$	$\frac{5}{2}\ \frac{5}{4}\ \frac{5}{8}\ \frac{5}{16}$	$\frac{7}{2}\ \frac{7}{4}\ \frac{7}{8}\ \frac{7}{16}$

Perhaps the most common simple meter is $\frac{4}{4}$, which sometimes appears as $\mathbf{c}$, a symbol for "common time." The symbol $\mathbf{\mathct}$ appears as a substitute for $\frac{2}{2}$, representing "cut time," or **alla breve.**

In a moderate tempo, Example 3.3a would represent duple meter with either the half note, quarter note, eighth note, or sixteenth note as a beat unit. Example 3.3b would represent a triple meter; 3.3c a quadruple meter; 3.3d a quintuple meter; and 3.3e a septuple meter. In addition, Examples 3.3d and 3.3e illustrate asymmetrical meters—that is, meters that cannot be divided into two or three equal parts. In $\frac{5}{4}$, for example, one may feel a grouping of 2 + 3 or 3 + 2. A more accurate signature might well be $\frac{3+2}{4}$ or $\frac{2+3}{4}$. The signature $\frac{7}{4}$ yields even further asymmetrical combinations such as $\frac{4+3}{4}$, or $\frac{3+4}{4}$, or $\frac{2+3+2}{4}$.

COMPOUND METER SIGNATURES

The terms "simple" and "compound," as they are applied to beat units in the previous chapter, also apply to meter signatures. A simple meter signature makes use of simple beats units—beat units that divide and subdivide normally into two, four, eight, and sixteen parts. Compound meter signatures employ compound beat units—dotted beat units that divide and subdivide normally into three, six, and twelve equal parts.

Let us examine $\frac{6}{8}$ as a model compound meter signature. In dealing with compound signatures one cannot apply the overly simplistic rule that states that the top number tells you how many beats are contained in the measure and the bottom number tells you the value of each beat. This is not the case in compound signatures. In a moderate tempo, a $\frac{6}{8}$ measure will normally contain two beats units, each the value of the dotted quarter note. Actually, the contemporary signature of $\frac{2}{\textgravedbldot}$ more accurately illustrates what is taking place. It conveys two important facts: (1) the number of beats in the measure and (2) the value of the beat unit.

In deciphering which are simple signatures and which are compound, a simple rule will enable you to quickly determine the answer:

> *If the upper number in the signature is six or larger, and is evenly divisible by three, the signature is compound.*

It is assumed that the classification of compound signatures calls for a moderate-to-fast tempo since at slow tempos even compound signatures are pulsed at the division of the beat rather than pulsed at the beat unit. For example, in a very slow tempo, a $\frac{6}{8}$ meter can be perceived as having six simple beat units, each unit being an eighth note. In a fast tempo, the same $\frac{6}{8}$ meter is described as having two beats, each unit being the dotted quarter note. Conversely, in a fast triple simple meter where the beat unit is represented by an eighth note or less ($\frac{3}{8}$ or $\frac{3}{16}$, etc.), all of the notes in the measure may be beamed together as if representing a single compound beat unit (Ex. 3.4).

Example 3.4

Symphony No. 2 (2nd movement), Beethoven

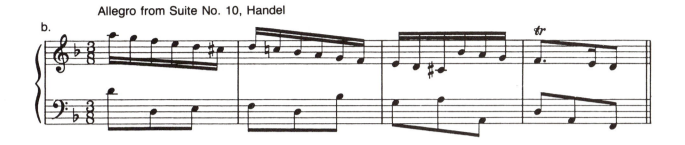

Allegro from Suite No. 10, Handel

Meter signatures having as an upper number a 6, 9, 12, or 15 are normally considered compound signatures. Meter signatures having as an upper number a 2, 3, 4, 5, or 7 are normally considered simple signatures. The chart in Example 3.5 can be useful in defining some of the more standard meter signatures.

METER CLASSIFICATIONS

Example 3.5			
METER	**BEAT UNIT**	**No. of Beats in Measure**	**CLASSIFICATION**
$\frac{3}{4}$	♩	3	Triple-simple
$\frac{4}{4}$	♩	4	Quadruple-simple
$\frac{5}{4}$	♩	5	Quintuple-simple
$\frac{6}{8}$	♩.	2	Duple-compound
$\frac{5}{8}$	♪	5	Quintuple-simple
$\frac{12}{4}$	♩.	4	Quadruple-compound
$\frac{9}{4}$	♩.	3	Triple-compound

In a compound meter signature, the number of beats in a measure (duple, triple, quadruple, quintuple) can be determined by dividing the top number in the meter signature by 3. The actual beat unit will be three times the duration represented by the bottom number. For example, in a given $\frac{6}{4}$ meter, the upper number (6) divided by 3 will yield two beats units (duple); the lower number (4) represents a quarter note value, which, multiplied by 3, yields the value of a dotted half note beat unit.

METER NOTATION: BEAT UNITS

The notation used in any given meter must reflect the beat unit.

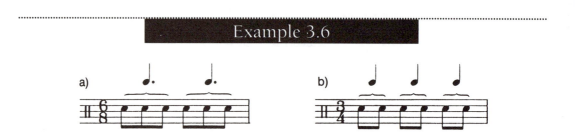

Example 3.6

Example 3.6a illustrates the appropriate notation for a $\frac{6}{8}$ measure. Since the beat unit is considered to be a dotted quarter note, the eighth notes must be beamed so the sum of their durations equals the duration of the beat unit—namely, the dotted quarter note. Example 3.6b illustrates the appropriate notation for a $\frac{3}{4}$ measure. Since the beat unit is the quarter note, the eighth notes (representing a division of the beat) must be beamed so that their grouping reflects the quarter note value. This rule of notation, in which beamed groups reflect the total duration of the beat unit, applies to all meter signatures and serves as an aid in determining the appropriate meter signature for any given measure of notation, regardless of its complication. For instance, in Example 3.7, each beat unit is clarified by the beaming. Each beat is made clear by its separation from other beats in the measure. All one has to do to identify the meter is to add up the total durations within each beamed beat unit. In doing so, it is discovered that each beamed unit contains a total of three eighth notes (or a dotted quarter note). There are three such beat units; therefore, the appropriate meter signature would be $\frac{9}{8}$.

Example 3.7

As a general rule, the notation may obscure one beat but may not obscure two or more consecutive beats in the measure. The term "obscure" implies that the notation may mask the exact point at which a beat begins.

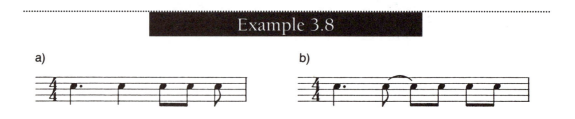

Example 3.8

Example 3.8a illustrates an incorrect notation in $\frac{4}{4}$. We can see that beats 2 and 3 are obscured by notation that would be difficult to play or read. The notation is further complicated by incorrect beaming or grouping of beat units. The same rhythm is correctly notated in Example 3.8b, which allows for the visual clarity of beat units. Note that beat 2 is obscured by the dotted quarter note, but this is acceptable since only one beat is obscured.

Two or more consecutive beat units, notated in division, may not be obscured by the notation. For example, in simple time, with the quarter note as the beat unit, the rhythmic pattern ♩ ♪ is frequently encountered and acceptable. However, the rhythmic pattern ♪ ♩. should be avoided since a ♩. must originate (in simple time) at the beginning of a beat.

The actual meter employed can determine how a certain rhythm should be notated. The chart in Example 3.9 illustrates awkwardly notated rhythmic patterns and shows what the correct notation should be in order to conform to the beat unit. It should be observed that correctly notated patterns do not change the sounding rhythms—only how they appear in notation.

Example 3.9

Meter	Pattern to avoid	Correct version	Reason (see list below)
$\frac{2}{4}$	♩⌣♩ (tied)	♩ (half note)	a
$\frac{6}{8}$	♩.⌣♩. (tied)	♩. (dotted half)	a
$\frac{2}{4}$	♪ ♩.	♪♪⌣♩	b
$\frac{6}{8}$	♩ ♩ (half)	♩ ♪⌣♩.	b, c
$\frac{2}{4}$	♪ ♩ ♪	♪♪⌣♪♪	b, c
$\frac{3}{4}$	♪ ♩ ♪	♪♪⌣♩.⌣♪	b, c
$\frac{3}{4}$	♪♪ ♩ ♩.	♪♪ ♪♪⌣♩	c, d
$\frac{6}{8}$	♪♪ ♪♪⌣♩	♪♪ ♪ ♩.	c, d, e
$\frac{2}{4}$	♫ ♩ ♪	♫⌣♫	c, e
$\frac{2}{4}$	♬♬ ♩	♩. ♪ ♩	d

Reasons for Corrections

a.   Complete consecutive beat units should not be tied together if a single larger note value can be used.

b.   An incomplete first beat must show the completion of that beat in notation.

c.   Beat units should be clearly visible and conform to the type of beat unit (simple or compound) being used.

d.   Any note values tied together within a beat unit must be replaced by the simplest notation (fewest number of notes) possible.

e.   Divisions of the beat must be representative of the beat unit.

BEAMING OF RESTS

Recent notational practice has included rests within the beaming of divisions and subdivisions of beat units. This practice offers the performer the option to more clearly see all of the notes and rests that occur within a single given beat. Some examples of this type of notation are given in Example 3.10.

Example 3.10

SYNCOPATION

Rhythmic patterns may be described as metric (or metrical) if they conform to the regular recurring stress patterns indicated by the meter signature. **Syncopation** exploits rhythmic patterns that do not conform to the regular metric accents, thereby stressing weak beats or weak portions of a beat. Syncopation can be achieved by tying or sustaining notes that occur on weak beats into strong ones or by using rests where strong beats normally occur (Ex. 3.11).

Example 3.11

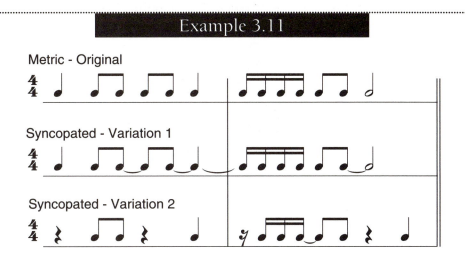

Meter must not be thought of as a set of molds into which musical ideas are poured. On the contrary, existing concepts of meter are applied to musical expression as a means of temporal organization. Many times, standard or traditional meters cannot serve the meter demands of more recent contemporary music. For instance, meter signatures might be changed or alternated from measure to measure to accommodate a musical idea. Meter, therefore, should be thought of as a secondary consideration (although a necessary one) in facilitating the written transmission of musical ideas.

Complete the chapter 3 drill sheets on the following pages before continuing. Also, see Appendix A and Appendix B for further study.

CHAPTER THREE DRILLS AND EXERCISES

1   Given the stress patterns below, determine the meter in the following examples:

a. > ᴗ ᴗ > ᴗ ᴗ	ex. TRIPLE	d. > ᴗ ᴗ ᴗ	
b. > ᴗ ᴗ ᴗ > ᴗ ᴗ		e. > ᴗ ᴗ > ᴗ	
c. > ᴗ > ᴗ		f. > ᴗ ᴗ ᴗ > ᴗ ᴗ	

2.   Insert bar lines where appropriate in the following examples:

Simple Meters

3. Insert bar lines where appropriate in the following examples:

Compound Meters

4. Insert an appropriate meter signature for each example given.

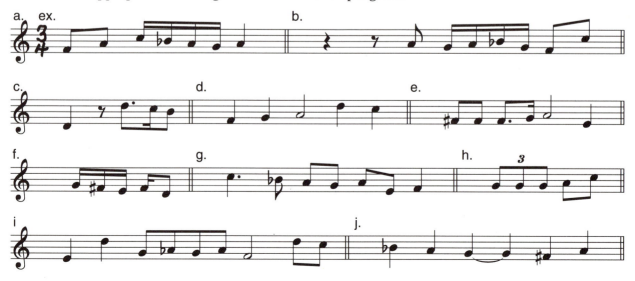

5. In the following examples, a note or rest is missing; add to the appropriate beat unit the one note, rest, or dot that will complete the measure.

6. Given the following signatures, complete the chart by supplying the appropriate beat unit, number of beats in the measure, and appropriate meter classification.

	METER	BEAT UNIT	NO. OF BEATS IN A MEASURE	CLASSIFICATION
ex.	$\frac{6}{8}$	♩.	2	Duple Compound
	$\frac{3}{2}$			
	$\frac{15}{4}$			
	$\frac{4}{2}$			
	$\frac{5}{8}$			
	$\frac{12}{2}$			
	$\frac{4}{1}$			
	$\frac{3}{8}$			
	$\frac{6}{16}$			
	$\frac{7}{4}$			
	$\frac{9}{4}$			
	$\frac{2}{2}$			
	$\frac{3}{16}$			
	¢			
	C			

7. Correctly beam the beat units in the following examples. Utilize ascending stems as in the first measure.

8. The following examples may contain notational errors—namely, incorrect groupings of beat units. Some of the beats may be correctly notated and not need revision. Renotate the errors while maintaining the integrity of the rhythms indicated. You may use the same staves, making corrections by notating on the fourth space of the staff.

Example:

j.

k.

9. Continue correcting notational errors where necessary.
   Compound Meters

Example:
a.

Compound Meters
b.

c.

d.

e.

f.

g.

h.

i.

j.

10. Continue correcting notational errors where necessary. The following examples are somewhat more challenging. Notate in the fourth space as in Exercises 8 and 9.

METER REVIEW (SELF-TEST: CHAPTER THREE)

1. Using the symbols > for strong or stressed beat and ∪ for weak or nonstressed beat, give the stress patterns of the meters indicated.

   a. Triple ____ ____ ____

   b. Duple ____ ____

c. Quintuple ____ ____ ____ ____ ____ or ____ ____ ____ ____ ____

d. Septuple ____ ____ ____ ____ ____ ____ ____

         or ____ ____ ____ ____ ____ ____ ____

         or ____ ____ ____ ____ ____ ____ ____

e. Quadruple ____ ____ ____ ____

2. The tempo of a composition may be the determining factor with regard to which note value will receive the beat. True _____ False _____

3. The lower number in the meter signature refers to a note value. True _____ False _____

4. A lower number one (1) in the meter signature refers to a _____ note (note value).

A lower number four (4) in the meter signature refers to a _____ note.

A lower number two (2) in the meter signature refers to a _____ note.

5. In all meter signatures, the upper number usually indicates the number of beats per measure. True _____ False _____

6. The meter signature for "common time" is indicated by the symbol _____.

7. The meter signature for "cut time" or alla breve is indicated by the symbol _____.

8. Meter signatures having as upper number _____, _____, _____, or _____ are normally considered to be compound meter signatures.

9. Meter signatures having an upper number _____, _____, _____, _____ or _____ are normally considered to be simple meter signatures.

10. "Cut time" or alla breve usually has a _____ (note value) as a beat unit.

11. The number of beats in a compound meter signature can be determined by dividing the top number in the signature (6, 9, 12, 15) by _____.

12. In a compound meter signature, the beat unit is three times the value (duration) of the note value represented by the bottom number. True _____ False _____

13. In compound meter, the beat unit is always a dotted note. True _____ False _____

14. Complete the following:

a. If the bottom number of a compound meter signature is a 4 (quarter note), the beat unit will be a _____note.

b. If the bottom number of a compound meter signature is an 8 (eighth note), the beat unit will be a _____ note.

c. If the bottom number of a compound meter signature is a 16 (16th note), the beat unit will be a _____ note.

d. If the bottom number of a compound meter signature is a 2 (half note), the beat unit will be a _____ note.

15. A fraction line always appears between the upper and lower numbers in the meter signature. True _____ False _____

16. In a compound meter signature, the top number usually indicates the number of beats per measure. True _____ False _____

Scale Structures

G O A L S

- The understanding of scale concepts as applied to basic, diatonic, chromatic, and whole-tone scales

- The understanding of major-scale structures

- The understanding of minor-scale structures and variation forms

- The ability to write and identify the above-mentioned types of scales, beginning on any pitch

SCALE

A **scale** may be defined as a series of incremental pitches, contained within an octave; however, to be more specific, one may say that most scales are constructed as a series of **diatonic** step increments. Scale pitches are assembled in either ascending or descending configurations without the repetition or omission of any letter names. The scale usually concludes with a repeated octave at the end of the series. Example 4.1 illustrates a basic (without chromatic alterations) diatonic scale.

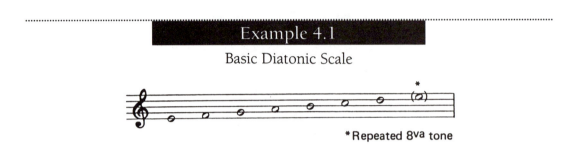

Example 4.1

Basic Diatonic Scale

*Repeated 8va tone

BASIC DIATONIC SCALES

The diatonic-scale configuration, with one exception to be discussed later, consists of specific patterns of whole and half steps. To construct a basic diatonic scale (without chromatic alterations), you may begin on any pitch and move in consecutive order, either ascending or descending, without omitting or repeating any notes, until all seven pitches have been presented. The eighth note will be an octave repetition (Ex. 4.2). Since there are seven basic diatonic pitches, this scale may begin on any one of them and end with the octave repetition.

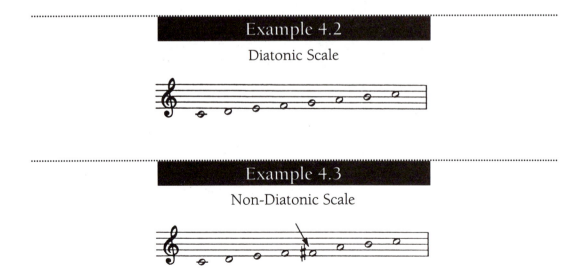

Example 4.2

Diatonic Scale

Example 4.3

Non-Diatonic Scale

Example 4.3 illustrates a nondiatonic scale structure because of the chromatically altered and repeated note, F, F♯. Since all basic diatonic scales encompass all seven unaltered tones, each scale would contain two sets of NOHS: the E–F as well as the B–C half step. Therefore, it may be stated that all basic diatonic scales contain two half steps, the remaining five scale steps being whole steps (Ex. 4.4).

Example 4.4

```
   1   1   *   1   1   1   *
 C - D - E * F - G - A - B * C
     D - E * F - G - A - B * C - D
         E * F - G - A - B * C - D - E
             F - G - A - B * C - D - E * F
                 G - A - B * C - D - E * F - G
                     A - B * C - D - E * F - G - A
                         B * C - D - E * F - G - A - B
                           *   1   1   *   1   1   1
```

*NOHS (Naturally Occurring Half Steps)

Since any of the seven basic pitches can serve as the beginning note of a scale, seven diatonic scales can be notated as basic scales (i.e., without any chromatic alterations). Each of these incorporates the two NOHS (naturally occurring half steps) in different locations within the scales. The ascending diatonic scale written from C to C positions the NOHS between the third and fourth scale degrees and also between the seventh and eighth (octave) scale degrees.

Example 4.5

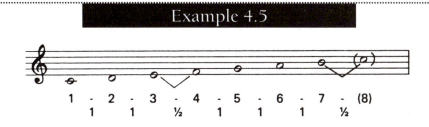

```
 1 - 2 - 3 - 4 - 5 - 6 - 7 - (8)
   1   1   ½   1   1   1   ½
```

Therefore, in the ascending scale from C to C, half steps occur between steps 3 and 4 and steps 7 and 8. This arrangement of whole and half steps creates what is known as a **major scale**.

MAJOR SCALES AND TETRACHORDS

In dealing with specific diatonic tonal scales, such as major and minor scales, the concept of **tetrachord** structure is quite helpful. A tetrachord is a four-note section or portion of a scale structure; it must be either the first, or lower, four notes of the scale or the last, or upper, four notes. Only four possible configurations exist for any given basic tetrachord (Ex. 4.6).

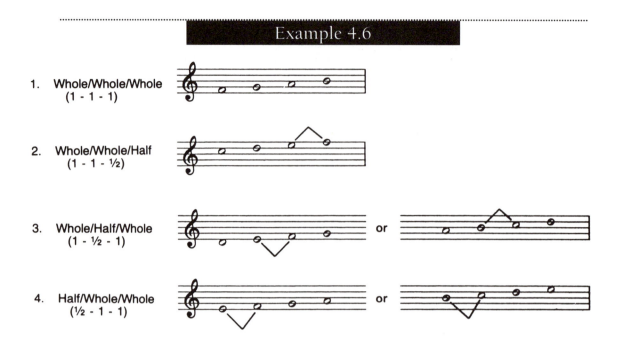

Every diatonic scale (seven tones plus the octave repetition) contains two tetra-chords, one upper and one lower tetrachord (Ex. 4.7).

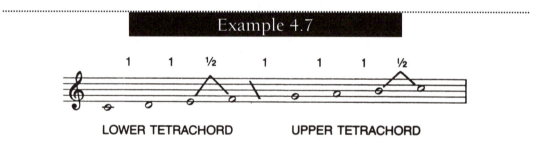

Note in Example 4.7 that the whole- and half-step configuration of the first, or lower, tetrachord is identical to the configuration in the second, or upper tetra-chord—namely, whole/whole/half. The two tetrachords in a major scale are sym-metrical in terms of whole- and half-step configurations. Also note that the two tetrachords are connected by a whole step. This connection of tetrachords will hold constant in all major and minor scales, that is, the two tetrachords will *always* con-nected by a whole step. Therefore, the configuration for any major scale is as shown in Example 4.8.

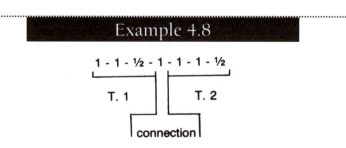

This whole/whole/half configuration is the only element that must be memorized for major scales. Since the tetrachords are symmetrical and connect by a whole step, any pitch can be selected as a starting note, and a major scale can be constructed quite easily by following these procedural steps (also see Ex. 4.9).

1. Given a starting pitch, construct a *basic* scale, including the octave repetition.
2. Number the scale degrees and divide them into two tetrachords.
3. Begin with the first tone and adjust, if necessary, the next (second) tone to conform with the step configuration (W–W–H). Continue in this manner through the fourth tone (last of the lower tetrachord).
4. Connect the first tetrachord to the second tetrachord by a whole step.
5. Repeat step 3 to complete the upper tetrachord of the scale.

Example 4.9

Procedure for Writing Out a Major Scale on *E*

STEP 1:   Construct Basic Scale

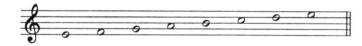

STEP 2:   Divide into Tetrachords

STEP 3:   Add Chromatic Signs to Lower Tetrachord

STEPS 4 & 5: Connect by Whole Step and Adjust Upper Tetrachord

The basic scale beginning on *C* has **NOHS** already between scale degrees 3 and 4 and between degrees 7 and 8; therefore, the *C*-major scale needs no further chromatic alteration (sharps or flats). It is the *only* major scale requiring no alterations. All others must have one or more chromatic sign(s) present.

MINOR SCALES AND TETRACHORDS

The basic scale beginning on *C,* as previously discussed, is the "model" for the major scale; likewise, the basic scale beginning on *A* becomes the "model" for minor scales. The basic scale beginning on *A* also contains no chromatic signs or alterations and forms what is known as the **minor scale.** The two tetrachords (lower and upper) *are not symmetrical* as they are in major scales; in fact, the upper tetrachord in minor has three possible variations, while the lower tetrachord remains constant. This variable upper tetrachord is a unique property of minor scales, unlike the consistent tetrachord structure of major scales (Ex. 4.10).

Examples 4.10

The Minor Scale with Variations

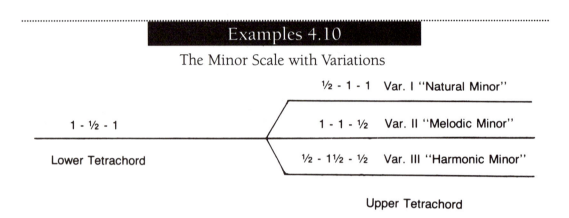

It would be incorrect to think of the minor as being three distinct minor scales; rather, one minor scale has three possible variations in the upper tetrachord. (The lower tetrachord will always be the configuration whole/half/whole.) Example 4.11 shows the notation of the upper tetrachord's three variations of the minor scale beginning on *A.*

Example 4.11

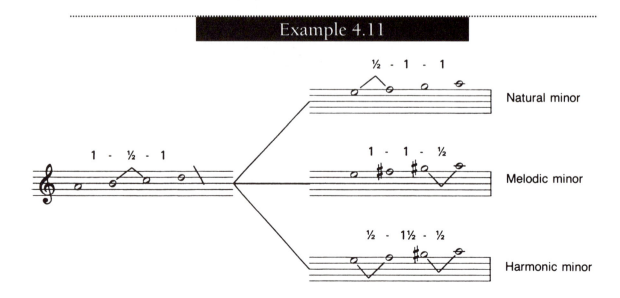

Harmonic Form of Minor

The harmonic form of minor incorporates the same lower tetrachord found in natural minor (whole/half/whole) and connects to its upper tetrachord by a whole step. The upper tetrachord begins with the same half step from the fifth to the sixth scale degrees as in natural minor but adds an additional half step between the seventh and eighth scale degrees by raising the seventh one half step. This results in a one-and-one-half-step increment between the sixth and seventh scale degrees. Thus the harmonic form of minor uses three sets of half steps, between scale degrees 2 and 3, 5 and 6, and 7 and 8 (refer back to Ex. 4.11).

Melodic Form of Minor

It must be noted that the whole- and half-step configurations for melodic minor refer to *only the ascending form*. The scale reverts to natural minor when it appears in *descending form*. All scales should be identifiable as major or minor by hearing or seeing in notation the first four notes (tetrachord) in either direction (ascending or descending). Only the upper tetrachord of the melodic minor form can be confusing, in that it is identical to the upper tetrachord configuration in a major scale (W–W–H). Since it can be confused with the upper tetrachord of major, and therefore its quality may not be determined until the lower tetrachord is notated or heard, melodic minor *always* descends as a natural minor scale; that is, it is altered so as to appear the same as the natural minor form. In other words, melodic minor has an ascending as well as a descending form (Ex. 4.12).

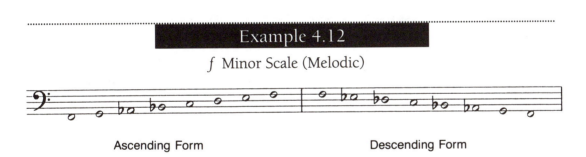

Example 4.12

ƒ Minor Scale (Melodic)

Ascending Form   Descending Form

It is interesting to note, as in Example 4.12, that the upper tetrachord in the melodic minor form of the scale has the same whole- and half-step configuration as does the upper tetrachord in major scales. It is also interesting to note that the upper tetrachord of the natural minor form contains the whole- and half-step configuration in exact reverse order of that found in the upper tetrachord of the melodic form of the minor scale (Ex. 4.13).

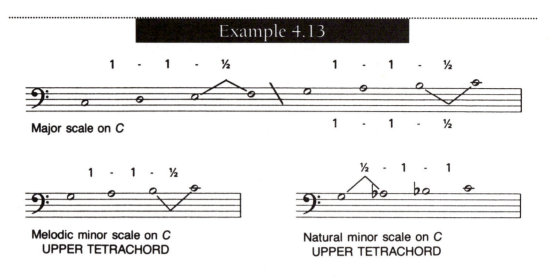

Example 4.13

1 - 1 - ½   1 - 1 - ½

1 - 1 - ½

Major scale on *C*

1 - 1 - ½

Melodic minor scale on *C*
UPPER TETRACHORD

½ - 1 - 1

Natural minor scale on *C*
UPPER TETRACHORD

CHROMATIC SCALE

A **chromatic scale** is constructed entirely of half steps. In each chromatic scale there are twelve half steps within the octave. The repetition of the octave creates the thirteenth note of the scale. Chromatic scales are represented by a combination of diatonic as well as chromatic half-step motion. If the scale were entirely structured in chromatic motion, then one would never change letter names within the scale (Ex. 4.14).

Example 4.14

All Chromatic Half Steps

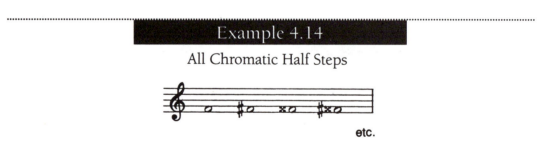

etc.

By alternating between diatonic and chromatic half-step motion, one can easily notate either an ascending or descending chromatic scale with a minimum amount of necessary chromatic signs (Ex. 4.15).

Example 4.15

Correct (minimal) Usage of Chromatic Signs

a.

b.

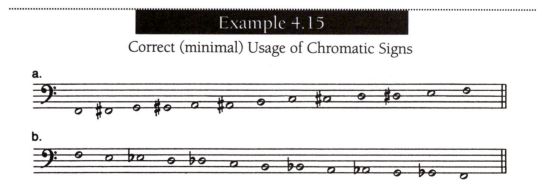

Note that, when ascending, sharps are used (Ex. 4.15a); conversely, when descending, flats are used (Ex. 4.15b). This practice avoids the redundant usage of natural signs, which would be required if flats were to be used in an ascending scale and sharps used in a descending scale (Exx. 4.16a and b).

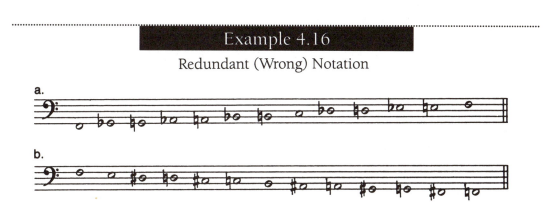

Example 4.16
Redundant (Wrong) Notation

a.

b.

WHOLE-TONE SCALES

The **whole-tone** scale is perhaps the simplest of all scale forms to understand. It is composed solely of whole steps and includes the repeated octave tone. Somewhere within the scale an enharmonic spelling must occur. In spelling these enharmonic whole steps, one letter of the diatonic musical alphabet is omitted between adjacent scale degrees; for example, E, G♭, or C♯, E♭, or B, D♭, and so on. Without this enharmonic spelling, the scale would not end on the same letter-name pitch with which it began (Exx. 4.17 and 4.18). The whole-tone scale is a perfectly symmetrical scale structure and has no half steps whatsoever.

Example 4.17

without enharmonic spelling

Example 4.18

**with* enharmonic spelling

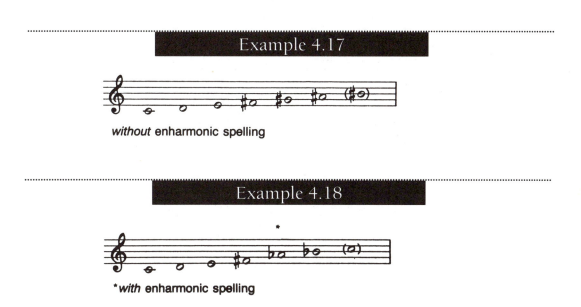

SUMMARY

To summarize the three types of scale configurations presented so far, let us use the following diagrams.

I. *DIATONIC* (seven-tone scale plus the octave repetition):

```
    1     1    ½    1    1    1    ½
 C - D -  E  * F -  G -  A -  B  * C
     D-   E  * F -  G -  A -  B  * C - D
          E  * F -  G -  A -  B  * C - D -  E
               F -  G -  A -  B  * C - D -  E  * F
                    G -  A -  B  * C - D -  E  * F - G
                         A -  B  * C - D -  E  * F - G -  A
                              B  * C - D -  E  * F - G -  A - B
 *NOHS                        ½    1    1    ½    1    1    1
```

II. *CHROMATIC* (12-tone scale plus the octave repetition).
It can begin and end on any pitch:

```
C - C♯ - D - D♯ - E*F - F♯ - G - G♯ - A - A♯ - B*C      Ascending
C*B - B♭ - A - A♭ - G - G♭ - F*E - E♭ - D - D♭ - C      Descending
```

III. *WHOLE-TONE* (Six-tone scale plus the octave repetition):

```
C - D - E - F♯ - A♭ - B♭ - C
(should contain an enharmonic spelling)
```

The major/minor scale system—a system known as **tonality**—governs the pitch content of music. The tonal center of a piece of music is considered the keynote (first scale degree) of the major or minor scale upon which both melody and harmony are based. This system is evident today in popular music and has been with us since the beginning of the eighteenth century. A **modal** system of scale structures predates the major/minor system. The basic scales not only provide us with the models for the major/minor system but also with the models for modal scale structures. (**Modal scale concepts are presented as an optional unit in Appendix E.**)

Complete the chapter 4 drill sheets on the following pages before continuing. Also, see Appendix A and Appendix B.

CHAPTER FOUR DRILLS AND EXERCISES

SCALES I

1. Write out the following *basic* scales, beginning on the given pitches, and indicate the half-step locations as shown.

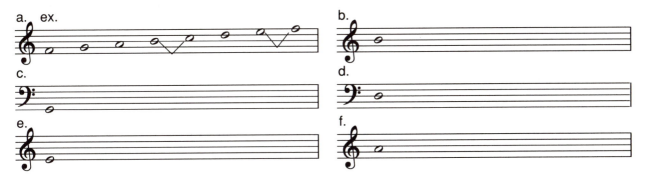

2. Given the whole- and half-step configurations below, name the basic diatonic scale represented by each one.

a. (ex.) 1-½-1-1-1-½-1 = basic scale on *D.*

b. 1-1-1-½-1-1-½- = _____.
c. ½-1-1-1-½-1-1- = _____.
d. ½-1-1-½-1-1-1- = _____.
e. 1-1-½-1-1-½-1- = _____.
f. 1-1-½-1-1-1-½- = _____.
g. 1-½-1-1-½-1-1- = _____.

3. Write out the following *chromatic* scales, beginning on the given pitches, in the direction indicated.

a.

(descending)

b.

(ascending)

c.

(ascending)

4. Notate WHOLE-TONE scales, begining on the indicated pitch:

a. (ascending)

b. (descending)

c. (ascending)

d. (descending)

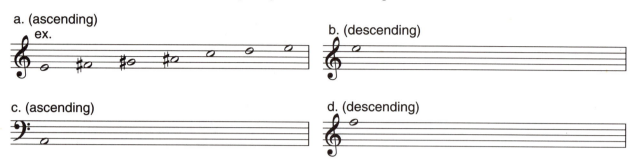

5. Given the following basic scales, convert each to major by adding the appropriate chromatic signs. Consider the starting pitch as tonic.

a. ex.

b.

c.

d.

e.

f.

g.

h.

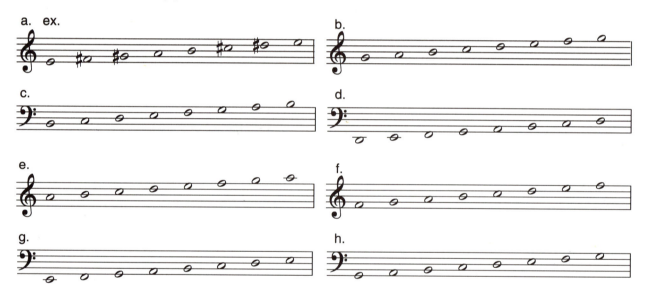

6. Given the following basic scales, convert each to natural minor by adding the appriopriate chromatic signs. Consider the starting pitch as tonic.

a. ex.

b.

c.

d.

e.

f.

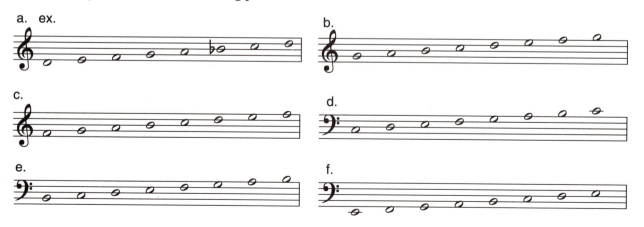

7. Given the natural minor scales below, convert each one to the requested form by adding the appropriate chromatic signs.

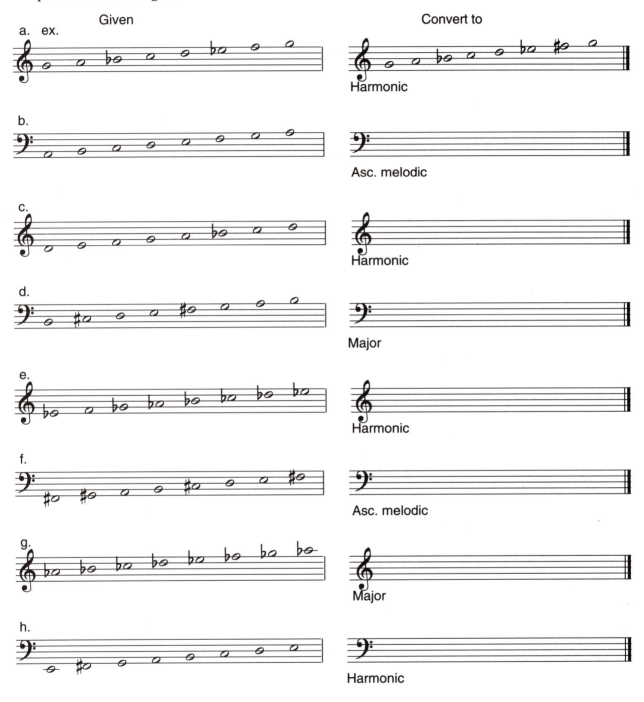

8. In each of the examples below, a tetrachord is given. Determine the whole- and half-step configuration of each tetrachord, decide whether to use the given tetrachord as a lower or an upper tetrachord, then incorporate it into either a major or minor scale in notation.

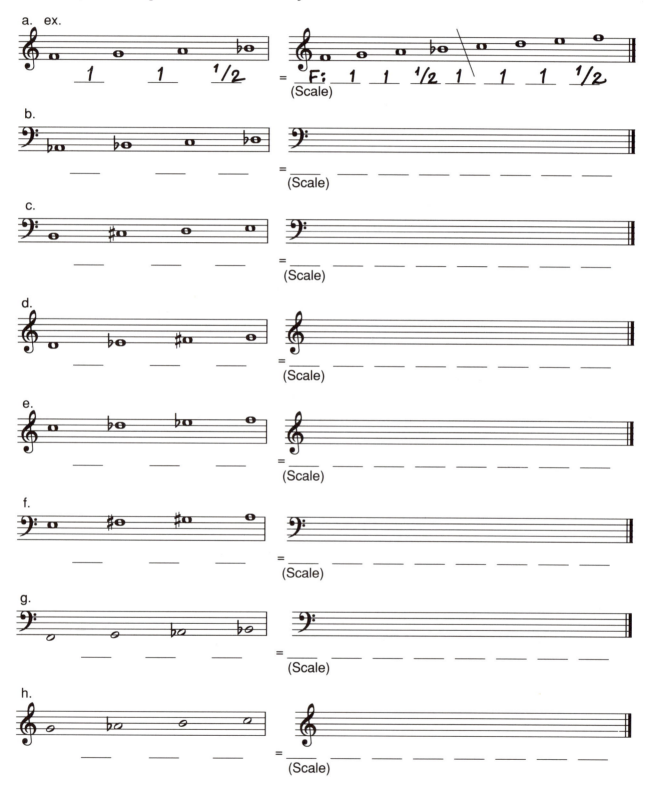

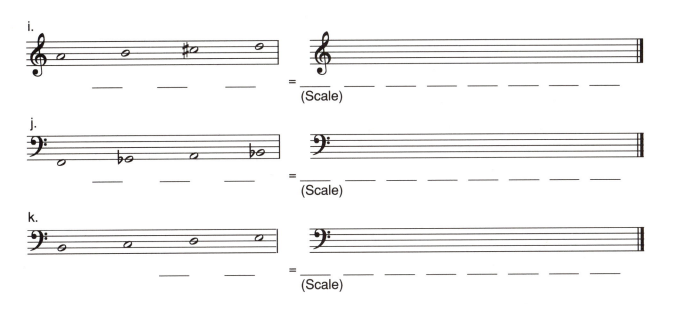

SCALES I REVIEW (SELF-TEST: CHAPTER FOUR)

1. There are _____ (number) basic diatonic scales.

2. Each basic diatonic scale contains _____ (number) half steps and _____ (number) whole steps.

3. In the basic diatonic scale beginning on *C*, half steps occur between _____ and _____ (scale-degree letters) and between _____ and _____.

4. In the basic diatonic scale beginning on *A*, half steps occur between _____ and _____ (scale degree numbers) and between _____ and _____.

5. In a basic diatonic scale, no chromaticism occurs between scale degrees. True _____ False _____

6. All basic diatonic scales contain _____ (number) different pitches with an octave repetition of the beginning pitch.

7. Naturally occurring half steps (NOHS) in basic diatonic scales occur between _____ and _____ (letters) and between _____ and _____.

8. A chromatic scale contains _____ (number) different pitches with an octave repetition of the beginning pitch.

9. In a chromatic scale, _____ (sharps or flats) are employed in the ascending form of the scale and _____ (sharps or flats) are used in the descending form of the scale.

10. Whole-tone scales contain _____ (number) different pitches plus an octave repetition of the beginning pitch.

11. Whole-tone scales contain at least one enharmonic whole step, for example *G♯–B♭*, *A♯–C*, *F♯–A♭*, in order for the scale to end an octave above (or below) the beginning pitch. True _____ False _____

12. Some whole-tone scales contain a half step between adjacent scale degrees. True _____ False _____

13. Any given major scale contains mostly whole steps and two sets of half steps, which always fall between _____ and _____ (scale-degree numbers) and between _____ and _____.

14. Tetrachords in major scales are always symmetrical (lower and upper the same). True _____ False _____

15. Tetrachords in minor scales (natural) are always symmetrical (lower and upper the same). True _____ False _____

16. All major and minor (all forms) scales have two sets of half steps. True _____ False _____

17. The descending form of the melodic minor scale has the same tetrachord configuration as _____ minor.

18. In all major and minor (all forms) scales, there is always a whole step between tetrachords. True _____ False _____

Major, Minor, and Pentatonic Scales (Scale Structures II)

G O A L S

• The understanding of relative and parallel major and minor scale relationships

• The ability to convert any major scale to any form of minor scale and vice versa

• The understanding of and ability to write anhemitonic and hemitonic pentatonic scale structures

• The understanding of terms naming diatonic scale degrees for major and minor scales

RELATIVE MAJOR AND MINOR SCALE STRUCTURES

Every major scale uses the same pitches or notes and chromatic signs as does a corresponding natural minor scale. These corresponding major and minor scales are identified as relative major and minor scales (Ex. 5.1).

Example 5.1

The notes and their order, or placement, in each of the above scales are the same. One could say that the only difference is where one begins and ends the spelling of the scale. The minor (natural form) is the same series of pitches, except that it begins on the sixth scale degree of the major scale (Ex. 5.2).

Example 5.2

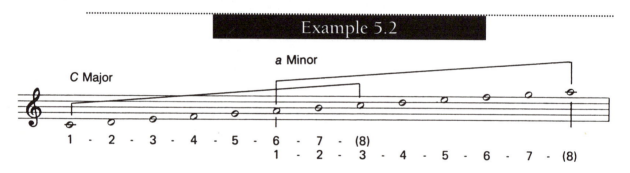

In Example 5.2, the scales used as illustration are *C* major and *a* minor. Note that lower-case letters are used when referring to minor scales while upper-case letters indicate major scales. Given any major scale, the **relative minor** scale always utilizes the same pitches, but it begins on the sixth scale degree of its major counterpart. Relative minor, therefore, can be defined as a minor scale having the same notes as its relative major, but with a different starting (and ending) pitch. Whatever chromatic signs appear in the major scale will also appear in the relative minor. These same chromatically altered pitches will, in the relative minor, have different placement with respect to scale degree (Ex. 5.3).

Example 5.3

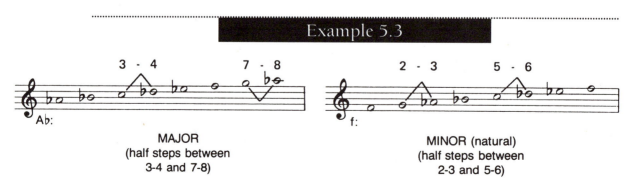

MAJOR
(half steps between
3-4 and 7-8)

MINOR (natural)
(half steps between
2-3 and 5-6)

Given any minor (natural form) scale, to find the **relative major**, merely use the same pitches found in the given minor scale and spell the scale beginning on the third scale degree. As in Example 5.4, only the numbering changes, and this, in turn, alters the position of whole and half steps. *The pitches remain the same as well as all chromatic alterations.*

Example 5.4

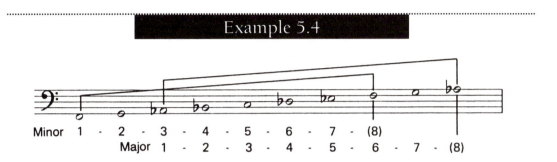

```
Minor   1 · 2 · 3 · 4 · 5 · 6 · 7 · (8)
              Major  1 · 2 · 3 · 4 · 5 · 6 · 7 · (8)
```

PARALLEL MAJOR AND MINOR SCALE STRUCTURES

The only other relationship between major and minor scale structures is the **parallel** relationship. In this respect, both major as well as minor scales begin and end on the same pitch. Having the identical starting pitch, the scales will differ in terms of chromatic signs. Since both scales begin on the same pitch, different chromatic alterations are necessary in order to conform to the standard whole- and half-step requirements of each scale (major = 1–1–1/2—1—1–1–1/2; and minor = 1–1/2–1—1—1/2–1–1). In other words, to convert a given major scale to a parallel minor (natural form): (1) begin on the same pitch as with the major; (2) spell the scale using the same chromatic alterations as they apply to the same pitches in the major scale; then (3) *lower* the third, sixth, and seventh scale degrees of the major scale by one chromatic half step (Ex. 5.5).

Example 5.5

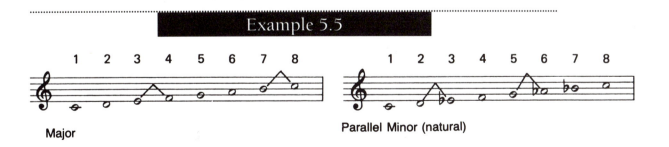

Major   Parallel Minor (natural)

Given a minor scale (natural form), to find the parallel major, do just the reverse: (1) begin the major scale on the same note as the minor; (2) spell the scale using the same pitches and chromatic alterations as they appear in the minor; then (3) *raise* the third, sixth, and seventh scale degrees by one chromatic half step.

When comparing and constructing major and minor scales, the chart in Example 5.6 should prove useful. It refers to parallel relationships (scales having the same starting note).

Example 5.6

GIVEN	TO FORM:			
	Major	Natural min.	Harmonic min.	Melodic min.
Major	—	lower 3, 6, 7	lower 3, 6	lower 3
Natural min.	raise 3, 6, 7	—	raise 7	raise 6, 7
Harmonic min.	raise 3, 6	lower 7	—	raise 6
Melodic min.	raise 3	lower 6, 7	lower 6	—

SCALE-DEGREE NAMES

Standard terminology exists to refer to specific scale-degree notes for major and minor scales. The terms are as follows:

Example 5.7

SCALE DEGREES   NAMES

1 . . . . TONIC
2 . . . . SUPERTONIC (one whole step above tonic)
3 . . . . MEDIANT (half way between 1 and 5) (third *above* tonic)
4 . . . . SUBDOMINANT (the fifth *below* tonic)
5 . . . . DOMINANT (the fifth *above* tonic)
6 . . . . SUBMEDIANT (the third *below* tonic)
7 . . . . LEADING TONE—when ½ step below tonic
SUBTONIC—when a whole-step below tonic (as in natural minor scales)

PENTATONIC SCALES

A **pentatonic** scale is a scale configuration that consists of only five tones plus the repeated octave tone. Any five tones within the octave may be used (Ex. 5.8); however, standard forms of pentatonic scales tend to spread out the tones of the scale throughout the octave (Ex. 5.9).

Example 5.8

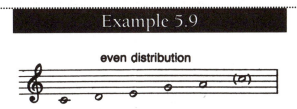

Example 5.9

even distribution

Example 5.8 represents a scale structure that exhibits a "cluster" or tight grouping of tones; Example 5.9 illustrates a more even distribution of tones within the octave. Standard forms of pentatonic scales include the **anhemitonic pentatonic** and the **hemitonic pentatonic** configurations. The anhemitonic form (which means without half steps) contains only whole-step and one-and-one-half-step increments. Examples 5.10 and 5.11 illustrate two types of anhemitonic structures.

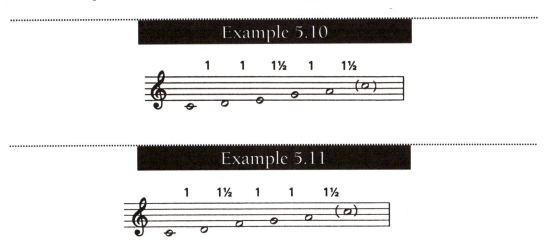

Example 5.10

Example 5.11

These two anhemitonic structures (Exx. 5.10 and 5.11) contain the same step configurations; that is, they both contain whole-step and one-and-one-half-step increments. Essentially, Example 5.11 is the same as Example 5.10 if you were to follow the configuration of increments beginning at the fourth tone of Example 5.10. Example 5.11 contains the same step-increment configuration as found in Example 5.10 if you were to begin on the third tone (*F*) instead of on *C* (Ex. 5.12).

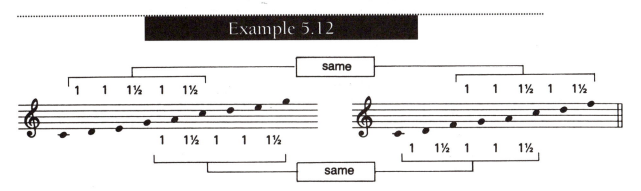

Example 5.12

The hemitonic forms consist of whole-, half-, and two-whole-step configurations (1–1/2–2) as illustrated in Examples 5.13 and 5.14.

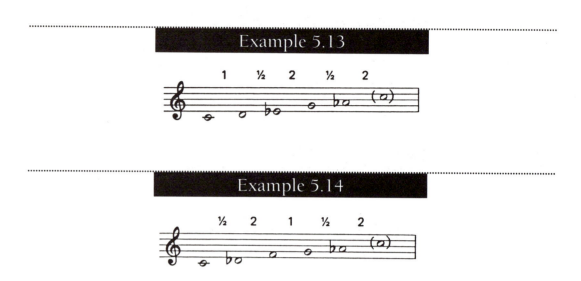

Again, you should note that Example 5.14 is essentially the same as Example 5.13, if you were to follow the configuration of increments beginning at the fourth note of Example 5.13; that is, Example 5.14 contains the same step increments as found in Example 5.13 when beginning on *F* instead of on *C* (Ex. 5.15).

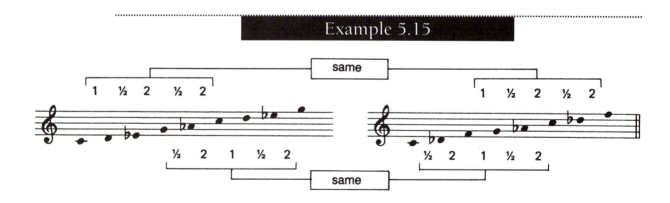

Another way to construct either anhemitonic or hemitonic pentatonic scales is to "extract" them from either major or natural minor scale systems. Given either a major or natural minor scale, with each of the scale degrees numbered (1 through 8), one can extract a pentatonic scale by selecting only the 1, 2, 3, 5, 6, and 1 (or 8) scale degrees from each scale. In other words, delete degrees 4 and 7. To illustrate this, the *C*-major and parallel *c*-minor scales are examined (Exx. 5.16a and b).

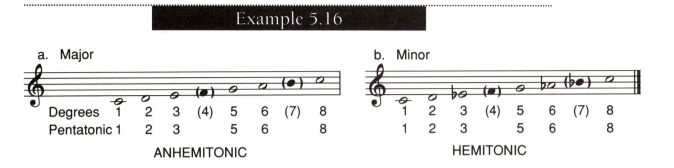

Example 5.16

a. Major

| Degrees | 1 | 2 | 3 | (4) | 5 | 6 | (7) | 8 |
| Pentatonic | 1 | 2 | 3 | | 5 | 6 | | 8 |

ANHEMITONIC

b. Minor

| Degrees | 1 | 2 | 3 | (4) | 5 | 6 | (7) | 8 |
| Pentatonic | 1 | 2 | 3 | | 5 | 6 | | 8 |

HEMITONIC

When selecting the pentatonic scale degrees (1, 2, 3, 5, 6, and 8) from the major scale system, no half steps occur, thus forming the anhemitonic pentatonic scale. When doing the same from the minor system (1, 2, 3, 5, 6, and 8), half steps will occur between 2 and 3, and between 5 and 6, as they would normally occur in natural minor, thus forming the hemitonic pentatonic scale.

This manner of constructing either anhemitonic or hemitonic pentatonic scales eliminates the necessity of counting whole-step, half-step, one-and-a-half-step, or two-whole-step increments in the scale's construction. You will have to rely upon your understanding of, and accuracy in writing, major and minor scales.

In summary, any anhemitonic pentatonic scale can be written on any given pitch by writing a major scale structure, then extracting and using *only* the scale degrees 1, 2, 3, 5, 6, and 8. Likewise, any hemitonic pentatonic scale can be written on any given pitch by writing a natural minor scale structure, then extracting and using only the same (1, 2, 3, 5, 6, and 8) scale degrees.

Pentatonic scale structures were at one time thought to have Asian origins, but in fact they sprang almost simultaneously from several different world cultures and are therefore equally indigenous to many musical cultures, including that of the native American Indian. One might say that the pentatonic scale structure is common to more world cultures than any other scale system.

In summary, pentatonic scales consist of five tones plus the octave repetition. The following charts illustrate the standard anhemitonic and hemitonic configurations beginning on *C*.

ANHEMITONIC	*HEMITONIC*
(C - D - E - - G - A - - C)	(C - D - E♭ - G - A♭ - C)
1 - 1 - 1½ - 1 - 1½	1 - ½ - 2 - ½ - 2
(or) ———————	(or) ———————
(C - D - - F - G - A - - C)	(C - D♭ - F - G - A♭ - C)
1 - 1½ - 1 - 1 - 1½	½ - 2 - 1 - ½ - 2

Complete the chapter 5 drill sheets on the following pages before continuing. Also, see Appendix A and Appendix B.

CHAPTER FIVE DRILLS AND EXERCISES

1. Given the following major scales, write out both the parallel as well as the relative minor scales (natural).

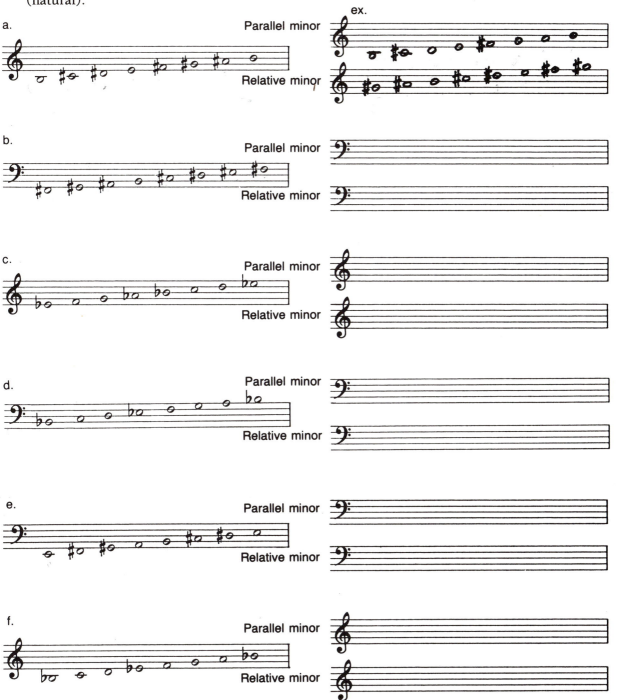

2. Given the scales notated below, analyze the whole- and half-step configurations in each and identify each scale.

a. ex. = E Major
(Scale)

b. = _____
(Scale)

c. = _____
(Scale)

d. = _____
(Scale)

e. = _____
(Scale)

f. = _____
(Scale)

g. = _____
(Scale)

h. = _____
(Scale)

i. = _____
(Scale)

j. = _____
(Scale)

3. Write out anhemitonic pentatonic scales beginning on the given pitches and label the step increments in each scale.

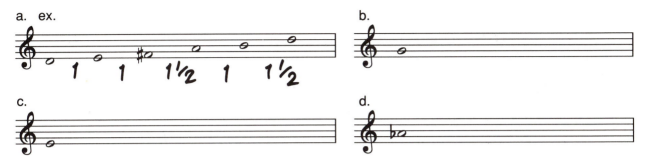

4. Write out hemitonic pentatonic scales beginning on the given pitches:

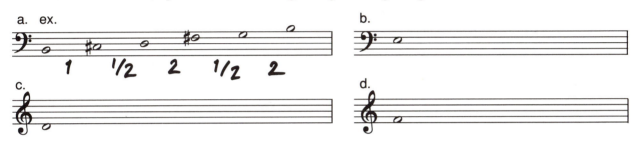

SCALES II REVIEW (SELF-TEST: CHAPTER FIVE)

1. In terms of whole and half steps, what is the upper tetrachord structure of:

    a. Natural minor _____.

    b. Ascending melodic minor _____.

    c. Harmonic minor _____.

    d. Major _____.

2. Half steps in major must occur between the _____ and _____ and between the _____ and _____ scale degrees.

3. All tetrachords in major and minor scales are connected by a whole step. True _____ False _____

4. Both upper and lower tetrachords in major scales have the same configuration of whole and half steps. True _____ False _____

5. The subdominants of any given major and its parallel minor (natural) are the same notes. True _____ False _____

6. The dominants of any given minor scale and its relative major are the same notes. True _____ False _____

7. A minor scale and its relative major have the same starting pitches. True _____ False _____

8. The mediant scale degree in major becomes the starting note for its relative minor. True _____ False _____

9. Naturally occurring half steps (NOHS) can be found between ____ and ____ and between ____ and ____.

10. A pentatonic scale contains _____ (number) different pitches plus an octave repetition of the beginning pitch.

11. A hemitonic pentatonic scale contains at least one _____ (whole step/half step).

12. An anhemitonic pentatonic scale contains no _____(whole steps/half steps).

13. A hemitonic pentatonic scale can be extracted from a major scale by omitting the fourth and seventh scale degrees. True _____ False _____

14. Pentatonic scales extracted from the minor scale will contain half steps. True _____ False _____

15. All forms of minor have a different descending structure. True _____ False _____

Intervals

GOALS

- The ability to write any interval on the staff

- The ability to identify any interval aurally

- The ability to sing any interval

- The ability to play any interval on the keyboard

- The ability to analyze intervals in a musical score

A knowledge of intervals is perhaps one of the most important skills that a musician must possess. For reading and analyzing music, performing, composing, studying harmony and counterpoint, or learning a new musical style, a complete knowledge of intervals is essential.

An **interval** is described as the distance, space, or difference in frequency between two pitches. An interval is labeled **melodic** if the two pitches are played in succession and is labeled **harmonic** if the two pitches are played simultaneously (Ex. 6.1).

Example 6.1

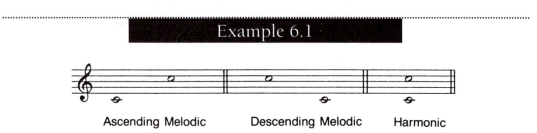

Ascending Melodic   Descending Melodic   Harmonic

In order to analyze an interval, it is necessary to determine both the numerical size and the quality.

NUMERICAL CLASSIFICATION

This procedure simply involves counting every line and space from one pitch up or down to the next pitch. The starting pitch (the first line or space) is always counted as number one.

Example 6.2 illustrates basic intervals (unaltered by chromatic signs) from the unison, or **prime**, to the octave.

Example 6.2

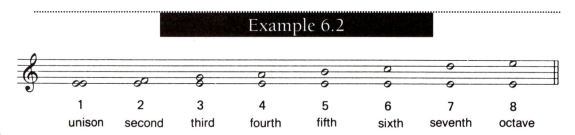

| 1 | 2 | 3 | 4 | 5 | 6 | 7 | 8 |
| unison | second | third | fourth | fifth | sixth | seventh | octave |

The addition of chromatic signs does not change the numerical classification. The intervals given in Example 6.3 are a seventh, unison, sixth, fourth, octave, third, second, and fifth.

Example 6.3

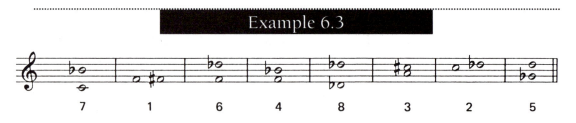

7   1   6   4   8   3   2   5

QUALITY CLASSIFICATION

The quality names for intervals are perfect, major, minor, augmented, and diminished. The capital or lower-case letters given below are used to identify the proper quality classification.

P = perfect   d = diminished
M = major   AA = doubly augmented
m = minor   dd = doubly diminished
A = augmented

Doubly augmented and doubly diminished intervals are rarely found in music.

PERFECT INTERVALS

Only the intervals of a unison, octave, fifth, and fourth can be termed **perfect intervals.**

A **perfect unison** is the repetition or the simultaneous playing of the same pitch with the same spelling. There is no space or distance between the pitches of a perfect unison (Ex. 6.4).

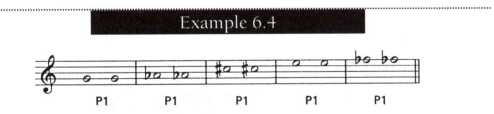

A **perfect octave** is an interval in which two tones have the same spelling but are separated by a distance of twelve half steps or six whole steps. In order to retain a perfect quality, both notes must have the same number and kind of chromatic signs (Ex. 6.5).

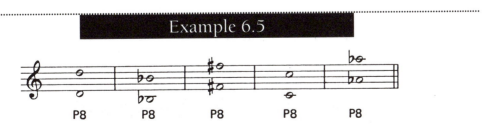

When determining the numerical classification of an interval, the first note (upper or lower) is always counted as number one. When determining the number of half steps or whole steps in an interval, the starting note is always counted as zero.

A **perfect fifth** contains seven half steps or three-and-a-half whole steps. Both notes of the interval of a fifth will be written either on lines or in spaces (Ex. 6.6).

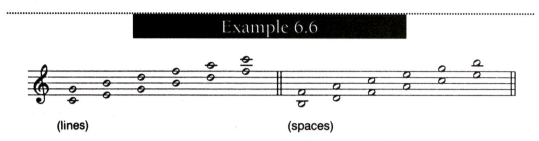

Example 6.6

(lines)   (spaces)

All basic fifths are perfect except the fifth *B* to *F*, which is one half step smaller than a perfect fifth. In order for it to be perfect, the interval must be expanded by one half step; that is, the *F* must be raised one half step with a sharp (*B–F♯*) or the *B* must be lowered to *B♭* (*B♭–F*) (Ex. 6.7).

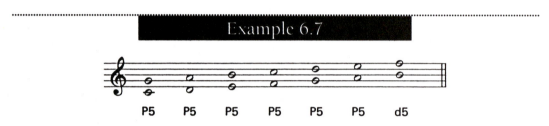

Example 6.7

P5   P5   P5   P5   P5   P5   d5

A fifth will be perfect if it spans one NOHS (naturally occurring half step). If the fifth spans two NOHS, it will be one half step smaller than a perfect fifth, thus making it diminished.

Example 6.8

(NOHS: Naturally Occurring Half Steps)

In Example 6.8, note that the interval *B* to *F* spans both the *B* to *C* as well as the *E* to *F* NOHS. As a result, this fifth is diminished.

An analysis of the basic fifths in Example 6.7 can provide a system of thinking that can make the spelling of perfect fifths relatively easy. In spelling perfect fifths, both the upper and lower notes will have the same number and kind of chromatic signs, except when *B* (or *B* altered) is the lower note. In this case, in order to retain a perfect quality, the upper note will be one chromatic sign higher than the lower note.

In each pair of notes in Example 6.9, both the upper and lower notes have the same number and kind of chromatic signs, and, as a result, all are perfect fifths.

Example 6.9

If **B** (or *B* altered) is the lower note of a perfect fifth, the upper note is always one chromatic sign higher than the lower note (Ex. 6.10).

Example 6.10

ALL MAJOR AND MINOR SCALES CONTAIN A PERFECT FIFTH (ASCENDING) FROM TONIC TO DOMINANT.

A **perfect fourth** contains five half steps or two-and-a-half whole steps. Note that a perfect fourth is one diatonic whole step smaller than a perfect fifth.

All basic fourths are perfect except the fourth from *F* to *B*, which is one half step larger than a perfect fourth. In order to make it perfect, the *B* must be lowered to *B*♭, or the *F* must be raised to *F*♯. A basic fourth will be perfect if it spans one NOHS. If it does not span one NOHS, it will be one half step larger than a perfect fourth, thus making it augmented (Ex. 6.11).

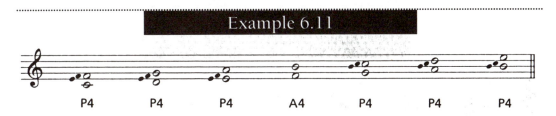

Example 6.11

P4   P4   P4   A4   P4   P4   P4

An analysis of the basic fourths in Example 6.11 can again provide a thought process that can aid in the spelling of perfect fourths. In spelling perfect fourths, both the upper and lower notes will have the same number and kind of chromatic signs, except when *F* (or *F* altered) is the lower note. In this case, the upper note will be one chromatic sign lower.

In the pairs of notes in Example 6.12, both the upper and lower notes have the same number and kind of chromatic signs, and, as a result, all are perfect fourths.

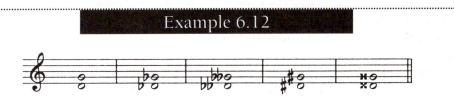

Example 6.12

If *F* (or *F* altered) is the lower note of a perfect fourth, the upper note is always one chromatic sign lower (Ex. 6.13).

Example 6.13

ALL MAJOR AND MINOR SCALES CONTAIN A PERFECT FOURTH (ASCENDING) FROM TONIC TO SUBDOMINANT.

MAJOR AND MINOR INTERVALS

Only the intervals of a second, third, sixth, and seventh can be termed major or minor intervals. (Ninths and other intervals larger than an octave will be discussed later in this chapter.)

A **minor second** contains one diatonic half step, and it is always spelled with adjacent letters in the musical alphabet.

A **major second** contains one diatonic whole step (or two half steps, one diatonic and one chromatic), and it is always spelled with adjacent letters in the musical alphabet. A major second is one chromatic half step larger than a minor second.

Of the seven basic seconds, five are major and two are minor. Note that all seconds are written on adjacent lines and spaces on the staff (Ex. 6.14).

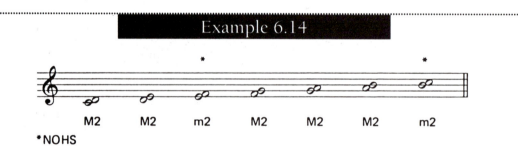

Example 6.14

M2   M2   m2   M2   M2   M2   m2

*NOHS

A **minor third** contains three half steps or one-and-a-half whole steps.

A **major third** contains four half steps or two whole steps. A major third is one chromatic half step larger than a minor third and one diatonic whole step larger than a major second. When spelling a third of any quality, always skip one letter of the musical alphabet between the lower and higher notes (Ex. 6.15).

Example 6.15

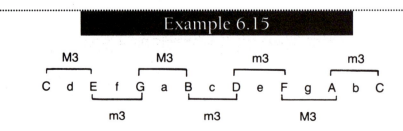

Of the basic thirds, three are major and four are minor. Note that all thirds are written either on two adjacent lines or on two adjacent spaces. A basic minor third spans one NOHS, and a basic major third spans no NOHS (Ex. 6.16).

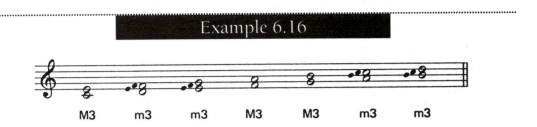

A **minor sixth** contains eight half steps or four whole steps. A minor sixth is one diatonic half step larger than a perfect fifth.

A **major sixth** contains nine half steps or four-and-a-half whole steps. A major sixth is one chromatic half step larger than a minor sixth and one diatonic whole step larger than a perfect fifth.

Of the seven basic sixths, four are major and three are minor. Note that a basic major sixth spans one NOHS and a basic minor sixth spans two NOHS (Ex. 6.17).

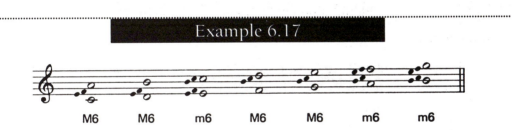

A **minor seventh** contains ten half steps or five whole steps. A minor seventh is a diatonic whole step smaller than a perfect octave and a diatonic half step larger than a major sixth.

A **major seventh** contains eleven half steps or five-and-a-half whole steps. A major seventh is one diatonic half step smaller than a perfect octave and one diatonic whole step larger than a major sixth.

Of the seven basic sevenths, two are major and five are minor. Note than a basic minor seventh spans two NOHS and a basic major seventh spans one NOHS (Ex. 6.18).

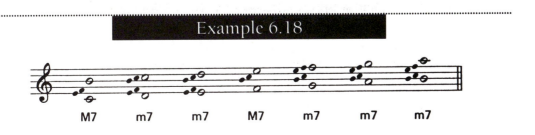

All major scales contain major seconds, major thirds, major sixths, and major sevenths ascending from tonic. In a minor scale (harmonic form) the ascending intervals (second, third, sixth, seventh) above the tonic are M2, m3, m6, and M7.

AUGMENTED AND DIMINISHED INTERVALS

All intervals can be written and classified as augmented or diminished, except for the unison, which can only be augmented. The chart in Example 6.19 shows how the classification of an interval can change by making it one half step larger or smaller. Read the chart from the middle to the right and then from the middle to the left. It is assumed that all changes will be chromatic half steps.

Example 6.19

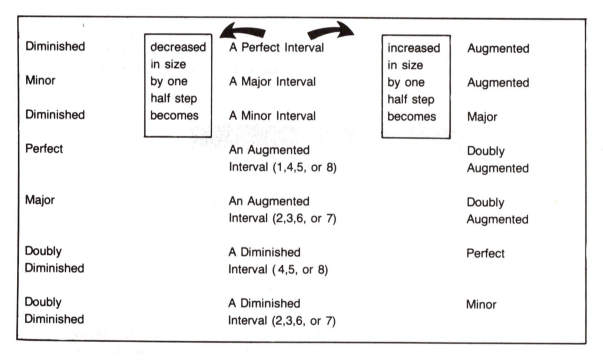

	decreased in size by one half step becomes	A Perfect Interval	increased in size by one half step becomes	Augmented
Diminished				
Minor		A Major Interval		Augmented
Diminished		A Minor Interval		Major
Perfect		An Augmented Interval (1,4,5, or 8)		Doubly Augmented
Major		An Augmented Interval (2,3,6, or 7)		Doubly Augmented
Doubly Diminished		A Diminished Interval (4,5, or 8)		Perfect
Doubly Diminished		A Diminished Interval (2,3,6, or 7)		Minor

Example 6.20 illustrates the use of the interval classification chart for augmented and diminished intervals.

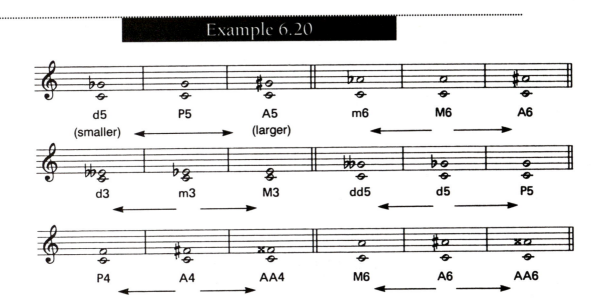

Note that the perfect unison becomes augmented when it is increased in size by one half step. A diminished unison cannot exist, since it merely results in an augmented unison in the opposite direction (Ex. 6.21). Diminished seconds are rarely encountered as they are enharmonic with a perfect unison.

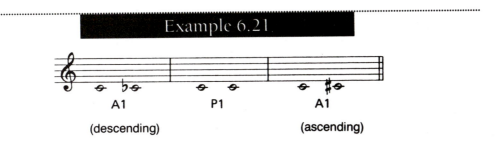

THE TRITONE

The interval of a **tritone** contains three whole steps (hence the name tritone) and may be written as an augmented fourth or as a diminished fifth. When identifying this interval by ear, it is impossible to distinguish between the two possibilities unless it is heard in a melodic or harmonic context. However, when analyzing or writing the interval of a tritone, it is necessary to be specific—that is, to identify or write the interval as an A4 or d5 (Ex. 6.22).

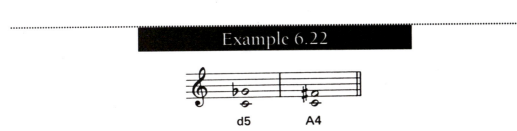

In all of the preceding examples in this unit, intervals have been measured from the lower note to the upper note. All of the principles given apply as well when measuring descending intervals (from the upper note down to the lower note).

INTERVAL CHART

Example 6.23 illustrates intervals that occur above and below middle C, with each interval being a half step larger than the previous one. The number of half steps contained in each interval is given, along with frequently used enharmonic equivalents.

Example 6.23

The intervals presented in Example 6.23 are defined by the number of whole steps, half steps, or both contained in each interval. Keep in mind that (1) half steps may be diatonic or chromatic and (2) whole steps may be diatonic, chromatic, or diminished thirds (enharmonic whole steps), for example, *E–G♭*, *C♯–E♭*, *B–D♭*, *A♯–C*.

Writing an interval is always a two-step process; you should first determine the basic letter-name spelling of the interval—the number of lines and spaces on the staff required for the interval. Do not try to write intervals by using only diatonic whole and half steps because, as mentioned above, half steps can be chromatic or diatonic, and whole steps can be diatonic, chromatic, or enharmonic diminished thirds (d3), thus causing you to arrive at an incorrect letter name, even though the whole- or half-step distance may be correct.

When analyzing a given interval, you should first determine the numerical classification by counting the number of lines and spaces involved; then, if necessary, you could determine the quality by counting the number of whole and half steps.

COMPOUND INTERVALS

Simple intervals are those that have a numerical classification of an octave or less; they include all intervals discussed thus far. **Compound intervals** have a numerical classification larger than an octave. Note: Augmented octaves (A8) are classified as simple intervals even though they are enharmonic with the interval of a minor ninth (m9).

Compound intervals may be analyzed with numbers such as 9, 10, 11, 12, and so on, up to the double octave, which would be a 15, and beyond. When analyzing compound intervals, reduce the interval to its simple form and insert the letter "C" (for compound) before the quality and numerical classification. Note that the quality classification remains the same when reducing a compound interval to a simple one (or vice versa) (Ex. 6.24).

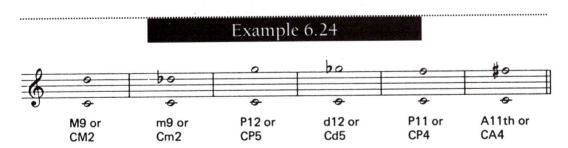

Example 6.24

| M9 or | m9 or | P12 or | d12 or | P11 or | A11th or |
| CM2 | Cm2 | CP5 | Cd5 | CP4 | CA4 |

Musicians are frequently careless about including the classification when discussing or analyzing compound intervals. It is common to hear or see the terms tenth, eleventh, twelfth, and so forth with the quality classification omitted. To be specific, the quality analysis must be included.

For extremely large intervals, the terms "doubly compound" (CC) and "triply compound" (CCC) may be used. Keep in mind that each capital C represents one octave (Ex. 6.25).

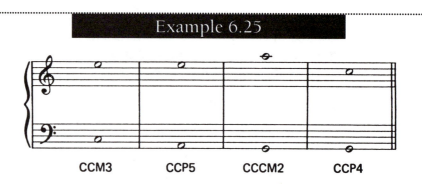

Example 6.25

CCM3   CCP5   CCCM2   CCP4

INVERSION OF INTERVALS

A knowledge of how intervals can be inverted can be helpful in writing and analyzing intervals.

Inversion of simple intervals at the octave merely means that the lower note is placed one octave higher while the upper note remains the same, or the upper note is placed one octave lower while the lower note remains the same (Ex. 6.26).

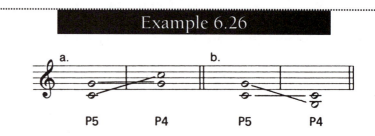

Example 6.26

a.   b.

P5   P4   P5   P4

In Example 6.26a, the note *C* was moved up one octave while the *G* remained the same. In Example 6.26b, the *G* was moved down one octave while the *C* remained the same.

GUIDELINES FOR INVERSION OF INTERVALS

The following guidelines, in the form of two statements, offer the knowledge needed to understand the inversion of intervals at the octave.

1. The numerical sum of a simple interval and its inversion will always equal nine (Ex. 6.27). This is because the note that remains stationary is counted twice.

    - A unison inverts to an octave (and an octave to a unison).
    - A second inverts to a seventh (and a seventh to a second).
    - A third inverts to a sixth (and a sixth to a third).
    - A fourth inverts to a fifth (and a fifth to a fourth).

P1   P8   M2   m7   M3   m6   P4   P5

2. Perfect intervals remain perfect when inverted. All others change quality when inversion takes place (Ex. 6.28).

- A major interval inverts to a minor interval (and minor to major).
- An augmented interval inverts to a diminished interval (and diminished to augmented).
- A doubly augmented interval inverts to a doubly diminished interval (and vice versa).

M3   m6   P4   P5   M2   m7   A2   d7   dd5   AA4

A knowledge of how intervals are inverted at the octave can be helpful in writing intervals and, in turn, serve as a means for checking the accuracy of a written interval. For instance, if the challenge is to write a minor seventh above *F*, you may choose to think of the interval that is found a major second down from *F*; then, notate this E♭ as an answer, one octave higher (above the *F*) (Ex. 6.29).

M2   m7

If the problem is to write a minor sixth above *F*, you may choose to think a major third down and then place this lower note up an octave (Ex. 6.30).

M3   m6

This thought process can apply to the writing of any interval, ascending or descending. It is particularly helpful with intervals larger than a perfect fifth or with complicated chromatic alterations in larger intervals.

Complete the chapter 6 drill sheets on the following pages before continuing. Also, see Appendix A and Appendix B.

CHAPTER SIX DRILLS AND EXERCISES

1. Write the basic intervals indicated above or below the note given (↑ above, ↓ below).

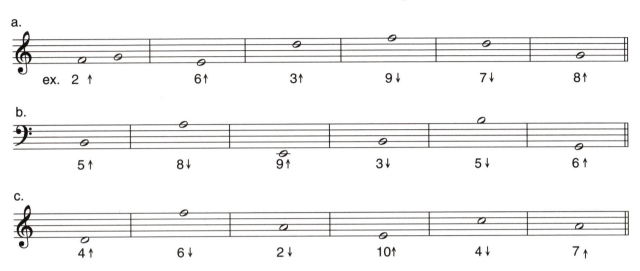

a.
ex. 2 ↑   6↑   3↑   9↓   7↓   8↑

b.
5↑   8↓   9↑   3↓   5↓   6↑

c.
4↑   6↓   2↓   10↑   4↓   7↑

2. Write the perfect intervals indicated.

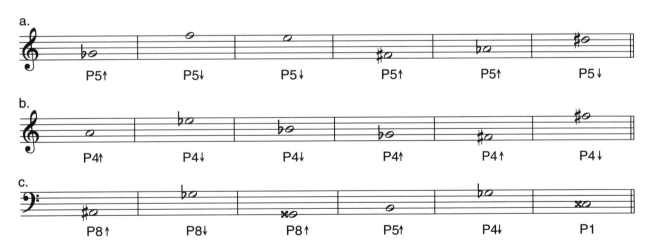

a.
P5↑   P5↓   P5↓   P5↑   P5↑   P5↓

b.
P4↑   P4↓   P4↓   P4↑   P4↑   P4↓

c.
P8↑   P8↓   P8↑   P5↑   P4↓   P1

3. Write the major or minor intervals indicated.

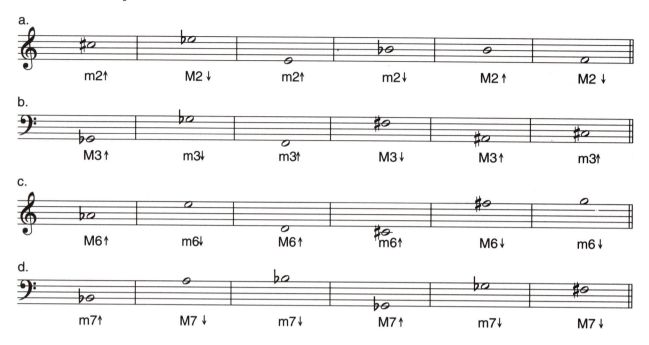

a.

m2↑   M2↓   m2↑   m2↓   M2↑   M2↓

b.

M3↑   m3↓   m3↑   M3↓   M3↑   m3↑

c.

M6↑   m6↓   M6↑   m6↑   M6↓   m6↓

d.

m7↑   M7↓   m7↓   M7↑   m7↓   M7↓

4. Write the augmented and diminished intervals indicated.

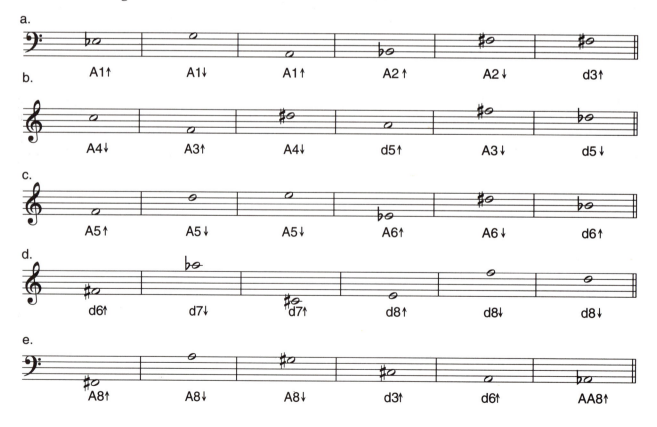

a.

A1↑   A1↓   A1↑   A2↑   A2↓   d3↑

b.

A4↓   A3↑   A4↓   d5↑   A3↓   d5↓

c.

A5↑   A5↓   A5↓   A6↑   A6↓   d6↑

d.

d6↑   d7↓   d7↑   d8↑   d8↓   d8↓

e.

A8↑   A8↓   A8↓   d3↑   d6↑   AA8↑

5. Analyze the intervals given.

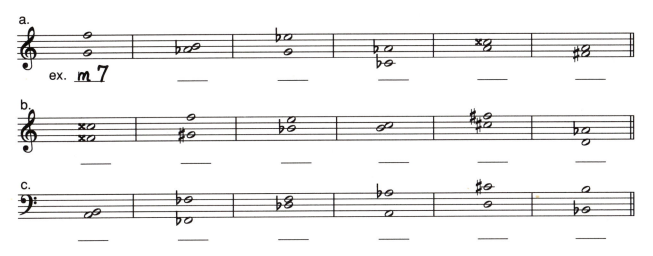

6. Write the compound intervals indicated.

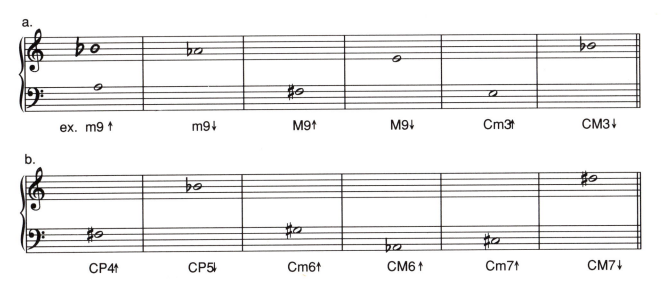

7.   Specify the melodic intervals contained in the melodies given.

Down in the Valley, American Folk Song

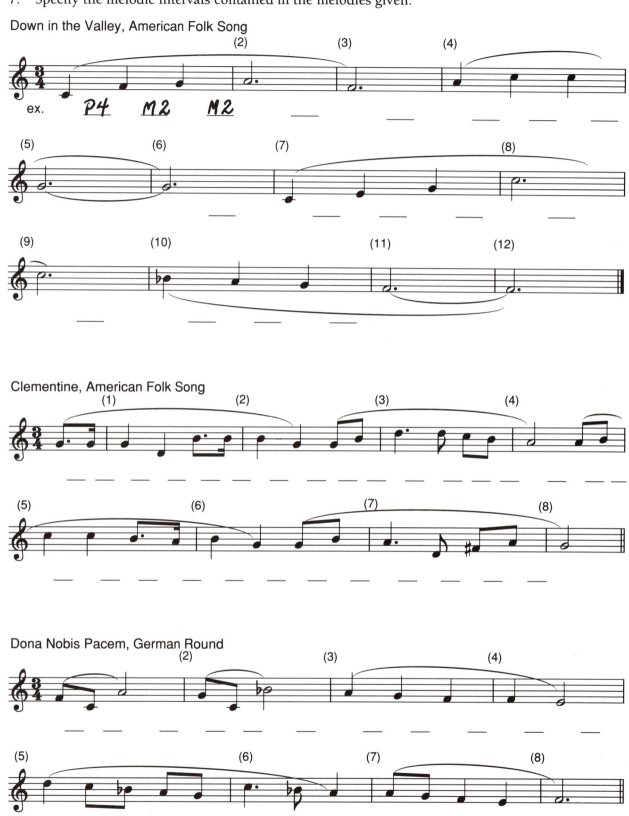

Brandenburg Concerto No. 6, Bach

The Well-Tempered Clavier, Book I, Fugue 10, Bach

Album for the Young, No. 14, Schumann

Chaconne (from Partita No. 2 in D minor), Bach
(m. 33 - 36)

8. Analyze the harmonic intervals (bracketed) in the example given.

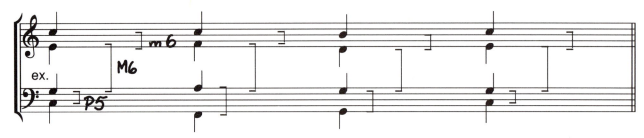

9. At the octave, invert the intervals given. The solid note heads indicate stationary pitches. Analyze
    both intervals.

e.

f.

g.

INTERVAL REVIEW (SELF-TEST: CHAPTER SIX)

1. The five common quality classifications for intervals are:

   a.

   b.

   c.

   d.

   e.

2. Complete the following:

   a. A perfect interval inverts to a _____ interval.

   b. A major interval inverts to a _____ interval.

   c. A minor interval inverts to a _____ interval.

   d. A diminished interval inverts to an _____ interval.

   e. An augmented interval inverts to a _____ interval.

3. Complete the following:

   a. A sixth inverts to a _____.

   b. A seventh inverts to a _____.

   c. A third inverts to a _____.

   d. A second inverts to a _____.

   e. A fourth inverts to a _____.

   f. A fifth inverts to a _____.

   g. An octave inverts to a _____.

   h. A unison inverts to a _____.

4. A harmonic interval is one in which the two pitches are sounding _____.

5. A melodic interval is one in which the two pitches are sounding _____.

6. Complete the following:

    a. A P8 contains _____ half steps or _____ whole steps.

    b. A m7 contains _____ half steps or _____ whole steps.

    c. A m6 contains _____ half steps or _____ whole steps.

    d. A M3 contains _____ half steps or _____ whole steps.

    e. A M2 contains _____ half steps or _____ whole steps.

    f. A m2 contains _____ half step.

    g. A d5 contains _____ half steps or _____ whole steps.

7. Complete the following:

    a. An A5 is enharmonic with a _____.

    b. A m7 is enharmonic with a _____.

    c. A m3 is enharmonic with a _____.

    d. An A1 is enharmonic with a _____.

    e. A M3 is enharmonic with a _____.

    f. A d5 is enharmonic with a _____.

    g. A M7 is enharmonic with a _____.

8. A tritone contains three whole steps and is written either as a _____ (interval) or a _____ (interval).

9. Complete the following:

    a. A m6 is one diatonic half step larger than a _____.

    b. A m7 is one diatonic half step larger than a _____.

    c. An A4 is one chromatic half step larger than a _____.

    d. A M7 is one diatonic half step smaller than a _____.

    e. A m3 is one chromatic half step smaller than a _____.

    f. A M2 is one chromatic half step smaller than an _____.

10. Complete the following:

    a. If a perfect interval is increased in size by one chromatic half step it becomes _____.

    b. If a major interval is increased in size by one chromatic half step it becomes _____.

    c. If a minor interval is increased in size by one chromatic half step it becomes _____.

    d. If an augmented interval is increased in size by one chromatic half step it becomes _____ _____.

e. If a diminished interval is increased in size by one chromatic half step it becomes _____ or _____.

f. If a perfect interval is decreased in size by one chromatic half step it becomes _____.

g. If a major interval is decreased in size by one chromatic half step it becomes _____.

h. If a minor interval is decreased in size by one chromatic half step it becomes _____.

i. If a diminished interval is decreased in size by one chromatic half step it becomes _____.

j. If an augmented interval is decreased in size by one chromatic half step it becomes _____ or _____.

11. Complete the following:

a. A major tenth can also be analyzed as a _____.

b. A minor tenth can also be analyzed as a _____.

c. A major thirteenth can also be analyzed as a _____.

d. A perfect twelfth can also be analyzed as a _____.

e. A minor fourteenth can also be analyzed as a _____.

f. A perfect eleventh can also be analyzed as a _____.

g. A diminished twelfth can also be analyzed as a _____.

Scales III (Revisited)

G O A L S

• The ability to recognize all diatonic intervals as they appear in major and minor scale structures

• The ability to relate concepts of scale structures to the melodic intervals comprising diatonic scales.

Up to this point, isolated skills have been presented chapter by chapter. We now begin to unify some of those concepts by revisiting major and minor scales, approaching them through intervallic structures. This facet of scale study, which should follow the unit on intervals, will provide a firmer, more stable basis for scale-structure comprehension while also reinforcing interval recognition. The two concepts (scales and intervals) are so complementary as to be almost inseparable; it is difficult to learn one without the other.

MAJOR SCALE

We can now view the major scale as constructed of either major or perfect intervals as measured up from the tonic. The scale increments are either major seconds or minor seconds. The second, third, sixth, and seventh scale degrees are major intervals when measured up from the tonic pitch. The fourth, fifth, and octave (again, measured up from the tonic) are perfect intervals (Ex. 7.1).

Example 7.1

D Major Scale

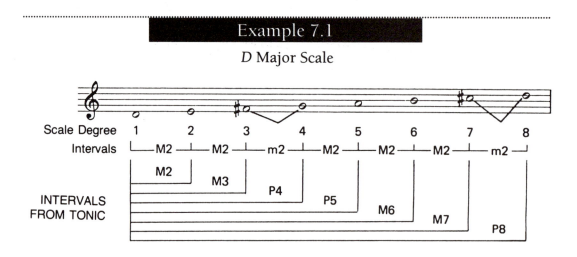

Note: Minor seconds are found between scale degrees 3 and 4 and between 7 and 8.

MINOR SCALE

In all minor scales, the ascending interval from the tonic to the mediant (third scale degree) is a minor third. In fact, the lower tetrachord is the same for all forms of the minor scale; that is, the intervals are major second, minor second, major second (Ex. 7.2). The *f* minor scale is used as a model in all of the following examples.

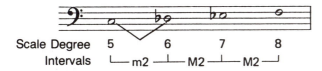

Scale Degree 1   2   3   4
Intervals   └─M2─┘ └─ m2 ─┘ └─M2─┘

Natural Minor Scale

In the upper tetrachord in natural minor we are dealing with a minor second (from the dominant up to the submediant), a major second (from the submediant up to the subtonic), and a major second (from the subtonic up to the tonic) (Ex. 7.3).

Example 7.3

Upper Tetrachord of a Natural Minor Scale

Scale Degree 5   6   7   8
Intervals   └─ m2 ─┘ └─ M2 ─┘ └─ M2 ─┘

Note: In all forms of minor as well as in major, the fourth, fifth, and octave are always perfect intervals and retain their perfect quality. They are, respectively, a perfect fourth, perfect fifth, and perfect octave up from the given tonic. Also, in all major as well as minor scales the connection between tetrachords is always a major second.

Both tetrachords of the natural minor scale combine to form the scale structure shown in Example 7.4.

Example 7.4

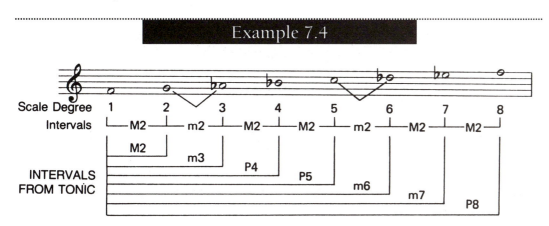

Scale Degree 1   2   3   4   5   6   7   8
Intervals   └─M2─┘ └─ m2 ─┘ └─M2─┘ └─M2─┘ └─ m2 ─┘ └─M2─┘ └─M2─┘

INTERVALS FROM TONIC

M2
m3
P4
P5
m6
m7
P8

Note: Minor seconds are found between scale degrees 2 and 3 and between 5 and 6.

Harmonic Minor Scale

As stated before, the lower tetrachord in the harmonic form of the minor scale is identical to the lower tetrachord in natural minor. The upper tetrachord, beginning on the dominant pitch of the scale, contains the following ascending intervals: minor second (from dominant up to submediant), augmented second (from submediant up to leading tone), and minor second (from leading tone up to tonic) (Ex. 7.5).

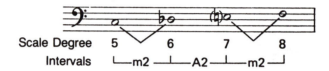

Example 7.5

Upper Tetrachord of f Harmonic Minor

Both tetrachords combine in harmonic minor to form the structure shown in Example 7.6.

Example 7.6

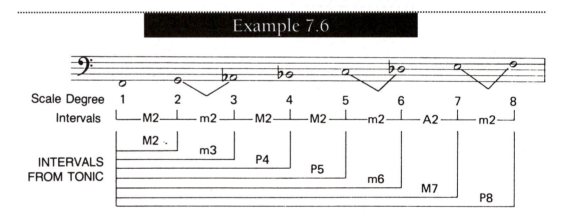

Note: Minor seconds are found between scale degrees 2 and 3, between 5 and 6, and between 7 and 8. This scale form represents the only diatonic scale having three sets of half steps.

Melodic Minor Scale

Again, the lower tetrachord is identical to the other two forms of the minor scale, having the characteristic minor third. The upper tetrachord in *ascending* melodic minor[1] contains the same intervals found in the upper tetrachord in major: a major second (from the dominant up to the submediant), a major second (from the sub-

---

[1] In actual music, it is fairly common to find the ascending form of the melodic minor scale in melodic lines, regardless of the direction of a melody; for instance, the ascending form may appear in a descending melodic line.

mediant up to the leading tone), and a minor second (from the leading tone up to the tonic). When descending, it follows the configuration of descending natural minor: major second (from tonic down to subtonic), major second (from subtonic down to submediant), and minor second (from submediant down to dominant) (Ex. 7.7).

Example 7.7

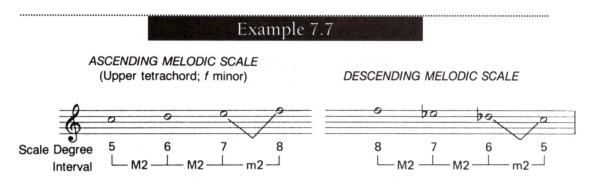

Both tetrachords combine to form the ascending and descending forms found in Example 7.8.

Example 7.8

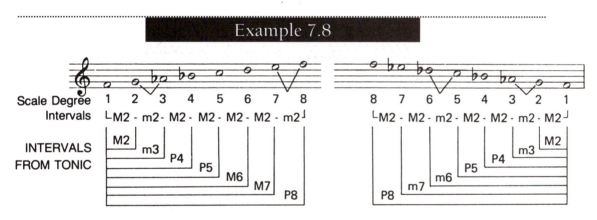

Complete the chapter 7 drill sheets on the following pages before continuing. Also, see Appendix A, and refer to Appendix D for a complete chart of major and minor scales.

CHAPTER SEVEN DRILLS AND EXERCISES

1. In each of the following, a scale is given. First, identify the given scale; second, extract, in notation, the requested interval; and third, label each interval.

a. ex.

= (scale) *E Major*

1. From the mediant up to the dominant.

m 3

2. From the subdominant up to the tonic.

P5

b.

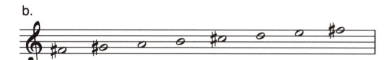

= (scale) _____

1. From the mediant up to the dominant.

_____

2. From the subdominant up to the tonic.

_____

3. From the supertonic up to the submediant.

_____

4. From the tonic down to the dominant.

_____

5. From the submediant down to the supertonic.

_____

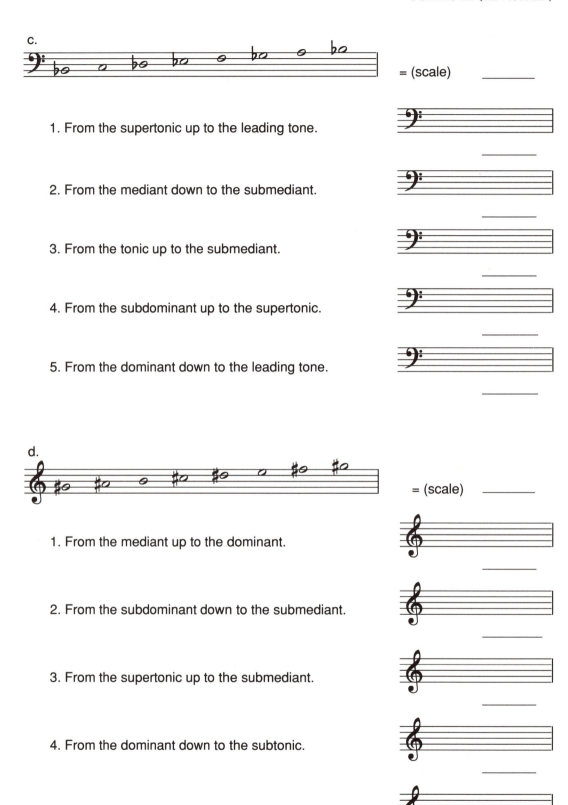

c.

= (scale) _____

1. From the supertonic up to the leading tone.

_____

2. From the mediant down to the submediant.

_____

3. From the tonic up to the submediant.

_____

4. From the subdominant up to the supertonic.

_____

5. From the dominant down to the leading tone.

_____

d.

= (scale) _____

1. From the mediant up to the dominant.

_____

2. From the subdominant down to the submediant.

_____

3. From the supertonic up to the submediant.

_____

4. From the dominant down to the subtonic.

_____

5. From the mediant up to the subtonic.

_____

e.

= (scale) _____

1. From the supertonic up to the leading tone.

_____

2. From the subdominant up to the mediant.

_____

3. From the tonic down to the submediant.

_____

4. From the leading tone down to the mediant.

_____

5. From the submediant up to the supertonic.

_____

SCALES III REVIEW (SELF-TEST: CHAPTER SEVEN)

1. The intervals found in a major scale (as measured up from the tonic) are either major or perfect.
   True _____ False _____

2. The intervals found in natural minor scales (as measured up from the tonic) are all either minor or perfect. True _____ False _____

3. Name the ascending interval found in major scales between:

   a. the mediant and the dominant. _____

   b. the subdominant and the tonic. _____

   c. the submediant and the mediant. _____

   d. the dominant and the leading tone. _____

   e. the supertonic and the dominant. _____

   f. the leading tone and the supertonic. _____

   g. the mediant and the tonic. _____

4. Name the ascending interval found in *natural* minor scales between:

    a. the supertonic and the subtonic. _____

    b. the mediant and the dominant. _____

    c. the submediant and the subdominant. _____

    d. the subdominant and the mediant. _____

    e. the mediant and the tonic. _____

5. Name the ascending interval found in *harmonic* minor scales between:

    a. the tonic and the submediant. _____

    b. the supertonic and the mediant. _____

    c. the mediant and the leading tone. _____

    d. the leading tone and the mediant. _____

    e. the supertonic and the submediant. _____

6. The only intervals up from tonic that remain constant when converting from major to the parallel minor (any form) are:

    _____, _____, _____, and _____.

7. The upper tetrachord in ascending melodic minor is the same as the _____ tetrachord in _____.

8. The upper tetrachord in descending melodic minor is the same as the _____ tetrachord in _____.

9. Of all major and minor (all forms) scales, only two scales have mixed chromatic signs (sharps along with flats). These two are _____ and _____.

10. Only the _____ scale, as a diatonic scale, has three sets of half steps within the scale.

11. Only the lower tetrachord varies from form to form in minor scales. True _____ False _____

12. The only diatonic scale containing an augmented second is the _____ scale.

13. When converting a major scale to its parallel natural minor, the _____ (scale degree(s)) must be (circle one):

    a. raised a half step.

    b. lowered a half step.

Key Signatures

GOALS

• The ability to write key signatures for every major and minor key in the treble and bass clefs

• The ability to identify the major or minor key represented by the key signature

In some contemporary compositions, composers have elected either to dispense with key signatures or to use unusual arrangements of sharps, flats, or both that best meet the needs of the music, performer, or scale resource being used. This chapter deals with traditional key signatures, which comprise the arrangement of chromatic signs that are either all sharps, all flats, or no chromatic signs at all.

Key signatures serve as a type of "shorthand" for the composer, copyist, or publisher. The beginning of most musical scores will provide the type of information in Example 8.1.

Example 8.1

(1) (2) (3)

1. The clef
2. The key signature
3. The meter signature

There are three things you must learn in order to write key signatures with fluency and accuracy:

1. the number of sharps or flats to employ
2. the correct order in which the sharps or flats appear in the key signature
3. the correct line or space on the staff for the placement of the sharps or flats

Because there are seven letters in the musical alphabet, a key signature may contain up to seven sharps or seven flats.

PLACEMENT AND SPACING OF FLATS

The order in which flats appear in a key signature is $B♭$, $E♭$, $A♭$, $D♭$, $G♭$, $C♭$, $F♭$. After the first flat ($B♭$), each additional flat is a perfect fourth above (Ex. 8.2).

Example 8.2

Note the exact line or space on which each flat appears as well as the interval pattern of "up a fourth, down a fifth" after the first B♭ is written.

If the flats in the key signature are spaced properly, it will be possible to draw diagonal lines through the seven flats as illustrated in Example 8.3.

Example 8.3

Staff placement of the flats is important. Do not insert a flat out of its proper sequence. Check to see that each flat is in its proper register.

Practice writing the key signature of seven flats in the treble and bass clefs before continuing.

PLACEMENT AND SPACING OF SHARPS

The order in which sharps appear in a key signature is F♯, C♯, G♯, D♯, A♯, E♯, B♯. After the first sharp (F♯), each additional sharp is a perfect fifth above (Ex. 8.4). This is the same ordering as flats, only backwards (Ex. 8.5).

Example 8.4

Flats:	B	E	A	D	G	C	F
Sharps:	F	C	G	D	A	E	B

Example 8.5

Note the exact line or space on which each sharp appears (Ex. 8.4). The interval pattern for the placement of sharps after the first sharp (F♯) is down a P4, up a P5, down a P4, down a P4, up a P5, and down a P4:

$$P4 \quad P5 \quad P4 \quad P4 \quad P5 \quad P4$$

If the sharps in the key signature are spaced properly, it will be possible to draw diagonal lines through the seven sharps as illustrated in Example 8.6.

Example 8.6

Practice writing the key signature of seven sharps in the treble and bass clefs before continuing.

MAJOR KEY SIGNATURES: SHARPS

When determining the major key when sharps are involved, the age-old method of finding the last sharp on the right and moving up to the next line or space to find the major key is one of the easiest systems.

1. Find the last sharp to the right in the key signature. This is always the leading tone of the major key.
2. Move up to the next adjacent line or space (a minor second) to find the tonic or keynote of the major key.

Example 8.7

In Example 8.7a, the last sharp to the right (and only sharp) is *F*♯. Considering *F*♯ as the leading tone, move up to the next adjacent space, and the letter name for that space (*G*) will be the major key represented by one sharp. The interval from the last sharp upward is always a minor second (leading tone to tonic).

The remaining major keys for the key signatures in Example 8.7 are: 8.7b, *D* major; 8.7c, *A* major; 8.7d, *E* major; and 8.7e, *F♯* major.

Note that if the line or space to which one moves has a previously placed sharp in that position, it must be included in the labeling of the key. Thus, Example 8.7e is *F♯* major (and not *F* major) because *F♯* appears previously in the key signature.

It should be mentioned that while individual chromatic signs apply only to the line or space on which they occur, a flat or sharp in the key signature applies to all lines and spaces with the same letter name, regardless of the octave.

The "line of fifths" in Example 8.8 gives the names of the major keys that have sharps in the key signature above the line, and the number of sharps in each key below the line.

Example 8.8

P5 higher

Key	C	G	D	A	E	B	F♯	C♯
Number of Sharps		1	2	3	4	5	6	7
		F♯	F♯	F♯	F♯	F♯	F♯	F♯
			C♯	C♯	C♯	C♯	C♯	C♯
				G♯	G♯	G♯	G♯	G♯
					D♯	D♯	D♯	D♯
						A♯	A♯	A♯
							E♯	E♯
								B♯

Each new key is a perfect fifth above the previous key, with one additional sharp being added to the key signature each time. Note that the number of sharps employed corresponds to the same number of perfect fifths above *C* that you must count in order to find the letter name of the key. For example, *B* is found by counting five perfect fifths above *C*. Therefore, the key of *B* major will contain five sharps.

MAJOR KEY SIGNATURES: FLATS

When determining the major key from a key signature of flats, the method of finding the second-to-last flat and labeling it as the major key is one of the systems used. Another method is to descend a perfect fourth from the last flat in the key signature and labeling that line or space as the tonic in the key. Either method will provide the same answer.

1. Find the second-to-last flat in the key signature.
2. The letter name of that flat is the major key.

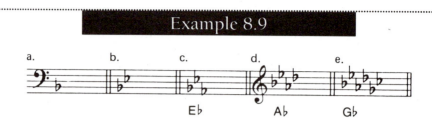

Example 8.9

In Example 8.9a, there is only one flat, so it is impossible to find the second flat from the right. In this case, you may count down a P4 from B♭ to find the key, which is F. F is the only plain-letter major key that employs flats. All other plain-letter names are major keys employing sharps, the exception being C major, which has no sharps or flats in its key signature.

In Example 8.9b, the second flat from the right is B♭, so B♭ would be the major key represented by a key signature of two flats. Example 8.9c would represent E♭ major, 8.9d is A♭ major, and 8.9e is G♭ major.

The "line of fifths" in Example 8.10 gives the names of the major keys that have flats in the key signature above the line and the number of flats in each key below the line.

Example 8.10

		P5 lower						
Key	C	F	B♭	E♭	A♭	D♭	G♭	C♭
Number of Flats		1	2	3	4	5	6	7
		B♭	B♭	B♭	B♭	B♭	B♭	B♭
			E♭	E♭	E♭	E♭	E♭	E♭
				A♭	A♭	A♭	A♭	A♭
					D♭	D♭	D♭	D♭
						G♭	G♭	G♭
							C♭	C♭
								F♭

Each new key is a perfect fifth below the previous key, with one additional flat being added to the key signature each time. Note that the number of flats employed corresponds to the same number of perfect fifths below C that you must count in order to find the letter name of the key. For example, A♭ is found by counting four perfect fifths below C. Therefore, the key of A♭ major will contain four flats.

MINOR KEY SIGNATURES

A minor key shares the same key signature with its relative major. For example, both C major and a minor (natural form) have the same key signature of no sharps or flats.

Determining the possible minor key, when presented with a key signature of sharps or flats, simply involves naming the major key represented and then finding the relative minor.

1. Determine the major key represented by the key signature.
2. Find the relative minor of the major key. The **relative minor** is a minor third below the tonic of the major key and is the submediant scale degree of the relative major.

Example 8.11

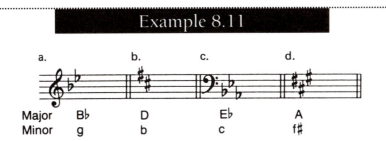

	a.	b.	c.	d.
Major	Bb	D	Eb	A
Minor	g	b	c	f#

In Example 8.11, the major key is indicated with a capital letter and the relative minor with a lower-case letter.

LINE OF FIFTHS AND CIRCLE OF FIFTHS

Example 8.12 gives the "line of fifths," which includes all major keys, the relative minor keys, and the number of flats or sharps in both types of keys.

Note that there are fifteen major keys and fifteen minor keys: seven of each with sharps, seven of each with flats, and *C* major and *a* minor, which contain no sharps or flats.

Example 8.12

							P5 below	P5 above							
Major	Cb	Gb	Db	Ab	Eb	Bb	F	C	G	D	A	E	B	F#	C#
Minor	ab	eb	bb	f	c	g	d	a	e	b	f#	c#	g#	d#	a#
	7b	6b	5b	4b	3b	2b	1b	0	1#	2#	3#	4#	5#	6#	7#
	Bb	Bb	Bb	Bb	Bb	Bb	Bb		F#	F#	F#	F#	F#	F#	F#
	Eb	Eb	Eb	Eb	Eb	Eb			C#	C#	C#	C#	C#	C#	C#
	Ab	Ab	Ab	Ab	Ab				G#	G#	G#	G#	G#	G#
	Db	Db	Db	Db						D#	D#	D#	D#	D#
	Gb	Gb	Gb								A#	A#	A#	A#
	Cb	Cb										E#	E#	E#
	Fb													B#

A key signature does not necessarily give you the key (keynote/tonic) of a composition. The key signature could represent a major key, minor key, or some other scale system. To determine the key, you must look beyond the signature and analyze the music. It is also important to note that key signatures for minor represent only the natural form; harmonic and melodic minor alterations always require the addition of chromatic signs to the music. These alterations for the harmonic and melodic forms of minor never appear as part of a key signature.

Example 8.13, the circle of fifths, is an alternate method of illustrating the continuum of key signatures. Both Examples 8.12 and 8.13 can enable you to visualize the logic of progressively adding either sharps or flats in the construction of key signatures using ascending or descending perfect fifths.

Example 8.13

The circle of fifths can be read clockwise or counterclockwise. The 1 o'clock mark represents the key of *G* major or *e* minor, and its signature contains one sharp. The 2 o'clock position represents the key of *D* major or *b* minor, and its signature contains two sharps, and so on.

When reading counterclockwise, instead of counting from 11 o'clock to 6 o'clock positions, you should think of "negative" 1 to negative 6 o'clock positions—that is, *F* major or *d* minor keys are found in the negative 1 o'clock position and are represented by the signature of one flat. Think of sharps as clockwise motion from *C* major (12 o'clock) and flats as counterclockwise motion from *C* major. By using this approach, the normal clock positions from 1 to 6 (positive or negative) directly correlate to the number of sharps or flats in the key signature, respectively.

The music in Example 8.14 illustrates the application of chromatic alterations to compositions in minor keys. The letter name of the minor key is given at the beginning of each composition, and each form of the minor scale is indicated in parentheses where it occurs.

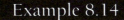

Example 8.14

Go Down, Moses, Spiritual

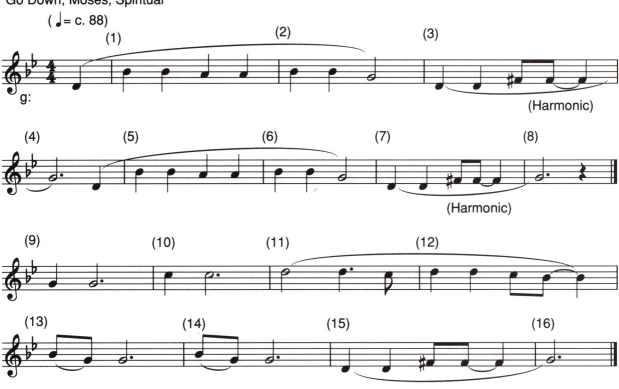

Shalom, Chaverim, Israeli Round

Ballade in G minor, Op. 118, No. 3, Brahms

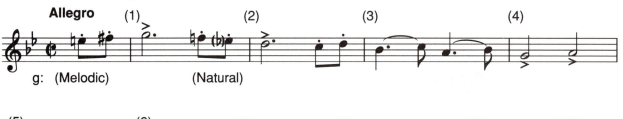

g: (Melodic)   (Natural)

(Melodic)   (♮7 ♮6)   (Natural)

Passacaglia in C Minor, Bach

c:

(Harmonic)

Canon, W. Billings

f♯   (Natural)

(Natural)

The Well-Tempered Clavier, Book 1, Fugue 2, Bach

c: (Harmonic)   (Melodic)

KEY SIGNATURES REVISITED

Another method that may be used for quickly determining the major or minor key is as follows:

1. For key signatures with sharps:

    •   find the last sharp to the right
    •   move up a minor second to find the possible major key; or move down a major second to find the possible minor key (Ex. 8.15).

Example 8.15

G major
e minor

In Example 8.15, the last sharp to the right is $F\sharp$. By moving up to the next space (a minor second) you find the major key represented by one sharp is G major. By moving down to the next space below the sharp (a major second) you find the minor key is *e* minor.

2. For key signatures with flats:

    •   find the last flat to the right
    •   if the last flat is in a space, ascend to the next space (a major third) to find the possible minor key, and ascend one more space (a minor third) to find the possible major key (Ex. 8.16a)
    •   if the last flat is on a line, ascend to the next line (a major third) to find the minor key, and ascend one more line (a minor third) to find the major key (Ex. 8.16b).

Example 8.16

a.  E♭ major
c minor

b.  D♭ major
b♭ minor

Remember that all minor keys represented by key signatures are natural form. Harmonic and melodic variations must be indicated by additional chromatic signs and placed individually in the music.

Complete the chapter 8 drill sheets on the following pages before continuing. Refer to Appendix D for a complete chart of major and minor key signatures.

CHAPTER EIGHT DRILLS AND EXERCISES

1. On the grand staff, write the major key signatures indicated.

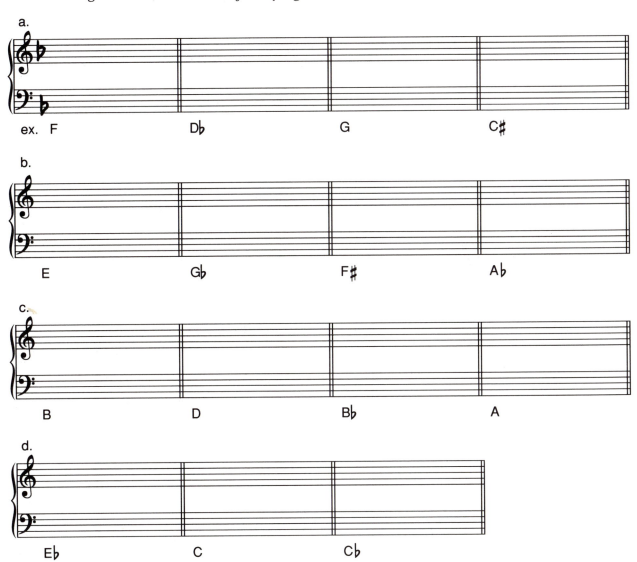

a.

ex. F   Db   G   C♯

b.

E   Gb   F♯   Ab

c.

B   D   Bb   A

d.

Eb   C   Cb

2.   On the grand staff, write the minor key signatures indicated.

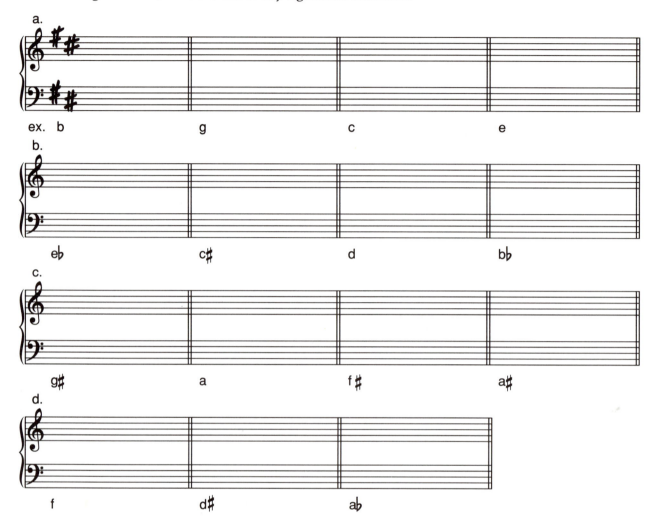

a.

ex. b   g   c   e

b.

eb   c#   d   bb

c.

g#   a   f#   a#

d.

f   d#   ab

3. Identify the major and minor keys for each example given.

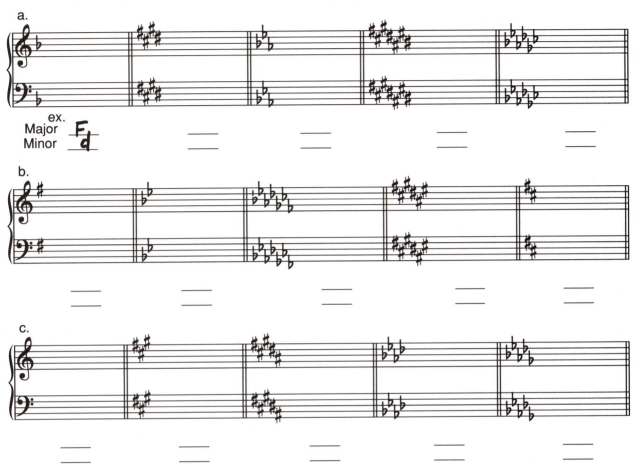

b.

c.

4. Identify the minor key as well as the form of the minor scale in the musical examples given.

Joshua Fought the Battle of Jericho, Spiritual

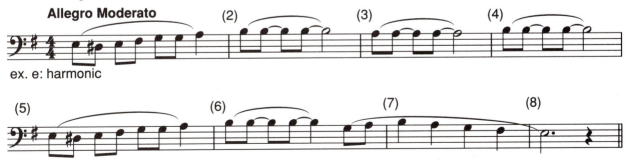

Boom Dali Da, Israeli Folk Song

Nocturne, Op. 9, No. 1, Chopin

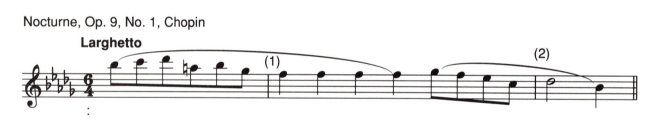

The Hebrew Children (variation), Spiritual

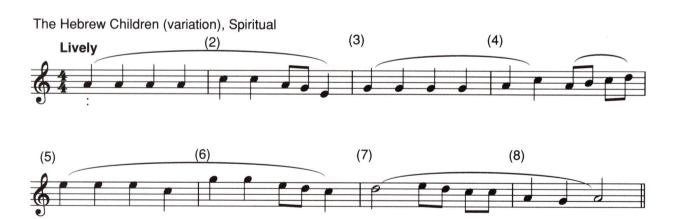

Two-Part Invention, No. 11, Bach

Le Bananier, L. M. Gottschalk

The Art of Fugue, Contrapunctus I, Bach

The Art of Fugue, Contrapunctus 3, Bach

Gavotta, D. Scarlatti

Sonata for Violin and Cembalo, Op. 5, No. 8, Corelli

KEY SIGNATURE REVIEW (SELF-TEST: CHAPTER EIGHT)

1. Complete the following:

    a. The key signature of *A* major contains _____ (number) _____ (sharps/flats).

    b. The key signature of *B♭* major contains _____ _____.

    c. The key signature of *B* major contains _____ _____.

    d. The key signature of *C♭* major contains _____ _____.

    e. The key signature of *F* major contains _____ _____.

    f. The key signature of *G♭* major contains _____ _____.

    g. The key signature of *E* major contains _____ _____.

    h. The key signature of *G* major contains _____ _____.

    i. The key signature of *D* major contains _____ _____.

    j. The key signature of *E♭* major contains _____ _____.

2. Complete the following:

    a. The key signature of *B* minor contains _____ (number) _____ (sharps/flats).

    b. The key signature of *G* minor contains _____ _____.

    c. The key signature of *A* minor contains _____ _____.

    d. The key signature of *E♭* minor contains _____ _____.

    e. The key signature of *C♯* minor contains _____ _____.

    f. The key signature of *F♯* minor contains _____ _____.

    g. The key signature of *B♭* minor contains _____ _____.

    h. The key signature of *G♯* minor contains _____ _____.

    i. The key signature of *D* minor contains _____ _____.

3. The order of flats as they appear in the key signature is _____ _____ _____ _____ _____ _____ and _____.

4. The order of sharps as they appear in the key signature is _____ _____ _____ _____ _____ _____ and _____.

5. Give the relative minor for each major key given. Use lower-case letters.

    A♭   *B*   *A*   *B♭*   *C♭*   *G*   *C*   *G♭*

    ex. ____   ____   ____   ____   ____   ____   ____   ____

6. Give the relative major for each minor key given. Use capital letters.

    b   *a♯*   *d*   *d♯*   *c*   *b♯*   *c♯*

    ex. ____   ____   ____   ____   ____   ____   ____

7. A system for determining the major key when the key signature contains sharps is to _____ _____ .

8. A system for determining the major key when the key signature contains flats is to _____

    _____.

9. The parallel minor of *D* major is _____.

10. The parallel major of *F* minor is _____.

11. Complete the following:

    a. In the treble clef, the fourth sharp in the key signature is placed on the _____ (number) _____ (line or space).

    b. In the treble clef, the sixth sharp in the key signature is placed on the _____ _____.

    c. In the bass clef, the third sharp in the key signature is placed on the _____ _____.

    d. In the treble clef, the fifth flat in the key signature is placed on the _____ _____.

    e. In the bass clef, the sixth flat in the key signature is placed on the _____ _____.

12. The key signature appears after the meter signature. True _____ False _____

13. All major keys with plain letter names (*A, B, C, D, E, F, G*) contain sharps. True _____ False _____

14. A flat or sharp in the key signature applies to all lines and spaces with the same letter name, regardless of the octave. True _____ False _____

15. Relative keys (major and minor) have the same key signature. True _____ False _____

16. Parallel keys (major and minor) have the same key signature. True _____ False _____

17. The tonic of a relative minor key is a minor third below the tonic of its relative major key. True _____ False _____

18. Key signatures for minor only represent the natural form of the minor scale. True _____ False _____

Triads

G O A L S

- The ability to spell and write any note as the root, third, or fifth of any major, minor, augmented, or diminished triad

- The ability to distinguish by ear the quality of triads

- The ability to perceive and sing the root of any sounding triad

- The ability to play on a keyboard any major, minor, augmented, or diminished triad

Any three or more different, simultaneously sounding tones may form what is commonly termed a **chord**. This chapter deals with **tertian** triads—chords that are vertical structures built by arranging any combination of two major or minor thirds above a given note. These structures (triads) have provided the harmonic foundation for many periods and styles of music.

A thorough knowledge of the intervals of the major and minor third, and the order in which the thirds are arranged above a given note, are the two skills that you must possess to write and identify any type of triad.

TRIAD STRUCTURE

Root Position

The three notes of a triad are referred to as the root, third, and fifth. If the structure is arranged exclusively in thirds, the lowest note is the root, and the chord is described as being in **root position**.

The middle note of the triad is called the "third" because it forms the interval of a third above the root. The uppermost note of the triad is called the "fifth" as it forms the interval of a fifth above the root of the triad (Ex. 9.1).

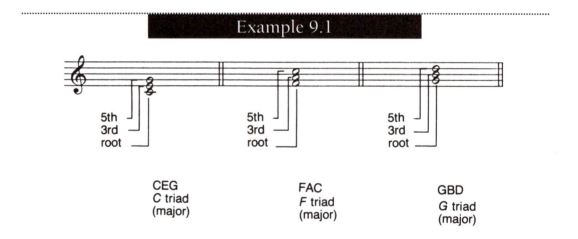

Example 9.1

5th
3rd
root

CEG
C triad
(major)

5th
3rd
root

FAC
F triad
(major)

5th
3rd
root

GBD
G triad
(major)

BASIC TRIADS

It is necessary to understand that the spelling of triads in root position involves skipping one letter of the musical alphabet between each note name in the triad. The use of chromatic signs does not change this rule. The seven **basic triads** (triads without chromatic signs), which may be constructed by using this procedure, are illustrated in Example 9.2.

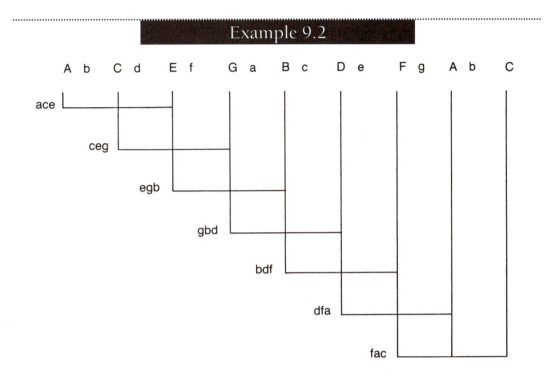

Example 9.2

You should be able to spell basic triads with fluency before continuing with the next concept.

TRIAD QUALITIES

The four qualities of triads found in traditional music literature are major, minor, augmented, and diminished. The arrangement of major and minor thirds, from root to third and third to fifth, in the four types of triads is as shown in Example 9.3.

Example 9.3

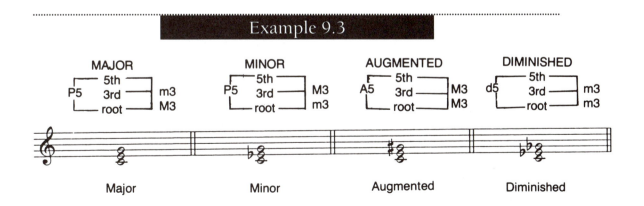

Arrangement of thirds above the roots of major, minor, augmented, and diminished triads are as follows.

• Major triads	A major third (root up to the third) and a minor third (third up to the fifth)
• Minor triads	A minor third (root up to the third) and a major third (third up to the fifth)
• Augmented triads	Two consecutive major thirds above the root
• Diminished triads	Two consecutive minor thirds above the root

When a triad is in root position, the interval between the root and the fifth in a major or minor triad is a perfect fifth. In an augmented triad the interval between the root and the fifth is an augmented fifth, and in a diminished triad the interval between the root and the fifth is a diminished fifth.

When analyzing triads, symbols are used to identify both the root as well as the quality (Ex. 9.4).

Example 9.4

A capital letter indicates a major triad (the actual letter indicates the root).

C

A capital letter with a superscript plus (+) indicates an augmented triad.

C+

A lower-case letter indicates a minor triad.

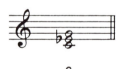

c

A lower-case letter with a superscript (o) indicates a diminished triad.

c °

In Example 9.4, the note *C* is the root of each triad.

When constructing triads in root position, the three notes will be written on all lines or all spaces. The use of chromatic signs does not change this rule (Ex. 9.5).

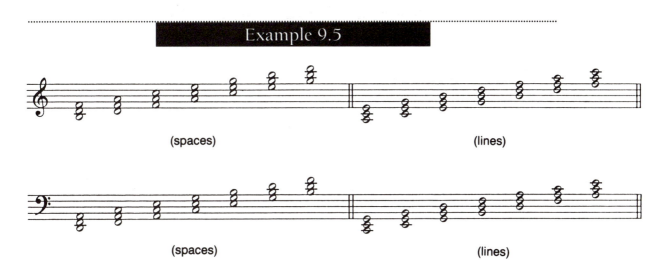

Seven Basic Triads

In Example 9.6, the seven basic triads are identified according to their qualities. Three are major (*C, F, G*), three are minor (*d, e, a*), and one is diminished (*b⁰*).

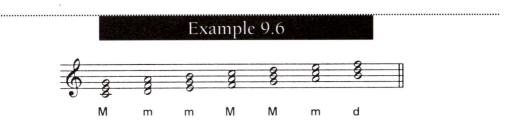

A thought process that is helpful when spelling major or minor triads is to divide the seven letters that can be used as roots into three groups, noting that (1) each note of the triad could have the same number and kind of chromatic signs, (2) the third could be one chromatic sign lower, or (3) the third and/or fifth could be one chromatic sign higher. This concept remains true even when the root is altered with a chromatic sign.

MAJOR TRIADS

Group 1	If *C, F,* or *G* is the root (natural or chromatically altered), all three notes have the same number and kind of chromatic signs.
Group 2	If *D, A,* or *E* is the root, the third of the triad is one chromatic sign higher than the root and fifth.
Group 3	If *B* is the root, the third and fifth are one chromatic sign higher than the root.

Example 9.7

Group 1: All notes have the same number and kind of chromatic signs.

Group 2: The third is one chromatic sign higher than the root and fifth.

Group 3: The third and fifth are one chromatic sign higher than the root.

MINOR TRIADS

Group 1	If *C, F,* or *G* is the root (natural or chromatically altered), the third of the triad is one chromatic sign lower than the root and fifth.
Group 2	If *D, A,* or *E* is the root, all three notes have the same number and kind of chromatic signs.
Group 3	If *B* is the root, the fifth is one chromatic sign higher than the root and third.

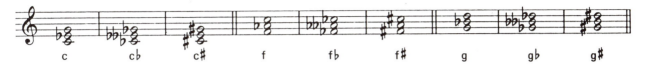

Group 1: The third is one chromatic sign lower than the root and fifth.

Group 2: All three notes have the same number and kind of chromatic signs.

Group 3: The fifth is one chromatic sign higher.

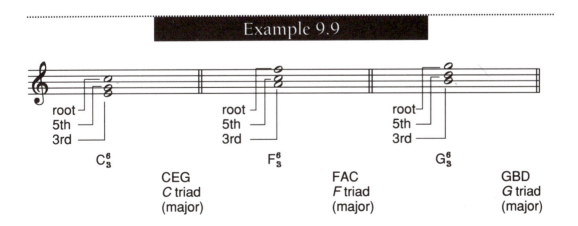

FIRST INVERSION

If the third is the lowest note in a chord, the triad is described as being in **first inversion**. The intervals above the bass (lowest voice) are now a third and a sixth. The symbol for first inversion is $^6_3$ (Ex. 9.9).

Example 9.9

SECOND INVERSION

If the fifth is the lowest note in a chord, the triad is described as being in **second inversion**. The intervals above the bass are now a fourth and a sixth. The symbol for second inversion is $^6_4$ (Ex. 9.10).

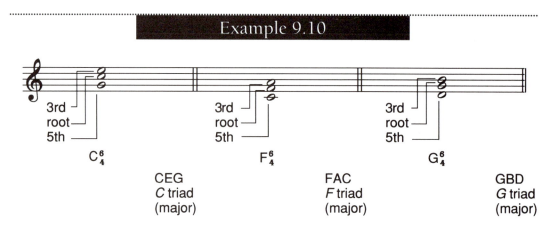

Example 9.10

C$^6_4$ F$^6_4$ G$^6_4$

CEG   FAC   GBD
C triad *F* triad *G* triad
(major) (major) (major)

Whether a triad is in root position, first inversion, or second inversion is determined by which part of the chord (root, third, fifth) is in the lowest voice. This applies to the three-voiced chords given in Examples 9.9 and 9.10 as well as to chords that contain four or more voices.

A triad in first or second inversion will have the interval of a fourth (the inversion of the fifth) present. The upper note of any appearing fourth is *always* the root of the triad.

Complete the chapter 9 drill sheets on the following pages before continuing. Also, see Appendix A and Appendix B. Refer to Appendix D for a complete chart of triads.

CHAPTER NINE DRILLS AND EXERCISES

1. Write the major triads indicated.

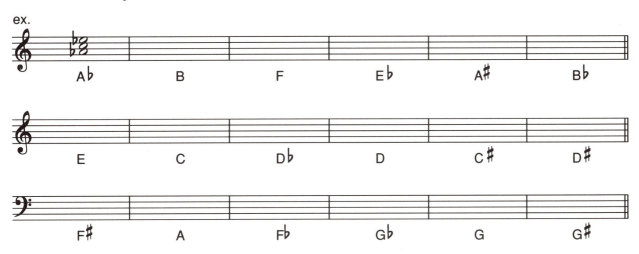

Ab   B   F   Eb   A#   Bb

E   C   Db   D   C#   D#

F#   A   Fb   Gb   G   G#

2. Write the minor triads indicated.

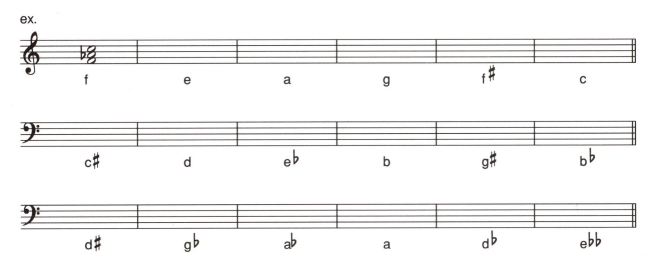

f   e   a   g   f#   c

c#   d   eb   b   g#   bb

d#   gb   ab   a   db   ebb

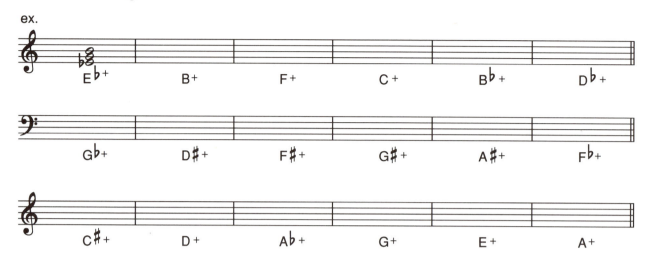

3. Write the augmented triads indicated.

ex.

Eb+   B+   F+   C+   Bb+   Db+

Gb+   D#+   F#+   G#+   A#+   Fb+

C#+   D+   Ab+   G+   E+   A+

4. Write the diminished triads indicated.

ex.

c#°   f#°   e°   b°   d°   f°

c°   d#°   a#°   a°   g°   b#°

5. Identify the root and quality of each triad given.

ex.

6. Identify the root and quality of the inverted triads given.

ex.

7. Write the chords indicated in (a) root position, (b) first inversion, and (c) second inversion. The superscript numbers (figured bass symbols) to the right of the chord name indicate the basic intervals above the lowest note in the chord. Chromatic signs need to be added according to the quality of the chord requested.

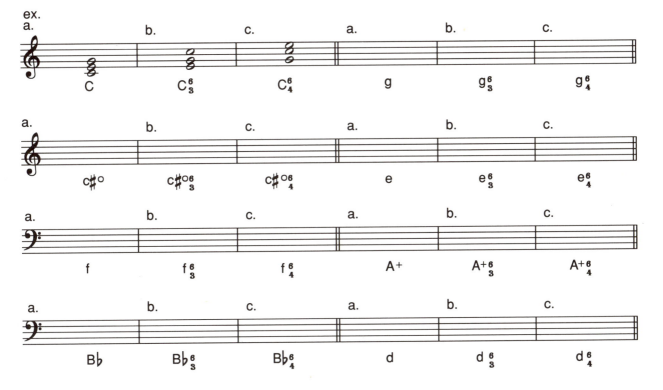

8. Write the triads indicated. The root, third, or fifth and quality of the triad is given. The symbol
    "3d" indicates the note is the third of a diminished triad; "1m" indicates the note is the root of a
    minor triad, and so on.

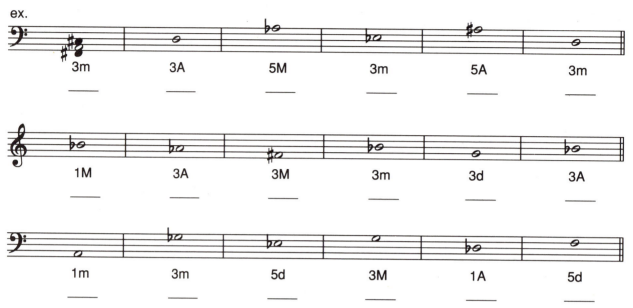

ex.

3m   3A   5M   3m   5A   3m

___   ___   ___   ___   ___   ___

1M   3A   3M   3m   3d   3A

___   ___   ___   ___   ___   ___

1m   3m   5d   3M   1A   5d

___   ___   ___   ___   ___   ___

9. Spell major triads with each letter given as the root, third, or fifth of a triad. Do not alter the given
    letters chromatically.

ex.

```
┌ E
│ C#          ┌ C
└ A (1)       │ A (3)    ┌ A (5)     ┌           ┌           ┌           ┌           ┌
              └ F        │ F#        └ C         └ C         └ C         └ D         │ D         ┌ D
                        └ D
```

```
┌           ┌           ┌           ┌           ┌           ┌           ┌           ┌           ┌
│ B         │ B         │ B         └ F#        │ F#        │ F#        └ G         │ G         │ G
```

10. Spell minor triads with each letter given as the root, third, or fifth of a triad. Do not alter the given letters chromatically.

ex.

```
 ⎡ B       ⎡ G#              ⎡        ⎡        ⎡        ⎡        ⎡        ⎡
 ⎢ G   ⎡ G# ⎢ E        ⎡ E   ⎢        ⎢        ⎢        ⎢        ⎢        ⎢
 ⎣ E   ⎢ E ⎣ C#        ⎢ C   ⎣ F    ⎣ F    ⎣ F    ⎣ B    ⎣ B    ⎣ B
       ⎣ C#            ⎣ A
```

```
 ⎡        ⎡        ⎡        ⎡        ⎡        ⎡        ⎡        ⎡        ⎡
 ⎢        ⎢        ⎢        ⎢        ⎢        ⎢        ⎢        ⎢        ⎢
 ⎣ C    ⎣ C    ⎣ C    ⎣ A    ⎣ A    ⎣ A    ⎣ G    ⎣ G    ⎣ G
```

11. Spell diminished triads with each letter given as the root, third, or fifth of a triad. Do not alter the given letters chromatically.

ex.

```
 ⎡ G      ⎡ E               ⎡        ⎡        ⎡        ⎡        ⎡        ⎡
 ⎢ E   ⎡ E ⎢ C#      ⎡ C#   ⎢        ⎢        ⎢        ⎢        ⎢        ⎢
 ⎣ C#  ⎢ C# ⎣ A#     ⎢ A#   ⎣ D    ⎣ D    ⎣ D    ⎣ B    ⎣ B    ⎣ B
       ⎣ A#           ⎣ Fx
```

```
 ⎡        ⎡        ⎡        ⎡        ⎡        ⎡        ⎡        ⎡        ⎡
 ⎢        ⎢        ⎢        ⎢        ⎢        ⎢        ⎢        ⎢        ⎢
 ⎣ E    ⎣ E    ⎣ E    ⎣ G#   ⎣ G#   ⎣ G#   ⎣ F    ⎣ F    ⎣ F
```

12. Spell augmented triads with each letter given as the root, third, or fifth of a triad. Do not alter the given letters chromatically.

ex.

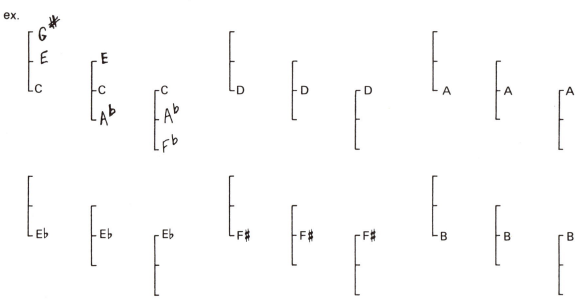

The following exercises provide additional drill with regard to triad quality classification. Note that in a four-voice texture one note of the triad is doubled; however, this does not alter the identification process.

To determine the root and quality of a four-voiced chord, the following guidelines will be helpful:

1. Identify all notes in the chord from the bass (lowest voice) to the soprano (uppermost voice). If desired, write the letter names beside each note.
2. Note which part of the chord (root, third, fifth) is doubled. Disregard the doubled tone.
3. Arrange the three remaining notes in thirds to determine the root and quality.

For example, if the notes in a chord from the bass to soprano are *G, G, E, B*, we note that the doubled note is *G* and that the three remaining notes are *G, E, B*. By arranging these three notes in thirds (E–G–B), we can determine the chord is E minor.

13. Identify the root and quality of each chord in the following Bach chorale excerpts. The circled notes are not part of the chord and should not be considered in the analysis.

a. O Ewigkeit, du Donnerwort

ex. ____

b. Ach was soll ich Sünder machen

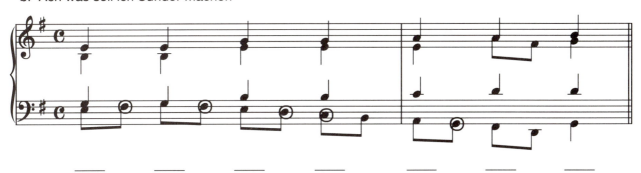

c. Ach Gott und Herr

d. Machs mit mir, Gott, nach deiner Güt

e. Vater unser im Himmelreich

f. Wer nur den lieben Gott

g.   Komm, heiliger Geist

h. Erhalt'uns, Herr, bei deinem Wort

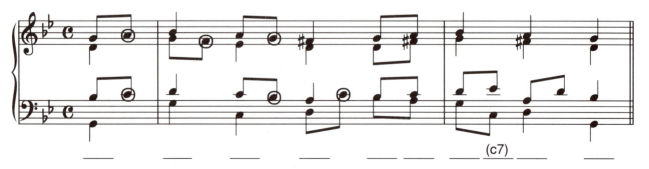

TRIAD REVIEW (SELF-TEST: CHAPTER NINE)

1. The four types of tertian triads are: _____, _____, _____ and _____.

2. The three parts (notes) of a triad are called the _____, _____, and _____.

3. The arrangement of thirds in a major triad in root position is:

   _____ (interval from root to third)

   _____ (interval from third to fifth)

4. The arrangement of thirds in a minor triad in root position is:

   _____ (interval from root to third)

   _____ (interval from third to fifth)

5. The arrangement of thirds in an augmented triad in root position is:

   _____ (interval from root to third)

   _____ (interval from third to fifth)

6. The arrangement of thirds in a diminished triad in root position is:

   _____ (interval from root to third)

   _____ (interval from third to fifth)

7. The interval between the root and fifth in a major or minor triad in root position is: _____ _____.

8. The interval between the root and fifth in an augmented triad in root position is: _____ _____.

9. The interval between the root and fifth in a diminished triad in root position is: _____ _____.

10. Triads in root position, whether basic or chromatically altered, are always spelled by omitting one letter of the musical alphabet between each note name in the triad. True _____ False _____

11. Circle the major triad(s): F, e°, G⁺, a, E♭, d.

12. Circle the minor triad(s): A⁺, G♯, a, c°, B♭, e♭.

13. Circle the augmented triad(s): B♭, d♯, D⁺, a°, D♭⁺, E.

14. Circle the diminished triad(s): B, c♯°, G⁺, E, b°, F.

15. If a triad is in first inversion, the _____ (root, third, fifth) of the chord is in the lowest voice.

16. If a triad is in second inversion, the _____ of the chord is in the lowest voice.

17. A diminished triad in root position will have two minor thirds arranged above the root. True _____ False _____

18. An augmented triad in root position will have a major third and minor third arranged above the root. True _____ False _____

19.   There are _____ (number) basic triads.

20.   Three of the basic triads are _____ (quality), three are _____, and one is _____.

21.   If *C, F,* or *G* (natural or chromatically altered) is the root of a major triad, all three notes will _____ will not _____ (check one) have the same number and kind of chromatic signs.

22.   If *D, E,* or *A* (natural or chromatically altered) is the root of a major triad, the third of the triad will be one chromatic sign _____ (higher or lower) than the root and fifth.

23.   If *B* (natural or chromatically altered) is the root of a major triad, the third and fifth will be one chromatic sign _____ (higher or lower) than the root.

24.   A minor triad can be altered to become a major triad by _____ (raising or lowering) the third a chromatic half step.

25.   A minor triad can be altered to become a diminished triad by _____ (raising or lowering) the fifth a chromatic half step.

26.   A major triad can be altered to become an augmented triad by _____ (raising or lowering) the fifth a chromatic half step.

Diatonic Triads

GOALS

- The ability to write the diatonic triads that occur in major and minor keys

- The ability to write and analyze isolated triads

- The ability to play at the keyboard all of the diatonic triads found in any major or minor key

- The ability to analyze diatonic triads in a musical score

- The ability to write, analyze, and play primary triads that occur in major and minor keys

- An understanding of the relationship of primary and secondary triads in major and minor keys

A combined knowledge of scales, key signatures, intervals, and triads is a necessary prerequisite in learning how diatonic triads are formed in major and minor keys. If a problem with the conceptualization arises, it will probably be due to a lack of a thorough understanding in one or more of the four skills mentioned above.

The concepts of diatonic triads form the foundation for the learning of seventh, ninth, and eleventh chords as well as other extended tertian structures. Diatonic triads frequently comprise the greatest number of chords found in a traditional composition. A knowledge of how they are formed and their function is indispensable to understanding the elementary aspects of harmony. A mechanical knowledge of triads truly becomes valuable when it can be applied to, and serves as a basis for, harmony and the succession of chords within a musical context.

DIATONIC TRIADS IN MAJOR

Writing the diatonic triads that occur in a major key involves the following steps.

1. Supply the correct key signature.
2. Write the major scale being considered.
3. Write two thirds vertically above each scale degree.
4. Analyze with Roman numerals, chord symbols, or both.

ROMAN NUMERAL IDENTIFICATION

Upper-case Roman numerals are commonly used to identify major triads; lower-case Roman numerals are used to identify minor triads. The addition of the superscript zero (^{0}) to the lower-case numeral and the addition of the superscript plus ($^+$) to the upper-case numeral indicate diminished and augmented triad qualities respectively. For example:

Major triads	I, III, IV, V, VI
Minor triads	i, ii, iii, iv, vi
Diminished triads	ii^0, vii^0
Augmented triads	III$^+$

Example 10.1 illustrates the seven diatonic triads found in the key of *C* major and the procedures for writing them.

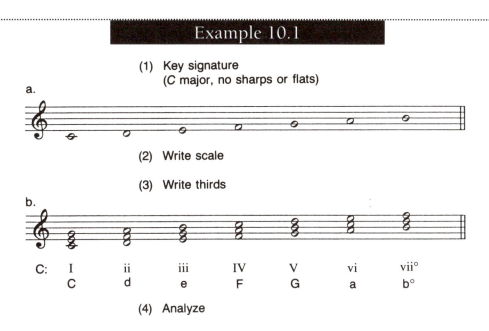

Example 10.1

(1) Key signature
(C major, no sharps or flats)

a.

(2) Write scale

(3) Write thirds

b.

C: I   ii   iii   IV   V   vi   vii°
     C   d   e   F   G   a   b°

(4) Analyze

The terms used to label diatonic triads found in major and minor are the same as those given to scale degrees on which they are constructed. The triad built on the first scale degree is called the tonic triad; the triad built on the second scale degree is called the supertonic triad; and so on through the scale degrees.

1. tonic	5. dominant
2. supertonic	6. submediant
3. mediant	7. leading tone or subtonic
4. subdominant	

Note that in a major key (Ex. 10.1b), three of the chords are major (I, IV, V), three chords are minor (ii, iii, vi), and one chord is diminished (vii°). These qualities will remain the same for *every set of diatonic triads constructed in a major key*. In a major key, the chord built on the seventh scale degree is called the leading-tone triad.

Practice writing the diatonic triads in several major keys (as in drill 1 at the end of this chapter) before continuing. Playing the triads at a keyboard will help to reinforce the understanding of this skill.

DIATONIC TRIADS IN MINOR

Harmonic Minor

Most compositions in minor keys exhibit, for the most part, the harmonic form of minor. However, it is rather common to find more than one form of minor in the same composition.

When writing diatonic triads in a minor key, the steps to follow are the same as for a major key.

1. Provide the key signature.
2. Write the scale.
3. Write triads on each scale degree.
4. Analyze.

The harmonic form of *c* minor is given in Example 10.2.

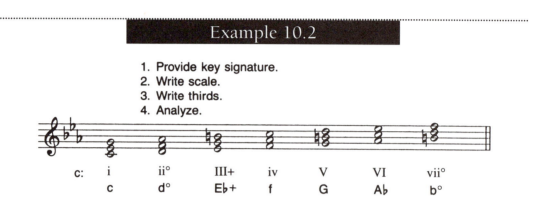

Example 10.2

1. Provide key signature.
2. Write scale.
3. Write thirds.
4. Analyze.

c:	i	ii°	III+	iv	V	VI	vii°
	c	d°	Eb+	f	G	Ab	b°

In the harmonic form of the minor scale, it is necessary to raise the seventh scale degree one chromatic half step. This will alter the quality of all triads containing the raised seventh scale degree as a root, third, or fifth—that is, the triads built on the third (III⁺), fifth (V), and seventh (vii°) scale degrees. The alterations found in the upper tetrachord of harmonic minor primarily function to accommodate a major triad built on the dominant as well as the diminished triad built on the leading tone.

Note that in harmonic minor, two chords are minor (i, iv), two chords are major (V, VI), two chords are diminished (ii°, vii°), and one is augmented (III⁺). This mediant triad appears as an augmented chord in the harmonic form of minor; however, in actual music practice, it often appears as a major chord (III). This quality is the result of the natural form of the minor scale.

The chord qualities presented in Example 10.2 will remain the *same for every minor key* (harmonic form).

Compare the similarities and differences between the chords that occur in a major key and its parallel minor key (harmonic form) (Ex. 10.3).

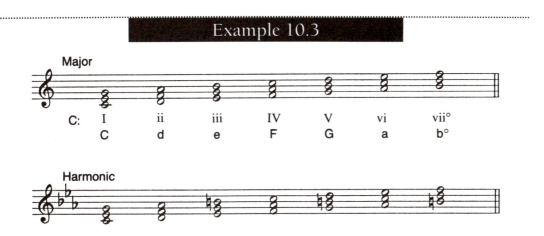

The names for the individual triads in a minor key (harmonic form) are the same as the triad names for a major key: tonic, supertonic, and so forth. Another acceptable way to label diatonic chords is to call the tonic triad the "one" chord, the supertonic triad the "two" chord, the mediant triad the "three" chord, and so on.

Practice writing diatonic triads in several minor keys (harmonic form) before continuing.

Natural Minor

When writing the diatonic triads that occur in the natural form of a minor key, the procedure is the same as before: provide the key signature; write the scale; write triads on each scale degree; analyze. The natural form of the c minor scale is given in Example 10.4.

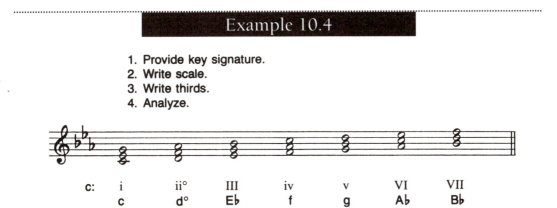

In natural minor no additional chromatic alterations are necessary. The names for the individual chords are the same as for major and the harmonic form of minor, except for the triad built on the seventh scale degree. In this case, it is called the **subtonic triad**, because the seventh scale degree is one diatonic whole step (M2) below the tonic.

Compare the similarities and differences between the triads in the natural form of the minor scale and those triads in major and in the harmonic form of the minor scale (Ex. 10.5).

Example 10.5

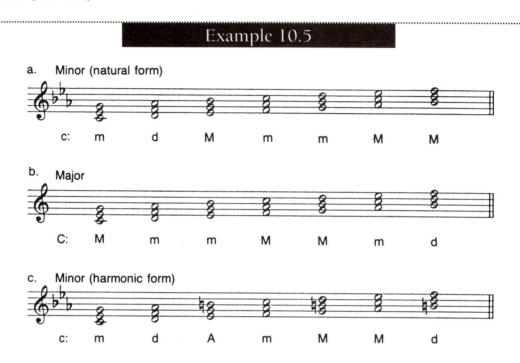

a. Minor (natural form)

c: m   d   M   m   m   M   M

b. Major

C: M   m   m   M   M   m   d

c. Minor (harmonic form)

c: m   d   A   m   M   M   d

Melodic Minor

When writing the diatonic triads that appear in the melodic form of the minor scale, there exists the possibility of having the choice of two different qualities of chords on each scale degree (except for tonic). This is due to the fact that the sixth and seventh degrees may be raised (as in major) or lowered (natural form). Example 10.6 illustrates these possibilities.

Example 10.6

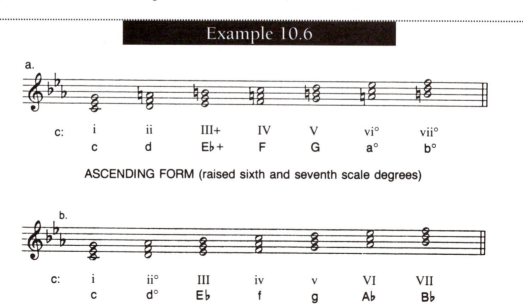

a.

c: i   ii   III+   IV   V   vi°   vii°
     c   d   Eb+   F   G   a°   b°

ASCENDING FORM (raised sixth and seventh scale degrees)

b.

c: i   ii°   III   iv   v   VI   VII
     c   d°   Eb   f   g   Ab   Bb

DESCENDING FORM (lowered sixth and seventh scale degrees, natural form)

Note that the triads that occur in the descending form of melodic minor, with the lowered sixth and seventh scale degrees (Ex. 10.6b), are the same as those triads that appear in the natural form of the minor scale (Ex. 10.4).

Practice writing the diatonic triads in several minor keys (melodic form) before continuing.

PRIMARY AND SECONDARY TRIADS

In major and minor keys, the triads that are built on the tonic, subdominant, and dominant scale degrees are called **primary triads**. These triads are termed primary because of their importance to tonality and their frequency of usage. Both the subdominant and dominant triads are in a perfect fifth relationship to the tonic (below and above respectively). Chords built on the remaining scale degrees are called **secondary triads**. The qualities of the primary triads found in major and minor are given in Example 10.7.

Example 10.7

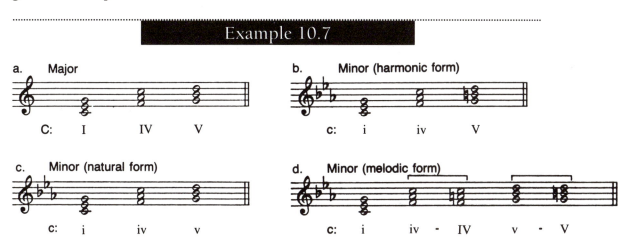

a. Major

C: I   IV   V

b. Minor (harmonic form)

c: i   iv   V

c. Minor (natural form)

c: i   iv   v

d. Minor (melodic form)

c: i   iv · IV   v · V

1. In a major key the three primary triads are major: I, IV, and V.
2. In the harmonic form of minor, i and iv are minor and V is major.
3. In the natural form of minor, all three chords are minor: i, iv, v.
4. In the melodic form of minor, the tonic triad is minor (i), and the two remaining triads can be either minor or major: iv/IV, or v/V.

PRIMARY AND SECONDARY TRIAD RELATIONSHIPS

Once the primary triads in either major or minor have been selected and identified, the remaining triads are referred to as secondary triads.

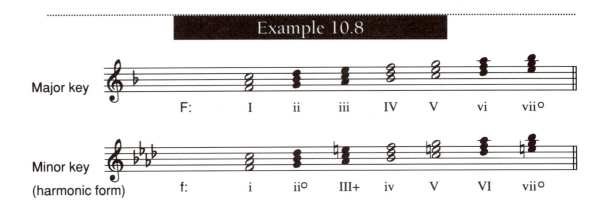

Example 10.8

Major key

F: I   ii   iii   IV   V   vi   vii°

Minor key
(harmonic form)

f: i   ii°   III+   iv   V   VI   vii°

In tonal music, each of the primary triads carries a specific function as a harmony. This refers to the normal or expected progression or resolution of a particular triad, as based upon actual practice in music literature. There are three basic functions:

1. The tonic triad serves as a tonic function chord (I or i). Its function is that of a chord free to move to any other diatonic chord; or it is one with little activity—a chord of repose, as in the final chord in a musical phrase.
2. The subdominant triad serves as a subdominant function chord (IV or iv). Its primary function is to resolve to the dominant. It may also resolve directly to the tonic.
3. The dominant triad serves as a dominant function chord (V). Its primary function is to resolve to the tonic chord.

Each of the secondary triads relates to a specific primary triad and may substitute for that particular triad.

1. Tonic as a primary triad relates to submediant as its related secondary triad (I–vi in major, or i–VI in minor).
2. Subdominant as a primary triad relates to the supertonic as its related secondary triad (IV–ii in major, iv–ii° in minor).
3. Dominant as a primary triad relates either to the mediant[1] or to the leading-tone triad as its secondary triad(s) (V–iii or V–vii° in major, or V–III+ or V–vii° in minor).

When substituted, the secondary triad carries the same function as does the primary (tonic, subdominant, or dominant). Example 10.9 illustrates each of the primary triads and their secondary triad relationships.

---

[1] Since the tonic, as a primary, also shares two common pitches with the mediant triad, the mediant is occasionally used as a secondary substitution for the tonic triad as well.

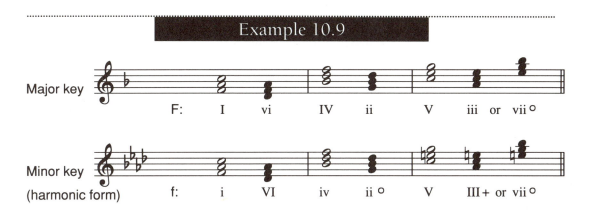

Example 10.9

It should be noted that each primary and related secondary triad share two common tones; in addition, each primary triad contains one pitch that the related secondary triad does not, and vice versa.

In a chord progression, or succession of triads, it is quite common for a given triad to be repeated, as, for example, in the common progression I, I, IV, V. In such a situation, the secondary substitution triad is often used in place of the repeated primary: I, vi, IV, V. In this case, the submediant (vi) triad substitutes for the repeated tonic chord and carries the same (tonic) function. It serves to provide more harmonic "color" and forward motion to the progression while maintaining the prolonged tonic function. This concept is explained in more detail in chapter 12, "Harmonization."

ISOLATED TRIADS IN MAJOR AND MINOR

The task of finding and labeling, by Roman numeral, a single, isolated chord in any of the possible major or minor keys involves a thorough knowledge of several skills that must be assembled to arrive at an accurate response. If, for example, the problem or question was to find the dominant triad (V) in the key of *a* minor (harmonic form), the thought process necessary in finding this isolated triad would involve the following steps:

1. Determine the key signature for *a* minor.
2. Find the fifth scale degree (dominant).
3. Spell the triad based on the quality of the Roman numeral indicated (M, m, d, A).
4. Check to see if any of the notes of the triad require a chromatic alteration because of the particular form of the minor scale being used (this will be necessary only with minor forms).

The correct answer to the problem is shown in Example 10.10.

a: V   (*E* major)

Complete the chapter 10 drill sheets on the following pages before continuing. Also, see Appendix A and Appendix B.

CHAPTER TEN DRILLS AND EXERCISES

1. Supply appropriate key signatures and write the diatonic triads that appear in the keys given. Analyze with Roman numerals and identify the root and quality of each triad. Use the harmonic form for all minor keys.

G: I ii iii IV V vi vii°
   G a b C D e f#°

Ab: __ __ __ __ __ __ __
    __ __ __ __ __ __ __

Eb: __ __ __ __ __ __ __
    __ __ __ __ __ __ __

E: __ __ __ __ __ __ __
   __ __ __ __ __ __ __

D: __ __ __ __ __ __ __
   __ __ __ __ __ __ __

B: __ __ __ __ __ __ __
   __ __ __ __ __ __ __

d: __ __ __ __ __ __ __
   __ __ __ __ __ __ __

f: __ __ __ __ __ __ __
   __ __ __ __ __ __ __

e: __ __ __ __ __ __ __
   __ __ __ __ __ __ __

g: __ __ __ __ __ __ __
   __ __ __ __ __ __ __

f#: __ __ __ __ __ __ __
    __ __ __ __ __ __ __

c: __ __ __ __ __ __ __
   __ __ __ __ __ __ __

2. Supply appropriate key signatures and write the primary triads that appear in the keys given. Analyze with Roman numerals and identify the root and quality of each triad. Use the harmonic form for all minor keys.

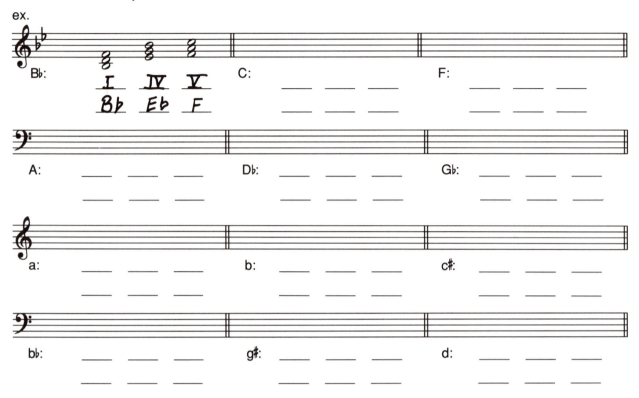

3. Using Roman numerals, identify each chord given. Indicate the root and quality of each triad.

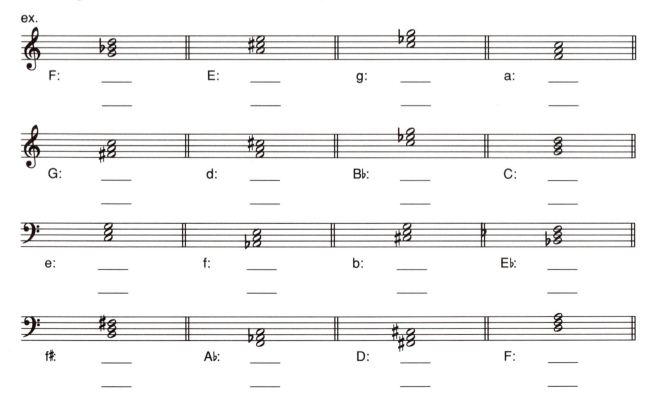

4. Write the diatonic triads indicated.

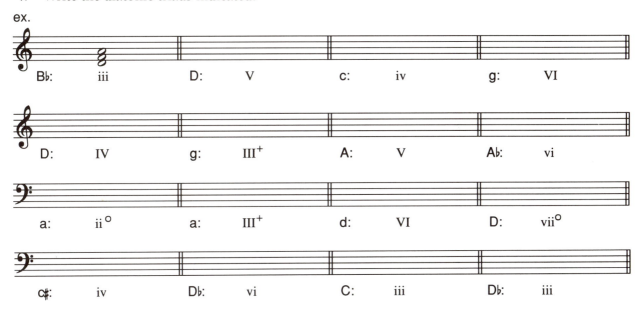

Bb: iii   D: V   c: iv   g: VI

D: IV   g: III⁺   A: V   Ab: vi

a: ii°   a: III⁺   d: VI   D: vii°

c#:   iv   Db: vi   C: iii   Db: iii

5. Write the secondary triad(s) for each primary triad given. Analyze with Roman numerals and indi-
    cate the root and quality of each chord. Use the harmonic form for all minor keys.

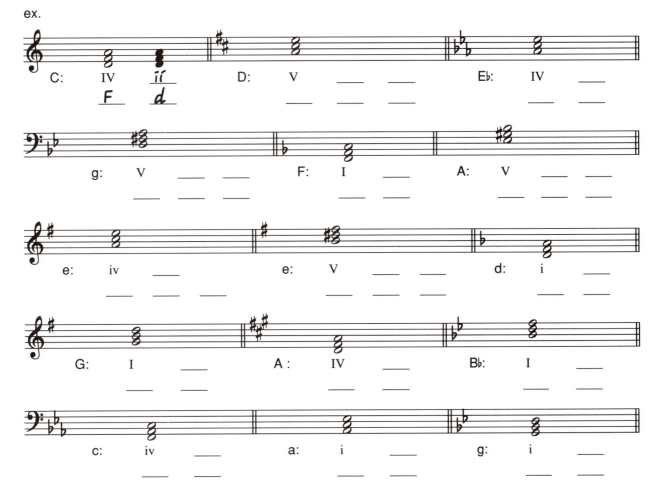

C: IV   ii   D: V   ___ ___   Eb: IV   ___ ___
      F   d

g: V   ___ ___   F: I   ___ ___   A: V   ___ ___
      ___ ___   ___ ___

e: iv   ___   e: V   ___ ___   d: i   ___
      ___ ___   ___ ___

G: I   ___   A: IV   ___   Bb: I   ___
      ___ ___

c: iv   ___   a: i   ___   g: i   ___
      ___ ___

6. Analyze each chord progression using Roman numerals. Identify the root and quality of each chord. The circled notes are not part of the chord and should not be considered in the analysis.

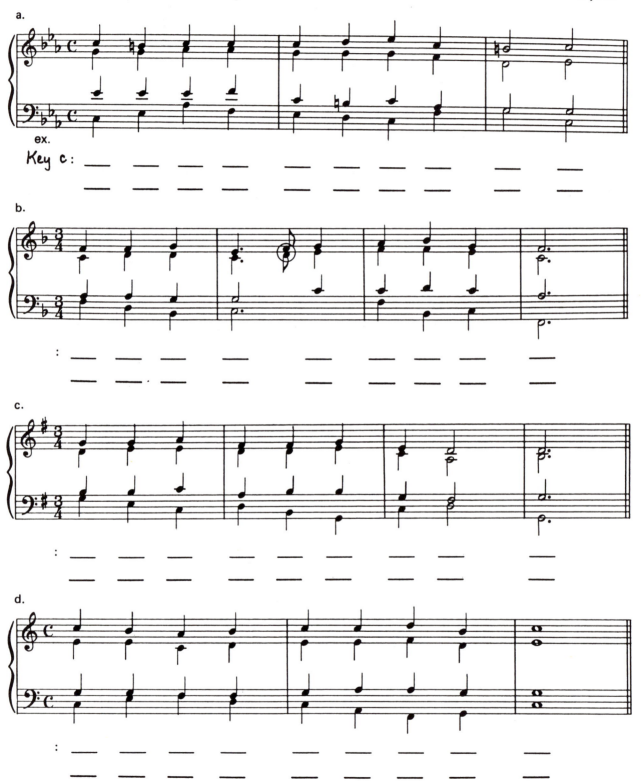

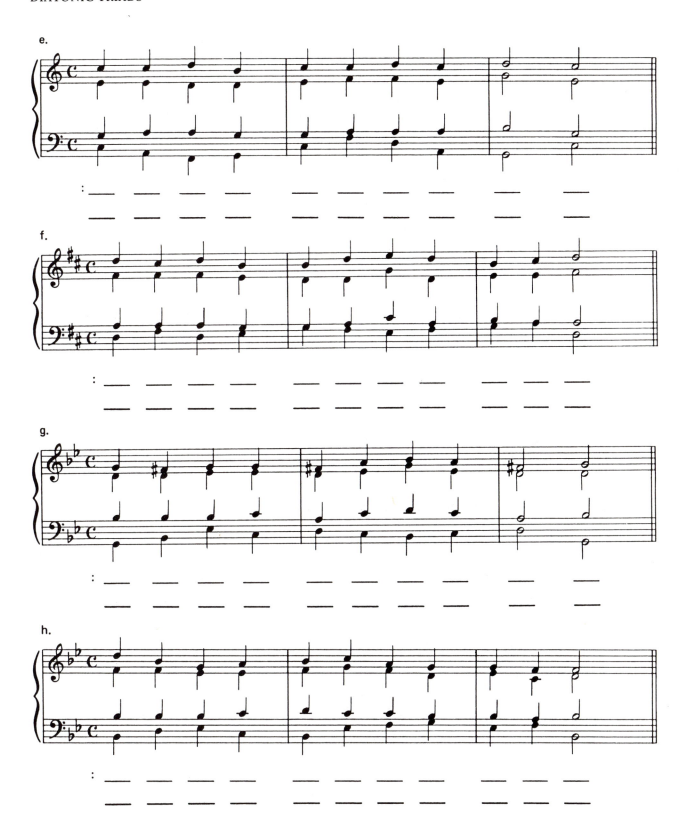

7. Analyze each chord progression using Roman numerals. Identify the root and quality of each chord. The circled notes are not part of the chord and should not be considered in the analysis.

Piano Concerto No. IV, Op. 58, Beethoven

a. Allegro moderato

Key G: I   _ _ _ _ _ _ _ _
        G   _ _ _ _ _ _ _ _

_   _   V⁷   _   _   _
_   _   D⁷   _   _   _

Preludio No. XI, J.S. Bach

b. Allegretto

Key   _ _ _ _ _ _ _ _ _ _ _
      _ _ _ _ _ _ _ _ _ _ _

The Wild Rider, Op. 68, No. 8, R. Schumann

c.   **Allegro con brio**

Key   :

fine

D.C. al fine*

*Repeat from the beginning to the word "fine."

Drink to Me Only with Thine Eyes, Old English Air

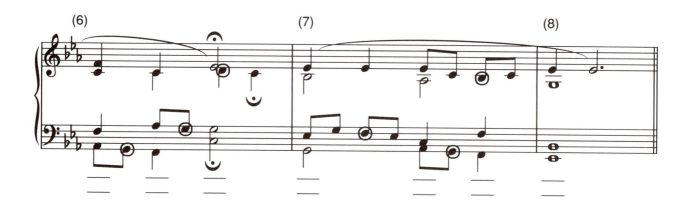

DIATONIC TRIADS REVIEW (SELF-TEST: CHAPTER TEN)

1. The three triads that are major in a major key are _____, _____, and _____ (Roman numerals).

2. The three triads that are minor in a major key are _____, _____, and _____.

3. The one triad that is diminished in a major key is _____.

4. The two triads that are minor in a minor key (harmonic form) are _____ and _____.

5. The two triads that are major in a minor key (harmonic form) are _____ and _____.

6. The two triads that are diminished in a minor key (harmonic form) are _____ and _____.

7. The one triad that is augmented in a minor key (harmonic form) is _____.

8. The names given to the diatonic triads found in major and minor (harmonic form) are (scale-degree names):

    a.

    b.

    c.

    d.

    e.

    f.

    g.

9. In minor (harmonic form), raising the seventh scale degree a chromatic half step alters the _____, _____, and _____ triads (Roman numerals).

10. The two triads in major and minor (harmonic form) that have similar qualities are _____ and _____ (Roman numerals).

11. In minor (natural form) the triad built on the seventh scale degree is called the _____ triad.

12. In minor (melodic form) the quality of the subdominant triad can be _____ or _____.

13. In a major key, the triad built on the seventh scale degree is called the _____ triad.

14. In minor (harmonic form), the triad built on the seventh scale degree is called the _____ _____triad.

15. Complete the following:

a. Upper-case Roman numerals are used to identify _____ triads (major, minor, augmented, diminished).

b. Lower-case Roman numerals are used to identify _____ triads.

c. An upper-case Roman numeral with a superscript plus ($^+$) is used to identify an_____ _____ triad.

d. A lower-case Roman numeral with a superscript zero (^{0}) is used to identify a_____ _____ triad.

16. The names for the diatonic triads (tonic, supertonic, mediant, etc.) built on the first six scale degrees in major and minor (all forms) are the same. True _____ False _____

17. The diatonic triads formed when using the lowered sixth and seventh scale degrees in minor (descending melodic) are the same as those formed when using the natural form of the minor scale. True _____ False _____

18. The first five notes (lower pentachord) of any form of a minor scale are the same. True _____ False _____

19. The three primary triads in a major key are _____, _____, and _____ (Roman numerals).

20. The three primary triads in a minor key (harmonic form) are _____, _____ and _____.

21. In a major key, the secondary triads are _____, _____, _____, and _____ (Roman numerals).

22. In a minor key (harmonic form), the secondary triads are _____, _____, _____, and _____.

23. In a minor key (harmonic form), there are two triads that are diminished and two triads that are augmented. True _____ False _____

Cadence Structures

GOALS

- The ability to identify any cadence

- The ability to classify any cadence

- The ability to write, in any key, an appropriate cadence pattern

The musical cadence is the means by which a musical phrase arrives at some type of closure. In many ways it is analogous to phrase punctuation in English. There are appropriate cadence types for interior phrases (phrases requiring an additional phrase for conclusion) and, likewise, appropriate closing or final cadence types. The term is from the Latin *cadere,* meaning "to fall," and is used today to describe the coming together or closing, either harmonically, melodically, or rhythmically, of musical expression.

A cadence can be determined by examining and analyzing the last two triads or sonorities in a musical phrase. The cadence can also be inferred from melodic patterns. Chapter 12, "Harmonization," will examine this concept in detail. This chapter approaches the study of cadence by classifying them as final and nonfinal types.[1]

FINAL CADENCE TYPES

Two specific chord progressions can serve as final cadences. Both of these progressions are conclusive and focus one's ear in the direction of the harmonic and melodic "home base," namely, tonic (Ex. 11.1).

Example 11.1

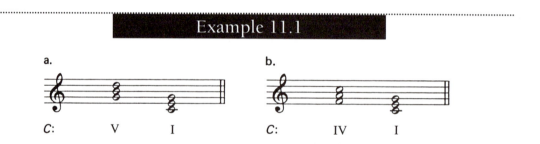

Authentic and Plagal Cadences

In order to be considered a final cadence, the last chord must be a tonic triad. The approach to the tonic may take two paths: (1) As in Example 11.1a, the tonic may be approached through the dominant triad (V–I); or (2) it may be approached, as in Example 11.1b, through the subdominant triad (IV–I). Example 11.1a (V–I) illustrates what is called an **authentic cadence.** Example 11.1b (IV–I) illustrates an example of a **plagal cadence.** The authentic cadence will sound very familiar to most students. The plagal cadence sound is also recognizable; it is the very typical "Amen" cadence concluding many hymns. Both of these cadences would appear in minor keys as shown in Example 11.2.

---

[1]The technical aspect of chord connection (voice leading/part writing) does not fall within the scope of this text, nor is it a consideration in these or any subsequent examples dealing with chord connection.

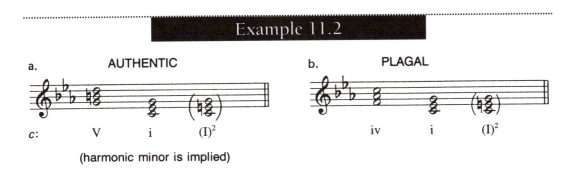

Example 11.2

a. AUTHENTIC   b. PLAGAL

c: V   i   (I)²   iv   i   (I)²

(harmonic minor is implied)

Perfect and Imperfect Cadences

Both of these final types of cadences may be additionally classified as **perfect** or **imperfect**. If the root of both chords is in the lowest voice (bass), and if the tonic (note) is in the highest voice of the final chord, the cadence is classified as perfect. If any of these factors is not present, the cadence is classified as imperfect.

NONFINAL CADENCE TYPES

There are two types of nonfinal cadences. Both are inconclusive; that is, they may not function as the last cadence in a phrase but rather serve to separate simple antecedent and consequent phrase structures. Both nonfinal types are intended for, and can be found in, analysis as interior-phrase closures (Ex. 11.3).

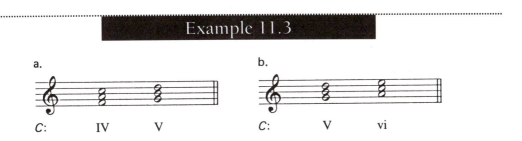

Example 11.3

a.   b.

C: IV   V   C: V   vi

Half Cadence and Deceptive Cadence

In Example 11.3a, the final chord is the dominant. In this example, it is approached through the subdominant; however, almost any chord can precede this

---

[2]From approximately the sixteenth through the mid-eighteenth centuries, a major tonic triad was commonly substituted for a final minor tonic triad; the raised third of this chord was termed a **Picardy third**.

dominant and the cadence type will remain intact. It is called a **half cadence** and can be described as a cadence on the dominant, approached by either a tonic or its secondary substitution (I or vi) or by a subdominant or its secondary substitution (IV or ii) triad. Example 11.3b illustrates what is known as a **deceptive cadence**. This is a cadence that is prepared by the dominant (V) triad. The ear fully expects the resolution to be to the tonic, but instead a secondary triad (vi) takes the place of the final chord. The result is a "deceived ear," accounting for the name of this cadence type. Although the V–vi progression is the most commonly occurring type of deceptive cadence, other progressions affecting such an "aural deception" are frequently encountered. These interior cadences could appear in minor keys, as shown in Example 11.4.

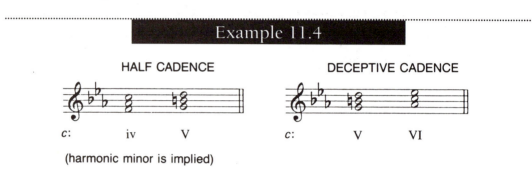

Example 11.4

HALF CADENCE

c: iv   V

DECEPTIVE CADENCE

c: V   VI

(harmonic minor is implied)

Note: In minor keys the Roman numerals for the approach and final chords in each of the four cadence types are the same for all cadences as they were in major keys. The only difference is that the key dictates the quality (major, minor, augmented, or diminished) of some of these triads.

CADENCE AS DETERMINED BY MELODIC DEMANDS

In a piece of music, cadence points are usually determined by several factors.

1. Usually the rhythmic values of the melody notes become somewhat elongated; that is, the melody seems to pause and "sit" momentarily.
2. In most Western tonal music, this pause usually occurs in the fourth, eighth, twelfth, or sixteenth measure.
3. The notes in the melody at these cadence points are actual chord-tone factors (root, third, or fifth) and can be found in the pairs of triads that form the above-described four stock cadence types.

A melody can therefore imply (sometimes dictate) the choice of cadence types. For example, if the final melodic note contains the root, third, or fifth found in the tonic chord, the tonic may be chosen to harmonize that final pitch of the melody. The penultimate (next-to-last) note would be found to be a factor in either the dominant triad (forming a V–I, or authentic, cadence—Ex. 11.5) or the subdominant triad (forming a IV–I, or plagal, cadence—Ex. 11.6).

Example 11.5

Melody Implying an Authentic Cadence

Example 11.6

Melody Implying a Plagal Cadence

If the final melodic note in an identified cadence is a factor (root, third, or fifth) in the dominant triad (V), then it must be determined which triad could serve as the penultimate or approach chord (Ex. 11.7).

Example 11.7

Melody Implying a Half Cadence

Finally, if the final melodic note in an identified cadence is a factor in the submediant triad (vi), it must be approached through the dominant chord; that is, the penultimate (approach) note in the melody must be a factor in the dominant triad (V—Ex. 11.8).

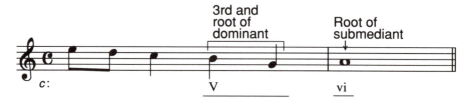

Example 11.8

Melody Implying a Deceptive Cadence

Armed with only these four "stock cadence types," one could effectively bring almost any tonal melodic phrase to a close, whether final or nonfinal.

Complete the chapter 11 drill sheets before continuing. Also, see Appendix A and Appendix B for further drills.

CHAPTER ELEVEN DRILLS AND EXERCISES

1. Analyze by Roman numeral the following cadential patterns. Then identify each cadence by specific type.

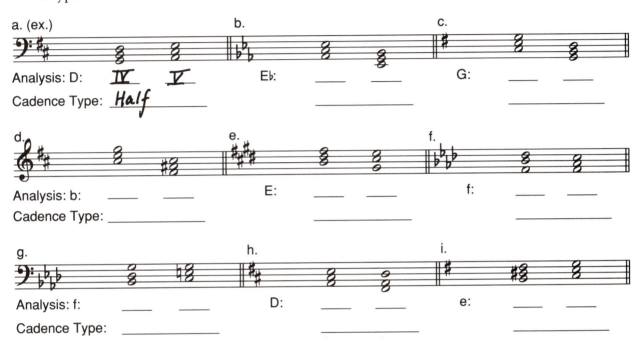

2. Notate the two chords (triads) representing the requested cadence type. Then analyze. Use the harmonic form for all examples in minor.

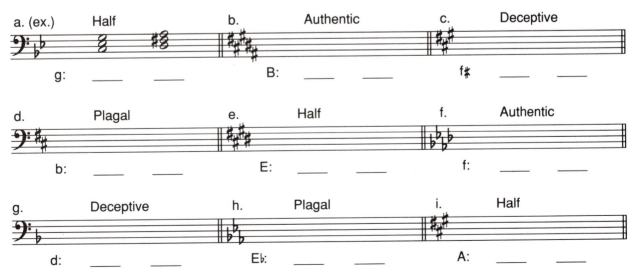

3. In the following examples, analyze the triads at the identified cadence points and label each type of cadence.

a.

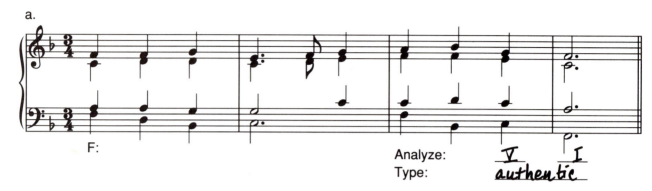

F:

Analyze: V I
Type: authentic

b.

b:

The Wild Rider, Op. 68, No. 8, R. Schumann

c. **Allegro con brio**

a:

d.

B♭:

e.

a:

f.

A:

g.

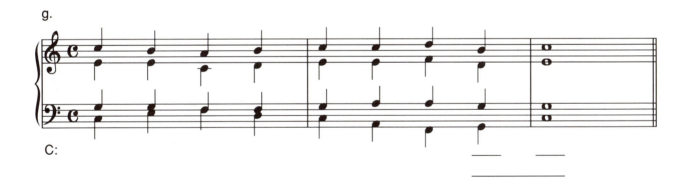

C:

4. Given the following melodic fragments, select the appropriate stock cadence type that best accommodates the melodic demands of each example. Use harmonic form for all minor keys.

CADENCE STRUCTURES REVIEW (SELF-TEST: CHAPTER ELEVEN)

1. The type of cadence employed can be determined by analyzing the last _____ (number) chords in a harmonic progression.

2. Two types of final cadences are the _____ and _____ cadences.

3. The chord progressions V–I (major) and V–i (minor, harmonic form) are classified as _____ cadences.

4. The chord progressions IV–I (major) and iv–i (minor, harmonic form) are classified as _____ cadences.

5. An authentic or plagal cadence is classified as perfect if _____ _____.

6. Two types of nonfinal cadences are the _____ and _____.

7. In a deceptive cadence in a major key, the dominant triad (V) resolves to _____ (Roman numeral).

8. In a deceptive cadence in a minor key (harmonic form), the dominant triad (V) resolves to _____ (Roman numeral).

9. In a half cadence, the final chord is usually _____ (Roman numeral).

10. Complete the following:

    a. The penultimate chord in an authentic cadence (major) is _____.

    b. The penultimate chord in a plagal cadence (major) is _____.

    c. The final chord in a deceptive cadence in a minor key (harmonic) is _____.

    d. The final chord in a half cadence (major) is usually _____.

11. If approaching a tonic triad as a final chord in a cadence, the penultimate, or approach, chord must be either a V or a vi. True _____ False _____

12. If approaching a submediant triad as a final chord in a cadence, the penultimate, or approach, chord must be a V. True _____ False _____

13. A dominant triad appearing as a penultimate triad can only resolve in a cadence to a _____ or a _____ (Roman numerals).

Harmonization

One of the most useful and interesting skills in theory is the harmonization of melody. This skill is the culmination of many previously learned concepts and requires you to use the skills acquired in previous units. Harmonization is the process of selecting appropriate harmonies for a given melody, deciding when to change those selected harmonies, and deciding which notes in a melody will be chord tones or **nonchord tones** (tones not accommodated by chords).

One might think that much of this skill is subjective—that is, dependent upon one's own taste and preferences; however, certain skills are necessary and can be learned in order to make logical decisions with regard to which melody notes to harmonize, when to change harmonies, and other matters.

HARMONIZING A MELODY

The following steps should be followed, in order, when selecting a simple harmony for a given melody.

1. Determine the key.[1]
2. Determine the cadence points (interior as well as final).
3. Determine the harmonic rhythm.
4. Sketch in primary triads.

These steps will provide you with a simple first-draft harmonization (more complex procedures will be discussed later in this chapter).

Step 4 will involve important decisions with respect to notes not accommodated by the selected triads. In making these decisions you will need to take into consideration factors such as:

1. harmonic rhythm
2. strong and weak beats in a given measure
3. prominent duration of notes
4. positioning of nonchord tones (nonharmonic tones).

Each step will now be discussed in detail. If any reference to a previously covered skill is not clear, you will need to refer to the appropriate unit for review. The following areas are assumed knowledge for this unit.

1. intervals   4. triads
2. scales   5. diatonic triads
3. rhythm and meter   6. cadence-type identification skills

---

[1]In many cases, steps 1 and 2 will be combined.

Step 1: Determine the Key

The key of any given melody can usually be accurately assessed by a few quick checks or observations. First, observe the key signature. This will tell you that the key indicated is either the major or the relative minor for that particular signature. For example, a two-sharp signature would imply either *D* major or *b* minor. At this point, observe the cadences (both interior and final), looking for "stock" cadence types. Usually, interior cadences will be some type of half cadence, and the final cadence will be either authentic or plagal.

In minor keys, somewhere within the melody, you may look for and notice chromatically altered leading tones (or altered submediant scale degrees). These chromatic alterations would be foreign to the major key yet are diatonic to the minor (Ex. 12.1).

Example 12.1
Determining the Key

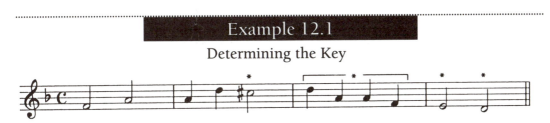

*Points which determine the key of *d* minor.

In Example 12.1, *C*♯ represents a leading tone in *d* minor with a cadence on *D*.

Step 2: Determine the Cadence Points

In order to complete this step, you must be able to identify where the cadence points occur. These points can be identified as "points of repose" in a melody and usually contain notes of longer durations. For example, if a melody is progressing in quarter and eighth notes, a cadence point might exhibit half notes.

If you are able to sing through the melody, or to play it, these cadence points will often stand out clearly. They will always conform to one of the "stock" cadence types presented previously since the notes of the melody will contain notes found in the triads of these cadences. They may be identified accordingly (Ex. 12.2).

Example 12.2
Determining the Cadence Points

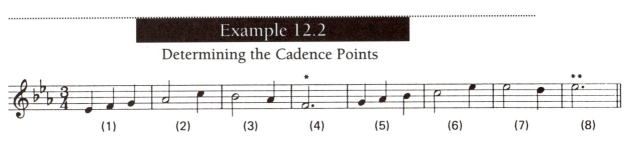

(1)   (2)   (3)   (4)   (5)   (6)   (7)   (8)

*Interior cadence point
**Final cadence point

In Example 12.2, E♭ major can be identified as the key, according to the procedures in step 1. The cadence points are identified as having longer note durations. The interior cadence (*) contains the note F, which is one of the notes of the dominant triad (B♭–D–F). This note can be harmonized with a V (dominant triad) and would thus fulfill the requirements for a half cadence.

The final cadence (**) has the final note of E♭ and could be accommodated by the tonic triad (E♭–G–B♭), thus constituting a cadence ending on the tonic (final). The approach to the tonic triad at the end could consider E♭ (third-to-last note) as a chord tone and could be harmonized by a plagal cadence (IV–I); or the D (penultimate note) could be considered as a chord tone, and it would accommodate a dominant-to-tonic, authentic cadence (V–I).

Either of these two choices would be logical and would depend upon the preference and personal taste of the person doing the harmonization. This process can *only lead you to logical choices—the final decision is ultimately subjective.* For a more complete discussion of how to select a chord for any given note, see step 4 in this process.

Step 3: Determine the Harmonic Rhythm

Harmonic rhythm is the rate at which harmonies change. It could be once per beat, once per measure, once every other measure, or almost any rate. It is primarily determined by the notes or tempo (or both) of the melody. Slow-moving melody notes might require a change on every beat, while rapidly moving melodic notes might call for changes less often, with more nonchord tones.

Looking back, Example 12.1 could have a harmonic rhythm of a half note since the melody seems to call for harmonic change every half note, or twice per measure. Example 12.2 could have a harmonic rhythm of a dotted half note as the melody seems to call for a harmonic change every dotted half note, or once per measure.

There is often a break or change in the harmonic rhythm when approaching a cadence, and it is not uncommon to find a harmonic rhythm, such as in measure 7 of Example 12.2, calling for quicker change of harmony at the cadence points.

Example 12.3 illustrates steps 1 and 2 completed: The key is determined as D major, the cadence types are identified (*) as a half cadence in measure 2, and a final (authentic) cadence in measure 4.

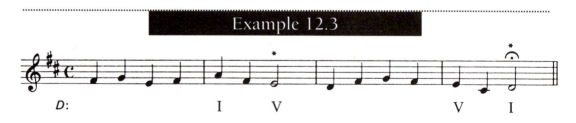

Example 12.3

The harmonic rhythm in this example would be the half note as changes in harmony seem to be called for on every other beat, or twice each measure.

Roman numerals are used in the example to identify the harmonies, and it is understood that the labeled harmony remains in place until changed. The placement of the numeral determines the point at which the change occurs. The key must be labeled in order for these Roman numerals to make sense. They must refer to diatonic harmonies within a certain key. An alternate method of notating harmonic change is given in step 4. Either method is acceptable; however, you should be consistent.

Step 4: Sketch in Primary Triads

Once the key of a melody is determined, you should recall, and jot down if necessary, the three primary triads found in that key. Almost any diatonic melody can be harmonized by using only these three chords. As a first draft, we will employ these; and later in the process we will make some substitutions that may sound more sophisticated and colorful. At this point, you need to know the information in steps 1 through 3, including the harmonic rhythm.

The melody should be examined, looking for rhythmically prominent thirds and fifths (or their inversions), since both notes contained in either of these two intervals can be found in the same chord. Keep in mind that triads are constructed in thirds and that we will be looking for melodic patterns that can be accommodated by primary triads.

Example 12.4

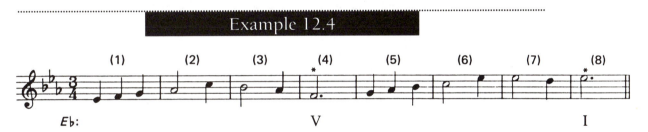

In Example 12.4 it has been determined that the key is $E^\flat$ major, and the cadence points have been identified (the first as a half cadence and the second as a final cadence). The harmonic rhythm in this example would be the dotted half note, or the full measure. Measure 4 has been identified as a cadence point because of the pause, or lack of melodic activity (the dotted half note).

Keeping in mind the primary triads (I: $E^\flat$–G–$B^\flat$; IV: $A^\flat$–C–$E^\flat$; V: $B^\flat$–D–F) we find that the pitch F in measure 4 is best accommodated by the dominant triad. This is the only primary triad containing an F.

As you can see, we are looking for the appropriate primary triad that contains the particular melodic note. Measure 1 contains the notes $E^\flat$, F, and G. Since triads are constructed in thirds and the harmonic rhythm is the dotted half note, we should attempt to accommodate only the $E^\flat$ and the G. The F will be considered a nonchord tone and will not be part of the sounding harmony. This decision is based on the following observations.

1. Two out of the three notes can be chord tones.
2. The F is in a rhythmically weak position in the measure.

Nonchord tones provide a necessary amount of dissonance or tension in a given situation. This balance between dissonance and consonance is a delicate one. Without dissonance, melodies could be boring and lack the tension–relaxation quality so common in the art form. In accommodating the $E^\flat$ and G, we find that the tonic triad is the most appropriate choice for measure 1. Measure 2 is a rather simple one in determining the chord choice. It contains only $A^\flat$ and C, both of which can be found in the subdominant (IV) triad.

Measure 3 contains the notes $B^\flat$ and $A^\flat$. It is also the measure that approaches the dominant triad in the half cadence. The $B^\flat$ is the more prominent note of the measure; therefore, the $A^\flat$ will be left as a nonchord tone. In approaching the harmonization of this $B^\flat$, one must consider the harmony already assigned to the following measure, namely the dominant. To harmonize measure 3 with the dominant would not only be redundant but would also take the "punch" out of measure 4; therefore, the only other primary triad containing $B^\flat$ would be the tonic. It would be the best choice in this situation.

Measure 5 contains three notes in stepwise motion. This type of motion is called **conjunct motion.** Once again, we need to determine which notes will be chord tones and which will be nonchord tones. Since the $A^\flat$ occurs between two notes forming a third, we will select G and $B^\flat$ as chord tones and the $A^\flat$ as a nonchord tone. G and $B^\flat$ are part of the tonic triad, and, therefore, it is the best choice in this instance.

Measure 6 is also a simple task. As in measure 2, it contains only two notes, a third apart. Both the C and $E^\flat$ can be found in the subdominant (IV) triad.

Measure 7 presents a more difficult situation in harmonization. We must look ahead and note that measure 8 is the final cadence, harmonized by the tonic. We would want to approach the tonic either through the dominant (V) or the subdominant (IV) to form one of our stock final cadences. Two possible solutions present themselves here, and both are viable:

Solution 1: Consider the $E^\flat$ in measure 7 as a chord tone and the D as a nonchord tone, and harmonize the measure with a subdominant, resulting in a plagal (IV–I) cadence.

Solution 2: Consider the D in measure 7 as a chord tone and the $E^\flat$ as a nonchord tone. This will result in the rhythmically more prominent note being a nonchord tone; however, this dramatic point of tension is appropriate at a cadence point since it amounts to the "final tension" before the final resolution. This will result in an *authentic cadence (V–I)*.

Either of these two solutions would work. Ideally, and until more experience is gained, you should play both solutions and select the one that is audibly more acceptable to you, keeping in mind that this is a subjective decision.

Solution 3: As an alternative, you could also break the harmonic rhythm in measure 7 and employ the tonic triad on the $E^\flat$, changing to the dominant on the D. This also would be acceptable since harmonic rhythm is often broken at the cadence points.

As mentioned in step 3, an alternate method of notating harmony for a given melody may be used (Ex. 12.5).

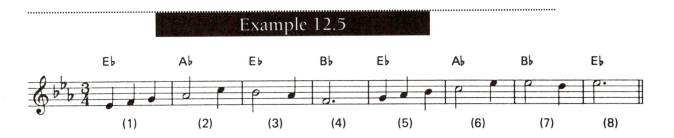

Example 12.5

Using the same melody, chords can be notated using letters above (or below) the given melody. These letters indicate the roots and qualities of the chords. This is commonly found in sheet music and is known as "lead-sheet" chord abbreviations. The letter abbreviations are not standardized. For example, "Am" as well as "a" can indicate an *a* minor chord. "A dim," "a dim," and "a⁰" can indicate an *a* diminished chord. In this style of notation, it is not necessary to indicate the key of the melody, although knowing the key is essential to harmonizing the melody.

SECONDARY SUBSTITUTION CHORDS: ADDING HARMONIC COLOR

Secondary triads (ii, iii, vi, vii⁰ in major, and ii⁰ III⁺, VI, vii⁰ in minor, harmonic form) may be used as substitution chords for their respective primaries. Substitution chords are located a diatonic third below the roots of the primary triads, the exception being the vii⁰, which is a diatonic third above the dominant (Ex. 12.6).

Example 12.6

Major

Primary:	I	IV	V
Substitution:	vi	ii	vii⁰
		iii	

Minor

Primary:	i	iv	V
Substitution:	VI	ii⁰	vii⁰
			III+

Secondary substitution chords have an important function in harmonization. When a certain primary triad is to be repeated, its secondary triad may be used on the repetition. This process allows for a change of harmonic color. For example, in *C* major, a repeated tonic chord may be replaced by a submediant (vi). This submediant differs from the tonic triad by one note (*A*), creating a minor harmonic quality while still retaining the tonic function. This change of harmonic quality can be helpful in extending harmonies over longer time spans.

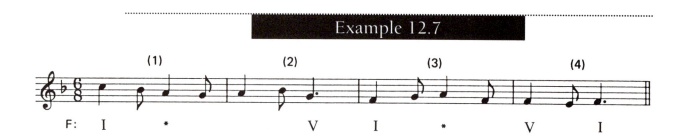

Example 12.7

In Example 12.7, the harmonic rhythm is felt as the dotted quarter note (two changes per measure), yet in places the melody dictates that the same harmony should be repeated (as in measures 1 and 3). In the second half of these measures, the secondary substitution chord for the tonic (vi) could effectively be used. Thus, inserting a *d* minor triad on the second beat of both the first and third measures provides a more colorful and active harmony, while it does not change the tonic function of those measures.

Note the dissonance on the dominant triad in the last measure (final cadence). An alternate harmonization here would be to break the harmonic rhythm and use a tonic on the first *F*, change to a dominant on the eighth note *E*, and return to the tonic on the final *F*.

Complete the chapter 12 drill sheets on the following pages before continuing. Also, see Appendix A, Appendix B, and Appendix F.

CHAPTER TWELVE DRILLS AND EXERCISES

Harmonize the following examples according to the procedures outlined in chapter 12. It is suggested that these melodies be played at the keyboard and that preliminary harmonization be attempted using only primary triads. Secondary substitution chords may be employed after the skeletal application of preliminary harmonies.

1.

ex. C: I   IV   V   I
        C   F   G   C

2.

3. The Art of Fugue, Contrapunctus 1, Bach

4. Piano Sonata, K. #332, Mozart

5.

6. Eine kleine Nachtmusik (3rd movement), Mozart

7.

8.

9.

10.

11. String Quartet, Op. 135 (3rd movement), Beethoven

12. "La Bandoline" from Pieces de Clavecin, Couperin

13.

14.

15.

See Appendix F for additional melodies to harmonize.

HARMONIZATION REVIEW (SELF-TEST: CHAPTER TWELVE)

1. Harmonic rhythm may be defined as _____
   _____.

2. Determining cadence points and selecting the types of cadences to be used should be one of the last procedures to consider when harmonizing a melody. True _____ False _____

3. Nonchord (or nonharmonic) tones may be defined as _____
   _____.

4. Complete the following:

   a. In a major key, the substitute chord for the tonic triad (I) is _____ (Roman numeral).

   b. In a major key, the substitute chord for the dominant triad (V) is _____ or _____.

   c. In a major key, the substitute chord for the subdominant triad (IV) is _____.

   d. In a minor key (harmonic form), the substitute chord for the tonic triad (i) is _____.

   e. In a minor key (harmonic form), the substitute chord for the subdominant triad (iv) is _____.

   f. In a minor key (harmonic form), the substitute chord for the dominant triad (V) is _____ or _____.

5. The key of a melody can usually be determined by _____
   _____.

6. Cadence points in a melody can usually be determined by observing where _____
   _____.

7. Most diatonic melodies can be harmonized by using only primary triads. True _____ False _____

8. The term "conjunct motion" is used to describe melodies that _____
_____.

9. In a melodic situation in which three stepwise notes appear, which of the three should not be considered as a chord tone if all three notes are being harmonized by the same chord? _____.

Form in Music

GOALS

• The ability to balance concepts of unity and contrast

• The understanding of motivic concepts and manipulations

• The ability to modify and extend, by manipulations, any given motive

• The ability to analyze the motivic structure of a musical phrase

• The ability to recognize and analyze simple melodic phrases and part forms in music

Form in music requires a delicate balance between contrast and unity. This balance can make the difference between a musical phrase that is interesting, yet understandable, and one in which ideas seem jumbled and unconnected. Form can be thought of in both macro and micro terms. The macro type of form is concerned with contrasting and similar phrase structure, overall contrast and repetition of thematic material, key relationships, and so on. The micro concepts of form deal specifically with small fragments and the manner in which the composer connects, interconnects, and, in general, manipulates these small ideas into larger musical phrases. This chapter will address both of these concepts of form and organization, beginning with the micro concepts, referring to the smallest unit, the "germ" idea, as **motive** or **motif**.

MOTIVE STRUCTURES

Motive is the smallest structure from which additional material may be generated. While the motive may, in fact, be harmonic or rhythmic, most motivic structures are considered and analyzed as melodic components. A motive may generally consist of two to eight notes. Once a motive is identified, you can trace various forms of it as it is manipulated through the process of musical creation.

In order to understand motivic concepts, each of the known manipulations will be discussed, explained, and illustrated by traditional notation as well as graphic representation. It is hoped that the graphic notation will help you establish a firmer grasp of the material and further serve as a memory aid.

The motive in Example 13.1 will be used throughout this chapter, along with its graphic representation.

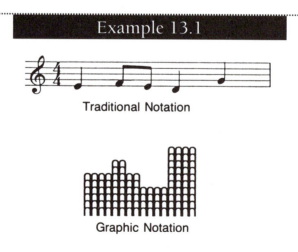

Example 13.1

Traditional Notation

Graphic Notation

REPETITION

The simplest of all manipulations would be the literal repetition of a motive (Ex. 13.2).

Example 13.2

While repetition might be the easiest to recognize and the simplest manipulation to write, you must be careful to avoid inducing boredom. This type of motivic extension quickly becomes tiresome, and great care must be exercised in choosing when and how often to use this device. Literal repetition, such as appears in Example 13.2, can be enhanced, however, by changes in dynamics, articulation, register, or orchestration.

TRANSPOSITION

A repeated motive may begin on a different pitch level. That is, the repeated motive would start on another pitch yet would follow accurately its original contour (Ex. 13.3). The transposition need not be immediate. There may be intervening material between the original and the transposition.

Example 13.3

1 Original
2 Transposition

Transposition affords the opportunity for a tremendous amount of variation. Many repetitions can be tolerated by the listener, as long as these repetitions appear at different pitch levels.

Two types of transposition are possible: (1) literal, exact transposition, in which the basic interval is retained and the exact quality of each successive interval is also retained; (2) approximate transposition, in which only the basic interval is maintained and the quality of the melodic intervals may vary (Ex. 13.4).

Example 13.4

Type 1: REAL TRANSPOSITION
of Example 13.3

Type 2: TONAL TRANSPOSITION
of Example 13.3

The terms used for these two types are given in Example 13.4: Exact (including interval quality) transposition, type 1, is called **real transposition**, and the approximate, type 2, is called **tonal transposition**. It follows that tonal transposition is consistent with the tonality as set forth in the key center (or signature). The real transposition may include chromatic signs in addition to those in the established key.

SEQUENCE

Sequence can be defined as two or more appearances of the motive, each at a different pitch level (transposed). To qualify as a sequence, at least two appearances are required, and these appearances *must be adjacent* to each other (Ex. 13.5). Most of the time, appearances of a motive in sequence begin on pitches that are also adjacent to each other, as in the beginning pitches in Example 13.5b (*E, D, C*).

Example 13.5

It is important to keep in mind that a sequence may continue through many transpositions. Sequence may be either tonal or real, depending upon whether or not the composer chooses to chromatically alter the melodic content. The sequence in Example 13.5b is tonal because the exact quality of some of the intervals is not maintained in the transpositions. Example 13.5b is therefore a tonal sequence.

RETROGRADE

The motive appearing backwards is a **retrograde**. Transposition and sequence may also apply to retrogrades (Ex. 13.6) as well as to all other manipulations.

Example 13.6

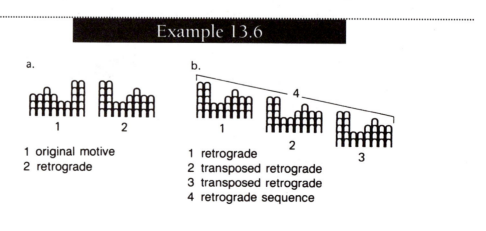

a.
1 original motive
2 retrograde

b.
1 retrograde
2 transposed retrograde
3 transposed retrograde
4 retrograde sequence

Retrograde appears as a vertical mirror image; that is, backwards. It should be noted that the rhythmic component, as well as pitches, are reflected in retrograde (Ex. 13.7).

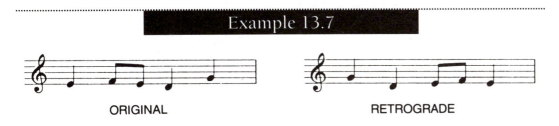

ORIGINAL   RETROGRADE

INVERSION

The **inversion** of a motive represents a horizontal mirror image. That is, it would appear upside down, as in a reflection in water. The motive will begin on the same pitch as the original; then, as the original descends, the inversion correspondingly ascends, following the same contour and intervals but in the opposite direction (Ex. 13.8).

1 Original
2 Inversion

Inversion can be either real or tonal. Example 13.9a illustrates a tonal inversion. In order to write a real inversion the D (second note) must appear as a D$\sharp$, and the F and C (fourth and fifth notes) must appear as F$\sharp$ and C$\sharp$ (Ex. 13.9b).

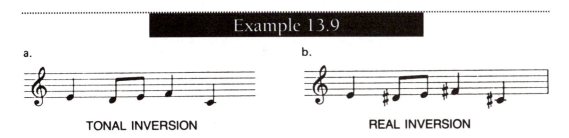

a.   b.

TONAL INVERSION   REAL INVERSION

RETROGRADE INVERSION

While any of the above manipulations may be used in combination (for example, a transposed retrograde), **retrograde inversion** is the only combination that has a formal term. It is best to think of this device as a "backwards inversion," or as a retrograde of the original inversion, since conceiving of this as an "inverted retrograde" is *not a legitimate label* for this manipulation.

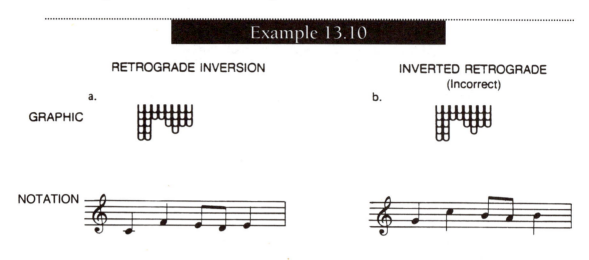

Example 13.10

RETROGRADE INVERSION   INVERTED RETROGRADE
                                                 (Incorrect)

a.   b.

GRAPHIC

NOTATION

While both the RI (retrograde inversion) and the IR (inverted retrograde) look identical in graphic representation, they appear quite different in actual notation. The notated example of the IR (Ex. 13:10b) appears merely as a transposition of the RI (Ex. 13.10a). The reason that the inverted retrograde is incorrect as a manipulation is that the IR merely forms a transposition of the retrograde inversion and is therefore a transposed RI. Example 13.10a is the correct version—the "backwards inversion" (RI).

AUGMENTATION AND DIMINUTION

These devices affect the durational aspect of a given motive. **Augmentation** is the term for increasing the durational values of the notes, while **diminution** is the label applied to decreasing durational values (Ex. 13.11).

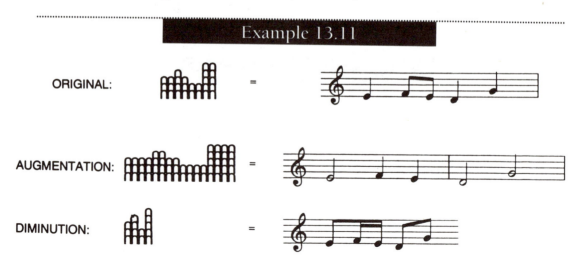

Example 13.11

ORIGINAL:

AUGMENTATION:

DIMINUTION:

Note that in Example 13.11, augmentation results in two measures (twice the duration of the original). While doubling or halving the durations represent the most common practices, any amount of durational adjustments may, in fact, result in augmentation or diminution.

DELETION AND EMBELLISHMENT

These devices, when applied to a given motive, either eliminate notes from the original (**deletion**) or append additional notes to the original (**embellishment**) (Ex. 13.12).

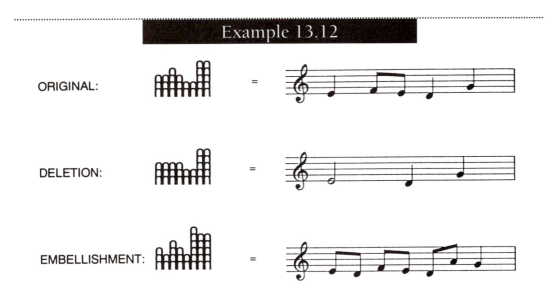

One can think of embellishment as a "filling-in" process that treats the original as a skeleton structure. Conversely, deletion "skeletalizes" the original, leaving only structural tones in place. In the process of deletion, some of the original notes of the motive may appear in longer durations, absorbing the durations of those notes omitted. Although this resembles augmentation, it does not extend the total duration of the motive as would augmentation.

INTERVALLIC EXPANSION AND CONTRACTION

These manipulations vary the size of intervals found in the original motive. **Intervallic expansion** increases the size of some (any number), while **intervallic contraction** decreases the size (Ex. 13.13).

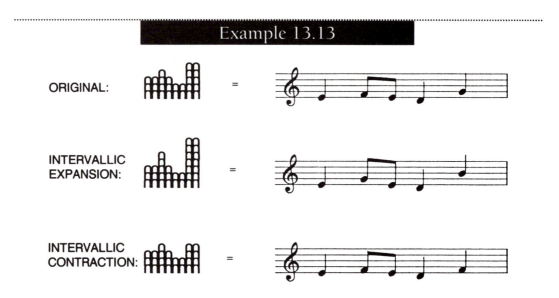

FRAGMENTATION

This device entails the isolation of sections of a given motive and the application of any combination of manipulations to these individual sections. Motivic fragments may be referred to as **submotives**, if the occurrence of these manipulated fragments is significant. Example 13.14 illustrates some of these fragmented manipulations.

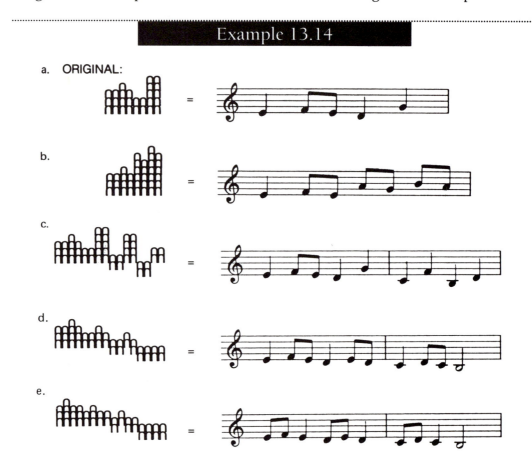

Example 13.14b illustrates the sequential treatment of the eighth-note fragment *F*, *E* (tonal sequence). Example 13.14c illustrates the sequential treatment of the perfect fourth of the original (*D–G*). Notice that the last appearance of transposition in the sequence also demonstrates the use of intervallic contraction (last two notes: *B–D*).

Example 13.14d treats the second, third, and fourth notes of the original (*F, E, D*) as a fragment or submotive and runs three transpositions as a sequence, cadencing on the final note (*B*). In the key of *C* major, this would imply a half cadence. Example 13.14e appears as a sequence, based on the retrograde of the first three notes of the original (*E, F, E*). Appearing three times in transposition (sequence), this phrase cadences on the leading tone (*B*), implying a half cadence. This manipulation may also be interpreted as a rhythmic variation of the first three notes of the original motive.

These illustrations represent only a small sampling of possible manipulations dealing specifically with fragmentation. It must be kept in mind that any of the manipulations discussed in this chapter may appear in any combinations.

When fragmentation is used extensively, one may choose, in analysis, to identify the motive as a combined submotive A and submotive B. Another possible identification might be to label these submotives individually as motive 1 and motive 2. These alternate identifying terms are employed based upon a somewhat subjective decision with regard to the submotives' subsequent appearances as structural elements. In other words, one chooses the appropriate terminology based upon careful observations of motivic appearances.

MUSICAL FORM

Phrase Structure

You have now covered all of the components needed to understand simple musical phrase structure and simple forms in music. While the study of musical form is an extremely complex endeavor, the understanding of simple phrase structure and simple part forms is easily within grasp and will greatly enhance your understanding of just how motivic manipulations contribute to the art of composition.

A **phrase** in tonal music consists of a given motive or motives, some form of manipulation of this motive, a rhythmic fabric and key context, and is framed by some type of cadence structure. While a musical phrase can stand alone, it usually appears in sets of phrases, some concluding with a type of nonfinal cadence (half cadence or deceptive cadence) and others bringing the musical statement to full closure (by using authentic or plagal cadences). Phrases in music are similar to phrases in any language. Most individual phrases rely upon others, or subsequent phrases, in order to form larger, more complete statements.

A phrase is said to be **regular** when it conforms to the standard (in Western tonal music) four- or eight-measure unit. An **irregular** phrase is one of any duration other than four or eight measures (for example, a three-measure or five-measure phrase). The melody in Example 13.15 illustrates a pair of regular, four-measure phrases.

Example 13.15

Symphony, No. 101   Haydn

Note that the first phrase, ending in measure 4, concludes as an implied half cadence, and in measure 8, the second phrase comes to full closure in the form of an authentic cadence. On further examination, you will see that the entire second phrase is a tonal transposition of the first four measures.

Period Form

The above example (Ex. 13.15) illustrates what is known as a **two-phrase period**. A period is any musical statement consisting of two or more phrases that form a more complete or coherent melodic statement. Most often, the first phrase in such a period ends on a nonfinal cadence, thus requiring the subsequent phrase in order to bring the melodic idea to conclusion. If two phrases comprise a given period, they may be similar phrases, as in Example 13.15, or contrasting phrases—that is, phrases that are structurally different from each other (Ex. 13.16).

Example 13.16

British

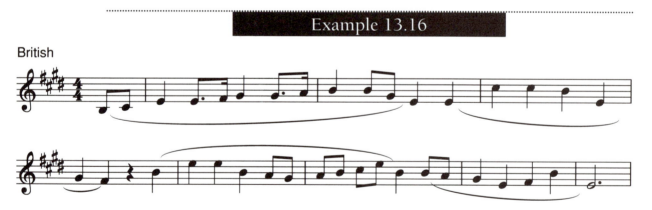

When phrases are melodically similar in construction, as in Example 13.15, the period is said to be a **parallel period**. When the phrases are different, as in Example 13.16, the structure is known as **a contrasting period**.

Two-Part and Three-Part Form

Most compositions consist of more than one phrase or even more than one period. When a second phrase or second period follows the first, it usually consists of different, or contrasting, material. This is known as **two-part form** and is sometimes termed **binary form**. It is usually represented, in analysis symbols, as an A–B form. Sometimes one or both of the contrasting phrases may be repeated (AA–BB), but it is still termed a binary or two-part form. The most common of all part forms is the **three-part form**, or **ternary form**.

This structure consists of the same A–B binary construction, with the addition of a restatement of the A material, resulting in an A–B–A form. You can think of this as a "B sandwich," or as a phrase, followed by a digression or contrasting phrase, followed by a restatement of the first phrase.

Example 13.17

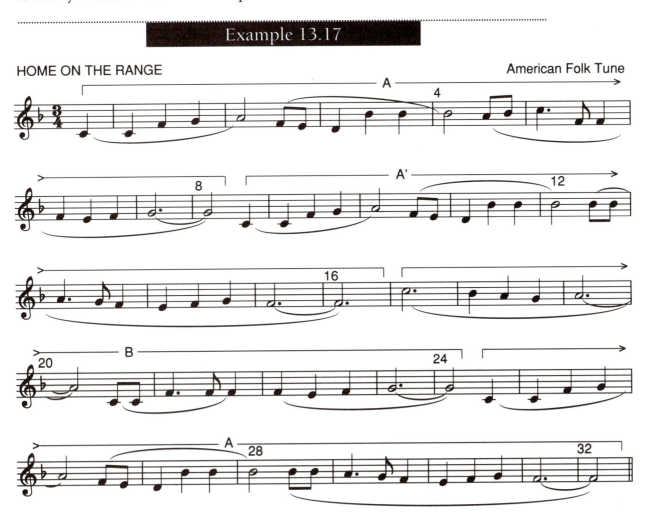

HOME ON THE RANGE   American Folk Tune

Example 13.17 is a ternary or A–B–A form with eight-measure phrases. Part A concludes in measure 8 with a melodically implied half cadence. Measures 9–16 repeat part A with slight cadential modification (the first four measures of the phrase are the same, with a different closing in the last four measures, which conclude in an implied authentic cadence). The first sixteen measures actually constitute a parallel period. Beginning in measure 17 and for the following eight measures (up to the cadence in measure 24) the melody is contrasting material, constituting a B section, ending in an implied half cadence. The restatement of the A material in the concluding eight measures represents a return to the A material, ending in an authentic (V–I) cadence.

This ternary form is also known as **song form** since it is, by far, the most common structure in popular Western tonal music.

Complete the chapter 13 drill sheets on the following pages before continuing. Also, see Appendix A and Appendix B, and refer to Appendix F for additional exercises in phrase and motivic analysis.

CHAPTER THIRTEEN DRILLS AND EXERCISES

1. Given the following motives, notate the requested manipulation on the staff provided.

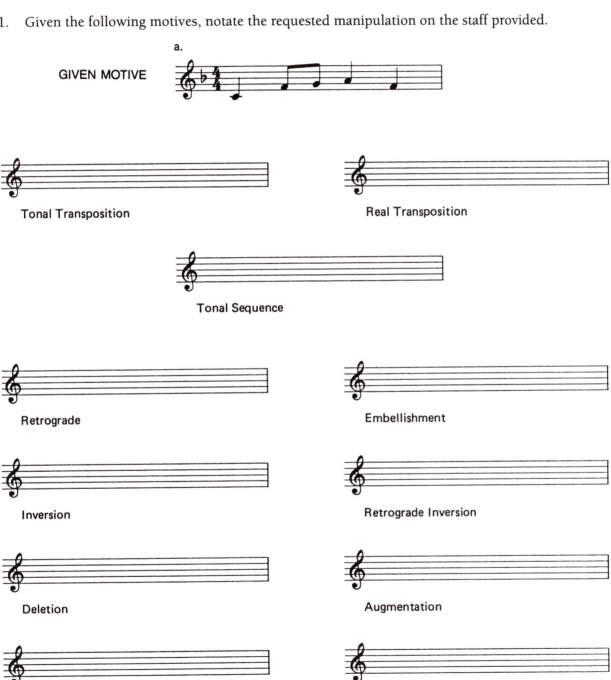

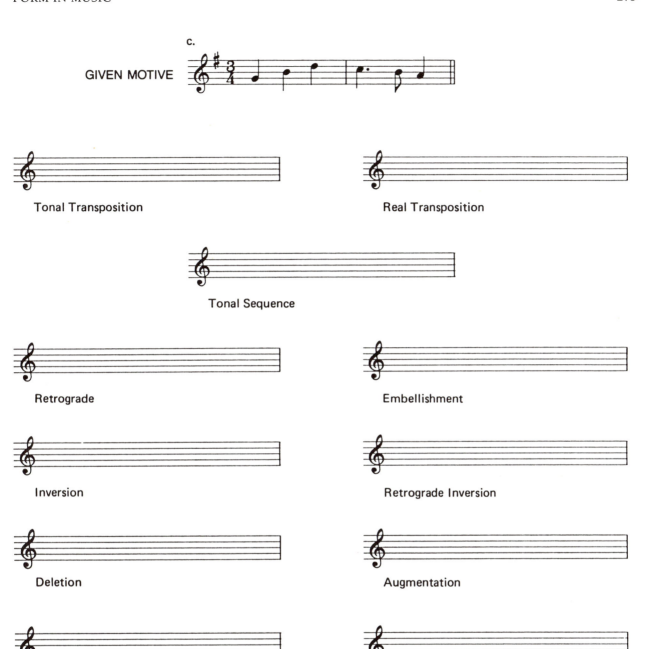

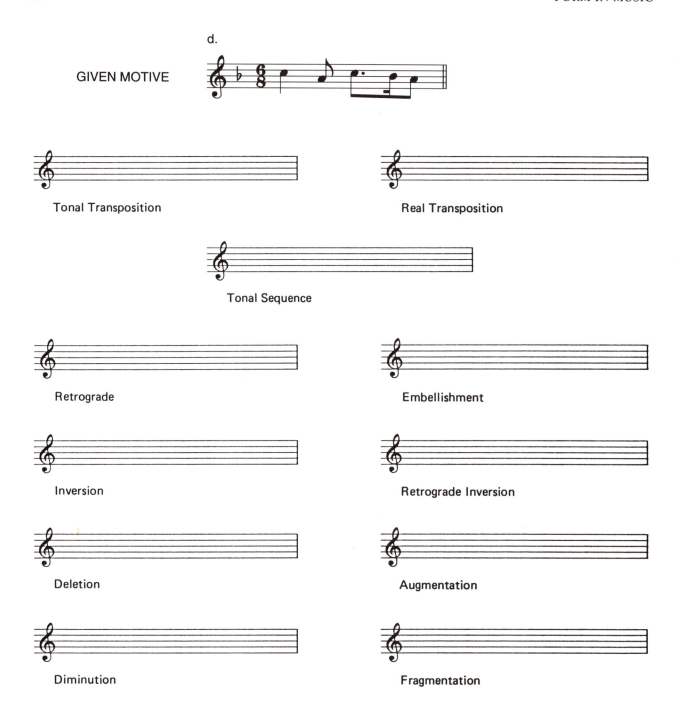

2. In the following examples an original motive is given, followed by several modifications. Identify each modification as it relates to the original.

a. Original

1.   ex. *retrograde* _____   2. _____   3. _____

4.   _____

b. Original

1.   _____   2. _____   3. _____

4.   _____

c. Original

d. Original

e. Original

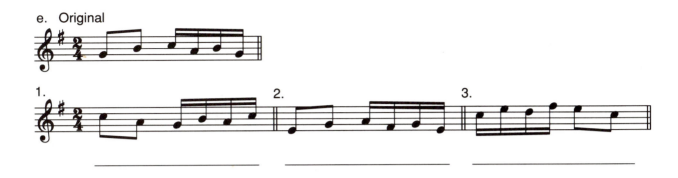

4.

f. Original

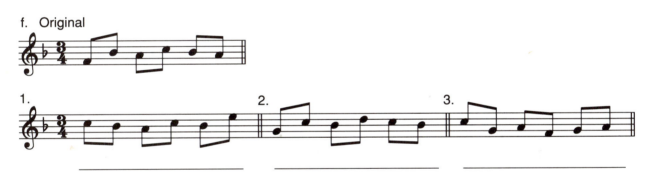

g. Original

1.   2.   3.

_____   _____   _____

4.

_____

h. Original

1.   2.   3.

_____   _____   _____

4.   5.

_____   _____

3. For each of the following excerpts, identify the motive(s) and each manipulation (account for every measure of music). Then analyze the phrase structure, identify (by bracketing) repeated, varied, or different phrases. Finally, state the overall form of each excerpt.

a.

Motive

Measure:	1. _____	9. _____	17. _____
	2. _____	10. _____	18. _____
	3. _____	11. _____	19. _____
	4. _____	12. _____	20. _____
	5. _____	13. _____	21. _____
	6. _____	14. _____	22. _____
	7. _____	15. _____	23. _____
	8. _____	16. _____	24. _____

The phrase structure in the above excerpt is _____.

b.

(1)   (2)   (3)   (4)   (5)

(6)   (7)   (8)   (9)   (10)   (11)

(12)   (13)   (14)   (15)   (16)

Motive

Measure: 1. _____   9. _____
           2. _____   10. _____
           3. _____   11. _____
           4. _____   12. _____
           5. _____   13. _____
           6. _____   14. _____
           7. _____   15. _____
           8. _____   16. _____

The phrase structure in the above excerpt is _____.

c.

Andante

German

Motive

Measure: 1. _____   9. _____

2. _____   10. _____

3. _____   11. _____

4. _____   12. _____

5. _____   13. _____

6. _____   14. _____

7. _____   15. _____

8. _____   16. _____

The phrase structure in the above excerpt is _____.

d.

(1)   (2)   (3)   (4)

(5)   (6)   (7)   (8)

Motive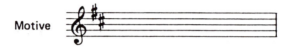

Measure: 1. _____
             2. _____
             3. _____
             4. _____
             5. _____
             6. _____
             7. _____
             8. _____

The phrase structure in the above excerpt is _____.

See Appendix F for additional melodies that can be used for motivic and phrase analysis.

Ear-Training Exercises

....

CHAPTER 1

1. WHOLE AND HALF STEP

Your instructor will play pairs of pitches. Identify them as either whole step (WS) or half step (HS). Each may be played either melodically or harmonically.

a. _____	f. _____	k. _____
b. _____	g. _____	l. _____
c. _____	h. _____	m. _____
d. _____	i. _____	n. _____
e. _____	j. _____	o. _____

p. _____	u. _____
q. _____	v. _____
r. _____	w. _____
s. _____	x. _____
t. _____	y. _____

Your instructor will predetermine the order of these examples for 1a–1y.

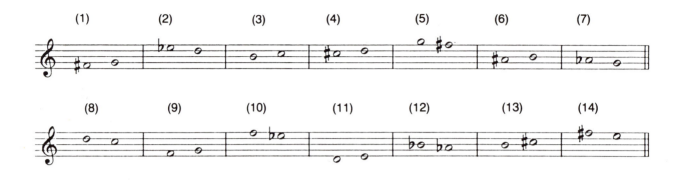

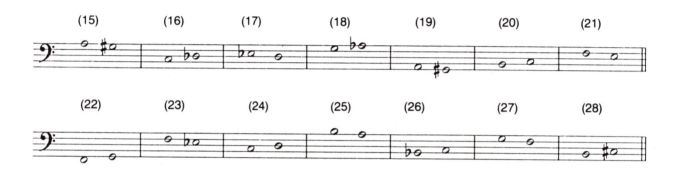

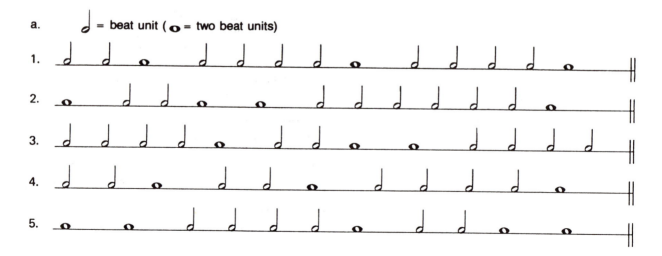

CHAPTER 2: RHYTHM

1. Practice tapping the following examples using the *simple beat unit* indicated as the pulse. Establish and retain a steady beat with one hand while tapping the example given with the other hand.

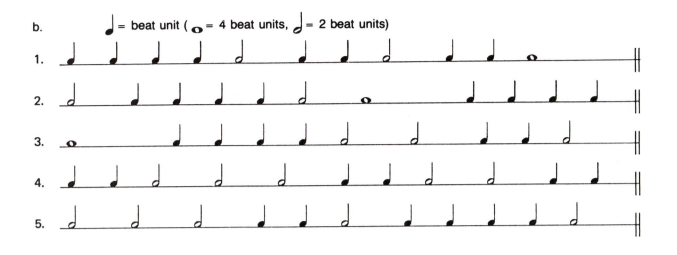

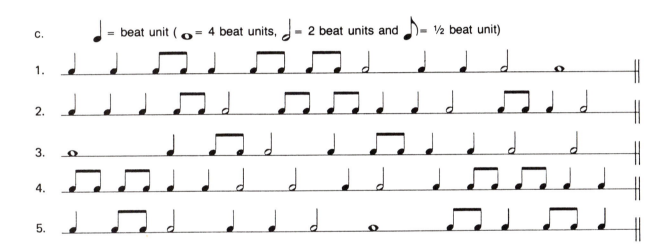

e.

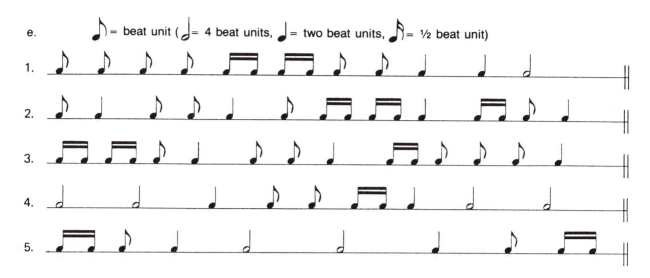

2.   Practice tapping the following examples using the *compound beat unit* indicated as the pulse. Establish and retain a steady beat with one hand while tapping the example given with the other hand.

a.

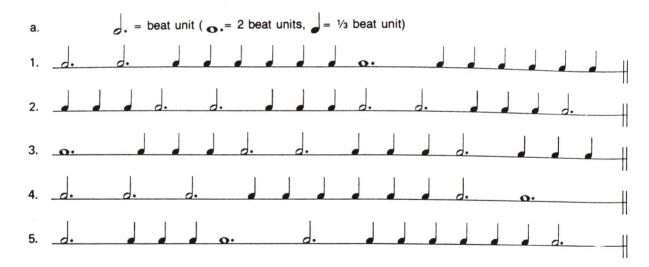

3. The following examples illustrate various rhythmic patterns that can appear when the quarter or dotted quarter notes are the beat unit. Establish a steady beat and practice tapping (or clapping) each pattern one, two, three, four, or five times until the series for each beat pattern is completed.

a.   *QUARTER NOTE BEAT UNIT PATTERNS*

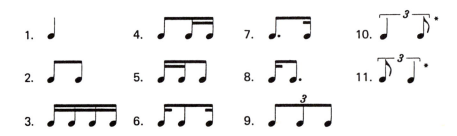

b.   *DOTTED QUARTER NOTE BEAT PATTERNS*

*Borrowed

CHAPTER 3: METER AND METER SIGNATURES

1. Your instructor will play ten examples from the selection below. As you listen to each two-measure example, determine whether it is simple or compound time (based on your perceptions of beat divisions) and the number of beats in each measure.

	TYPE OF DIVISION	BEATS/MEASURE	POSSIBLE METER
ex.	simple	2	2/4
a.			
b.			
c.			
d.			
e.			
f.			
g.			
h.			
i.			
j.			
k.			

Your instructor will predetermine the order of the examples for 1a–1k.

2.   Circle your choice (a, b, c, or d) as the correct metered rhythm played by your instructor.

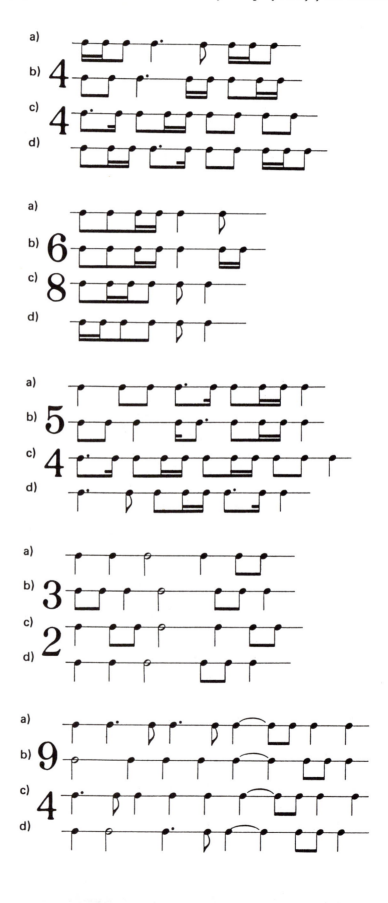

3.   The following examples are either two or three measures in length and include patterns consisting of the beat unit, division, subdivision (borrowed division), as well as beat multiples (durations larger than the beat unit). As your instructor plays each example, notate as accurately as possible.

CHAPTER 4: SCALES I: SCALE STRUCTURES

1. Your instructor will play scales in groups of five. Label each one played according to the abbreviations below:

> DIA–diatonic (seven-tone) scale
> CH–chromatic scale
> WT–whole-tone scale

1. _____	6. _____	11. _____
2. _____	7. _____	12. _____
3. _____	8. _____	13. _____
4. _____	9. _____	14. _____
5. _____	10. _____	15. _____
16. _____	21. _____	26. _____
17. _____	22. _____	27. _____
18. _____	23. _____	28. _____
19. _____	24. _____	29. _____
20. _____	25. _____	30. _____

CHAPTER 5: SCALES II: MAJOR, MINOR, AND PENTATONIC SCALES

It is suggested that students first become familiar with the sound of major scales, since this is the scale form given primary exposure. In listening for major scales, pay particular attention to the position and "gravitational" effect of the half steps.

1. Your instructor will play two different scales; one will be either major or natural minor; the other will be either the relative or the parallel scale. You must determine (1) what the first scale is (major or minor) and (2) whether the second scale is the parallel or relative major or minor. One of the two scales played will be major.

	FIRST SCALE (quality)	SECOND SCALE (quality)	RELATIONSHIP
a.	_____	_____	_____
b.	_____	_____	_____
c.	_____	_____	_____
d.	_____	_____	_____
e.	_____	_____	_____
f.	_____	_____	_____
g.	_____	_____	_____
h.	_____	_____	_____
i.	_____	_____	_____
j.	_____	_____	_____
k.	_____	_____	_____
l.	_____	_____	_____
m.	_____	_____	_____
n.	_____	_____	_____

2. Your instructor will play minor scales; determine the form of minor played and identify it as natural, harmonic, or melodic minor.

a.	_____	n.	_____
b.	_____	o.	_____
c.	_____	p.	_____
d.	_____	q.	_____
e.	_____	r.	_____
f.	_____	s.	_____
g.	_____	t.	_____
h.	_____	u.	_____
i.	_____	v.	_____
j.	_____	w.	_____
k.	_____	x.	_____
l.	_____	y.	_____
m.	_____	z.	_____

CHAPTER 6: INTERVALS

Students, over time, have thought of many ear-training aids in order to identify a played interval. Some of the more effective ones are listed below:

1. Some students will identify a melodic interval by associating the sound within a major or minor scale context.
2. Most students find that associating an interval with a familiar song opening (i.e., first two notes of a song) to be very successful. For example, a P5 is easily identified as the first two pitches in "Twinkle, Twinkle, Little Star."
3. Some students can narrow down choices of possible intervals by degree of consonance or dissonance and further narrow possibilities by the span or distance of the interval. For example, if a M7 is played, it is classified as a sharp dissonance, yet spread very wide.

Any of the above techniques might be effective as a learning tool for you. Most students will use more than one technique, employing a given one in dealing with certain intervals and perhaps a differing one on other occasions. It may be beneficial to learn several methods in order to use them most advantageously.

It is suggested that intervals be learned in groups rather than all at the same time.

1. Begin by distinguishing the difference between like pairs of intervals such as M2 and m2, M3 and m3, P4 and P5, M6 and m6, or M7 and m7.
2. Next, proceed to identify a mixture of the four perfect intervals, then the four major intervals, then the four minor intervals. *The tritone should be treated as an interval that could appear with any group.*
3. Only after the above has been mastered should dictation of all intervals be undertaken.

Your instructor will play at least ten or fifteen intervals for identification each time interval dictation is given. Take the dictation first row, left to right, then second row, left to right. Your instructor dictates while you write:

ex. <u>M2</u>   <u>m2</u>   <u>m2</u>   <u>M2</u>   <u>M2</u>

    <u>m2</u>   <u>m2</u>   <u>M2</u>   <u>M2</u>   <u>M2</u>

Be sure to make a clear distinction between the upper-case M (for major) and the lower-case m (for minor). Use the spaces provided on the following pages for interval dictation.

1. INTERVAL PAIR DICTATION

(M2 and m2) a. _____ _____ _____ _____ _____   b. _____ _____ _____ _____ _____
                _____ _____ _____ _____ _____   _____ _____ _____ _____ _____

           c. _____ _____ _____ _____ _____   d. _____ _____ _____ _____ _____
                _____ _____ _____ _____ _____   _____ _____ _____ _____ _____

           e. _____ _____ _____ _____ _____   f. _____ _____ _____ _____ _____
                _____ _____ _____ _____ _____   _____ _____ _____ _____ _____

(M3 and m3) a. _____ _____ _____ _____ _____   b. _____ _____ _____ _____ _____
                _____ _____ _____ _____ _____   _____ _____ _____ _____ _____

           c. _____ _____ _____ _____ _____   d. _____ _____ _____ _____ _____
                _____ _____ _____ _____ _____   _____ _____ _____ _____ _____

           e. _____ _____ _____ _____ _____   f. _____ _____ _____ _____ _____
                _____ _____ _____ _____ _____   _____ _____ _____ _____ _____

           g. _____ _____ _____ _____ _____   h. _____ _____ _____ _____ _____
                _____ _____ _____ _____ _____   _____ _____ _____ _____ _____

(P5 and P4) a. _____ _____ _____ _____ _____   b. _____ _____ _____ _____ _____
                _____ _____ _____ _____ _____   _____ _____ _____ _____ _____

           c. _____ _____ _____ _____ _____   d. _____ _____ _____ _____ _____
                _____ _____ _____ _____ _____   _____ _____ _____ _____ _____

           e. _____ _____ _____ _____ _____   f. _____ _____ _____ _____ _____
                _____ _____ _____ _____ _____   _____ _____ _____ _____ _____

           g. _____ _____ _____ _____ _____   h. _____ _____ _____ _____ _____
                _____ _____ _____ _____ _____   _____ _____ _____ _____ _____

(M6 and m6) a. _____ _____ _____ _____ _____   b. _____ _____ _____ _____ _____
                _____ _____ _____ _____ _____   _____ _____ _____ _____ _____

           c. _____ _____ _____ _____ _____   d. _____ _____ _____ _____ _____
                _____ _____ _____ _____ _____   _____ _____ _____ _____ _____

           e. _____ _____ _____ _____ _____   f. _____ _____ _____ _____ _____
                _____ _____ _____ _____ _____   _____ _____ _____ _____ _____

           g. _____ _____ _____ _____ _____   h. _____ _____ _____ _____ _____
                _____ _____ _____ _____ _____   _____ _____ _____ _____ _____

(M7 and m7) a. ____ ____ ____ ____ ____   b. ____ ____ ____ ____ ____
                 ____ ____ ____ ____ ____   ____ ____ ____ ____ ____

          c. ____ ____ ____ ____ ____   d. ____ ____ ____ ____ ____
                 ____ ____ ____ ____ ____   ____ ____ ____ ____ ____

          e. ____ ____ ____ ____ ____   f. ____ ____ ____ ____ ____
                 ____ ____ ____ ____ ____   ____ ____ ____ ____ ____

          g. ____ ____ ____ ____ ____   h. ____ ____ ____ ____ ____
                 ____ ____ ____ ____ ____   ____ ____ ____ ____ ____

2. INTERVAL GROUP DICTATION (P1, P4, P5, P8)
                            (m2, m3, m6, m7)
                            (M2, M3, M6, M7)

          a. ____ ____ ____ ____ ____   b. ____ ____ ____ ____ ____
                 ____ ____ ____ ____ ____   ____ ____ ____ ____ ____

          c. ____ ____ ____ ____ ____   d. ____ ____ ____ ____ ____
                 ____ ____ ____ ____ ____   ____ ____ ____ ____ ____

          e. ____ ____ ____ ____ ____   f. ____ ____ ____ ____ ____
                 ____ ____ ____ ____ ____   ____ ____ ____ ____ ____

3. ALL INTERVALS, MIXED

          a. ____ ____ ____ ____ ____   b. ____ ____ ____ ____ ____
                 ____ ____ ____ ____ ____   ____ ____ ____ ____ ____
                 ____ ____ ____ ____ ____   ____ ____ ____ ____ ____

          c. ____ ____ ____ ____ ____   d. ____ ____ ____ ____ ____
                 ____ ____ ____ ____ ____   ____ ____ ____ ____ ____
                 ____ ____ ____ ____ ____   ____ ____ ____ ____ ____

          e. ____ ____ ____ ____ ____   f. ____ ____ ____ ____ ____
                 ____ ____ ____ ____ ____   ____ ____ ____ ____ ____
                 ____ ____ ____ ____ ____   ____ ____ ____ ____ ____

g. _____ _____ _____ _____ _____   h. _____ _____ _____ _____ _____
   _____ _____ _____ _____ _____   _____ _____ _____ _____ _____
   _____ _____ _____ _____ _____   _____ _____ _____ _____ _____

i. _____ _____ _____ _____ _____   j. _____ _____ _____ _____ _____
   _____ _____ _____ _____ _____   _____ _____ _____ _____ _____
   _____ _____ _____ _____ _____   _____ _____ _____ _____ _____

k. _____ _____ _____ _____ _____   l. _____ _____ _____ _____ _____
   _____ _____ _____ _____ _____   _____ _____ _____ _____ _____
   _____ _____ _____ _____ _____   _____ _____ _____ _____ _____

m. _____ _____ _____ _____ _____   n. _____ _____ _____ _____ _____
   _____ _____ _____ _____ _____   _____ _____ _____ _____ _____
   _____ _____ _____ _____ _____   _____ _____ _____ _____ _____

o. _____ _____ _____ _____ _____   p. _____ _____ _____ _____ _____
   _____ _____ _____ _____ _____   _____ _____ _____ _____ _____
   _____ _____ _____ _____ _____   _____ _____ _____ _____ _____

4.   ERROR DETECTION

The instructor will play the melodies while inserting chromatic signs (not shown) or different pitches. Make corrections where needed.

Your instructor will determine specific alterations beforehand.

5.   CLASSIFICATION OF INTERVALS

Classify all intervals, from a P1 to a P8, from what you believe to be the most consonant to the most dissonant interval. (Intervals are sometimes placed into groups such as those listed below. This grouping may help you in establishing the rather subjective arrangement of intervals from consonant to dissonant.)

1. perfect consonances: P1, P4, P5, and P8
2. imperfect consonances: m3, M3, m6, and M6
3. mildly dissonant: M2 and m7
4. sharp dissonances: m2 and M7
5. unclassified (or appearing in one or more groups: tritone)
   CONSONANT ◄————————————————————► DISSONANT

— — — — — — — — — — — — — —

PROCEDURE

1. Play or sing the intervals in item 1 above (P1, P4, P5, and P8). Decide for yourself which is the purest consonance and enter that interval on the response line (consonant side).
2. Working backwards, play or sing the intervals in item 4 above (m2 and M7). Decide which is the harshest dissonance and enter that interval on the response line (dissonant side).
3. Fill in the interior intervals, after either singing or playing them, to represent a continuum of consonant-to-dissonant sound.

CHAPTER 7: SCALES III: SCALES REVISITED

Practice singing the intervals found in various scales by using the following procedure:

1. Play the tonic of the scale.
2. Sing (match) the tonic.[1]
3. Think of the selected diatonic interval and try to sing it.
4. Check your accuracy by playing the interval at the keyboard.
5. Approach each interval in order from small to large (seconds, thirds, fourths, etc.).

---

[1]It is not necessary to sing these in the exact octave in which they are notated. They can be sung in any comfortable octave.

On the following staves, the hollow note heads indicate pitches played; the solid note heads indicate pitches to be sung. Begin with intervals found in major scales.

MAJOR DIATONIC INTERVALS

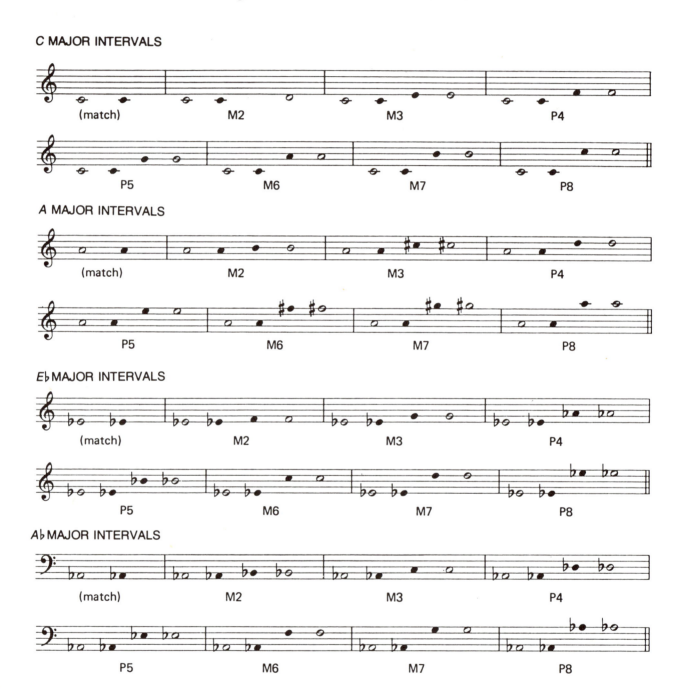

MINOR DIATONIC INTERVALS

With practice, the above exercises can be performed quite rapidly, singing just before playing the pitches. *It is important to sing each pitch first,* using the keyboard only as reinforcement.

CHAPTER 9: TRIADS

After playing and singing triads at the keyboard, begin to identify the quality of the isolated triads by ear. In the initial stages it may be helpful to concentrate on pairs of triad qualities, for instance, major and minor, major and augmented, minor and diminished, and so forth, before including all four triads.

Initially, triads may be played as broken chords (arpeggiated), but eventually one should be able to identify the quality of a triad played in block (simultaneously) fashion. Ten to fifteen chords for triad identification should be drilled as a "set" each time this is practiced.

Take dictation first row left to right, then second row, left to right. Your instructor will dictate while you write:

ex.   M   m   M   m   m
        M   M   m   m   m

1.   TRIAD QUALITIES IN PAIRS

Your instructor will determine the order of triads beforehand.

(Major and Minor)

a. _____ _____ _____ _____   b. _____ _____ _____ _____ _____
   _____ _____ _____ _____   _____ _____ _____ _____
   _____ _____ _____ _____   _____ _____ _____ _____

c. _____ _____ _____ _____   d. _____ _____ _____ _____ _____
   _____ _____ _____ _____   _____ _____ _____ _____
   _____ _____ _____ _____   _____ _____ _____ _____

(Major and Augmented)

a. _____ _____ _____ _____   b. _____ _____ _____ _____ _____
   _____ _____ _____ _____   _____ _____ _____ _____
   _____ _____ _____ _____   _____ _____ _____ _____

c. _____ _____ _____ _____   d. _____ _____ _____ _____ _____
   _____ _____ _____ _____   _____ _____ _____ _____
   _____ _____ _____ _____   _____ _____ _____ _____

(Minor and Augmented)

a. ____ ____ ____ ____ ____   b. ____ ____ ____ ____ ____
   ____ ____ ____ ____ ____   ____ ____ ____ ____ ____
   ____ ____ ____ ____ ____   ____ ____ ____ ____ ____

c. ____ ____ ____ ____ ____   d. ____ ____ ____ ____ ____
   ____ ____ ____ ____ ____   ____ ____ ____ ____ ____
   ____ ____ ____ ____ ____   ____ ____ ____ ____ ____

(Augmented and Diminished)

a. ____ ____ ____ ____ ____   b. ____ ____ ____ ____ ____
   ____ ____ ____ ____ ____   ____ ____ ____ ____ ____
   ____ ____ ____ ____ ____   ____ ____ ____ ____ ____

c. ____ ____ ____ ____ ____   d. ____ ____ ____ ____ ____
   ____ ____ ____ ____ ____   ____ ____ ____ ____ ____
   ____ ____ ____ ____ ____   ____ ____ ____ ____ ____

2. ALL TRIAD QUALITIES

a. Try to perceive a triad as a possible chord to end a composition. If so, the chord will probably be major or minor. If the triad cannot be perceived as a final chord, the quality will probably be augmented or diminished.

(Major, Minor, Augmented and Diminished)

a. ____ ____ ____ ____ ____   b. ____ ____ ____ ____ ____
   ____ ____ ____ ____ ____   ____ ____ ____ ____ ____
   ____ ____ ____ ____ ____   ____ ____ ____ ____ ____

c. ____ ____ ____ ____ ____   d. ____ ____ ____ ____ ____
   ____ ____ ____ ____ ____   ____ ____ ____ ____ ____
   ____ ____ ____ ____ ____   ____ ____ ____ ____ ____

e. ____ ____ ____ ____ ____   f. ____ ____ ____ ____ ____
   ____ ____ ____ ____ ____   ____ ____ ____ ____ ____
   ____ ____ ____ ____ ____   ____ ____ ____ ____ ____

g. ____ ____ ____ ____ ____   h. ____ ____ ____ ____ ____
   ____ ____ ____ ____ ____   ____ ____ ____ ____ ____
   ____ ____ ____ ____ ____   ____ ____ ____ ____ ____

i. ____ ____ ____ ____ ____   j. ____ ____ ____ ____ ____
   ____ ____ ____ ____ ____   ____ ____ ____ ____ ____
   ____ ____ ____ ____ ____   ____ ____ ____ ____ ____

b.   Your instructor will play a triad (any of the four qualities). You will:

> 1.   listen to determine the root;
> 2.   sing the root;
> 3.   sing the triad.

· ·

CHAPTER 10: DIATONIC TRIADS

1.   Sing the following chord progressions, as illustrated, in several major and minor keys.

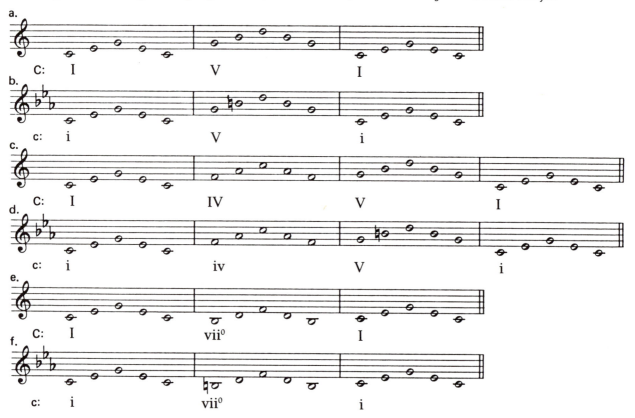

CHAPTER 11: CADENCE STRUCTURES

Your instructor will play cadence structures from the examples given. Identify each stock cadence type and label. Your instructor will determine the order of the examples beforehand.

1. _____	1. _____	1. _____
2. _____	2. _____	2. _____
3. _____	3. _____	3. _____
4. _____	4. _____	4. _____
5. _____	5. _____	5. _____
6. _____	6. _____	6. _____
7. _____	7. _____	7. _____
8. _____	8. _____	8. _____
9. _____	9. _____	9. _____
10. _____	10. _____	10. _____

1.

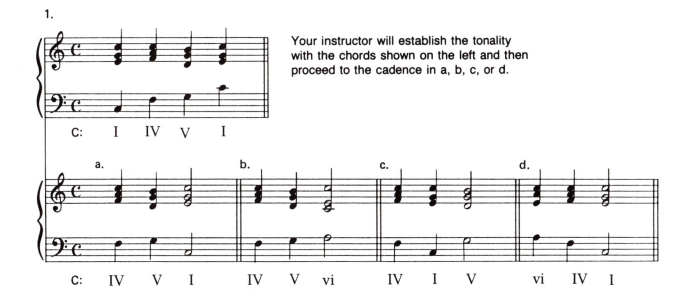

Your instructor will establish the tonality with the chords shown on the left and then proceed to the cadence in a, b, c, or d.

2.

d: i V i iv

a. b. c. d.

d: V i V i V i i V VI i iv i

3.

B♭: I iii IV V

a. b. c. d.

B♭: I IV V I IV I I V I I V vi

CHAPTER 12: HARMONIZATION

The harmonization process is, at best, a subjective one that not only requires the ability to employ primary and secondary harmonies but also demands some elementary keyboard skills in order to hear a given triad along with its melodic component. Accompaniment patterns aid in maintaining a given harmony by providing motion to carry and sustain the harmony. Since keyboard applications are necessary for any ear training at this juncture, refer to "Chapter 12: Harmonization" in Appendix B.

After playing through the various accompaniment patterns and typical harmonic progressions, refer to the collection of melodies, Appendix F, for specific melodic examples.

Fill in an appropriate harmony, paying particular attention to items such as harmonic rhythm, cadence patterns, primary and secondary triad relationships, and so on. In most situations, a choice of two or possibly three different harmonies might be possible. It is at this juncture that one's personal taste or sound choice becomes critical. Follow the prescribed procedure in order to determine areas where choices are to be made:

1. Write in all possible triad choices.
2. Play each triad in succession and *listen*.
3. Decide which triad creates forward motion and smooth connection both to and from the harmony in question.

The following example illustrates the above procedure and the possible choices that can be made in harmonizing a particular melody.

Battle Hymn of the Republic

C:

Choice 1		I		I		I		I
Choice 2		V		I		I		IV
Choice 3	(V)	I		I		vi		vi
Choice 4		I		vi		iii		vi
Choice 5		iii		I		vi	iii	IV
Choice 6		I	V	iii	IV	I	vi	IV

CHAPTER 13: FORM IN MUSIC (MOTIVIC) AND PHRASE STRUCTURES)

In each of the following examples you will hear the given motive followed by various manipulations. Identify each of the manipulations as your instructor plays them. Your instructor will predetermine their order.

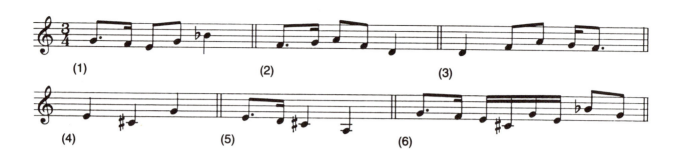

(1)   (2)   (3)

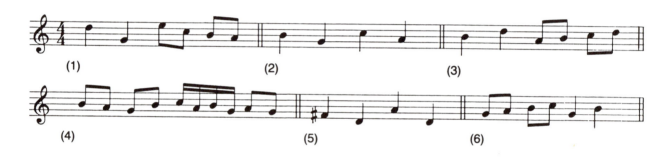

(4)   (5)   (6)

4. MOTIVE:

a. _____   d. _____

b. _____   e. _____

c. _____   f. _____

(1)   (2)   (3)

(4)   (5)   (6)

5. MOTIVE: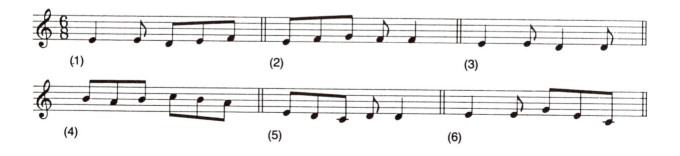

a. _____   d. _____

b. _____   e. _____

c. _____   f. _____

(1)   (2)   (3)

(4)   (5)   (6)

Keyboard Exercises and Drills

....

CHAPTER 1: PROPERTIES OF SOUND—BASIC NOTATION

1.   Become familiar with the letter names of the keys and their relative position on the keyboard.
2.   Practice labeling keys on the keyboard with enharmonic spellings.
3.   Become familiar with the different registers of the keyboard. Practice finding isolated notes such as a^1, b^3, and so on.

LOCATE AND PLAY DRILLS

1.   Locate and play isolated keys on the keyboard. For example, locate and play all *As*, then all *Bs*, and so forth.

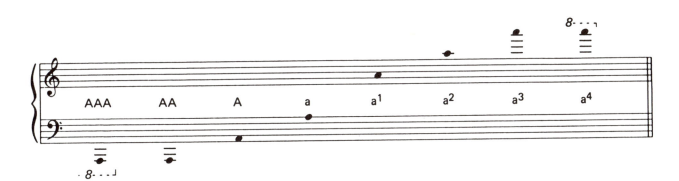

2. Locate and play all NOHS (naturally occurring half steps) on the keyboard.

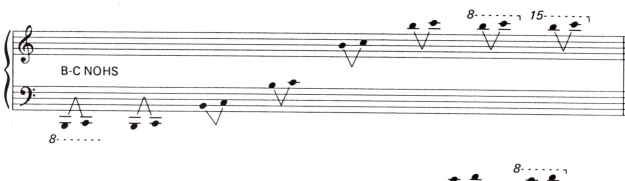

3. Referring to written exercises at the end of chapter 1, locate and play these pitches at the keyboard.

4. Locate and play half steps, whole steps, and octaves above and below every key on the keyboard.

5. Locate and play the isolated notes given.

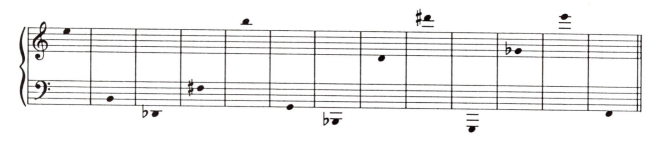

6. Locate and play the keys that represent the lines and spaces of the treble and bass clefs. Play in succession and as a block chord.

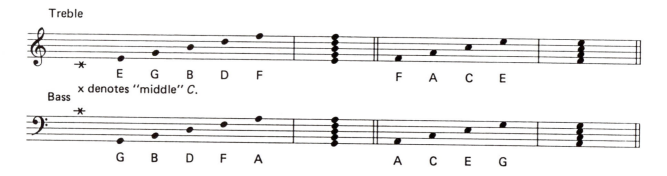

7. Name all white keys on the keyboard going from low to high and from high to low. Name all black keys in the same manner.

Note: If an actual keyboard instrument is not available for practice, use the keyboard insert located in the inside back-cover pocket of this book for some of the exercises.

CHAPTER 3: METER AND METER SIGNATURES

The following examples may be played on the piano, on any two pitches (octaves are suggested), using the right hand for the upper part and the left hand for the lower part. They may also be tapped, clapped, or sung on a neutral syllable by two or more people.

CHAPTER 4: SCALES I: SCALE STRUCTURES

Locate and play the following scales on the keyboard.

1. All basic diatonic scales, noting the position of the NOHS (naturally occurring half steps) within each scale.

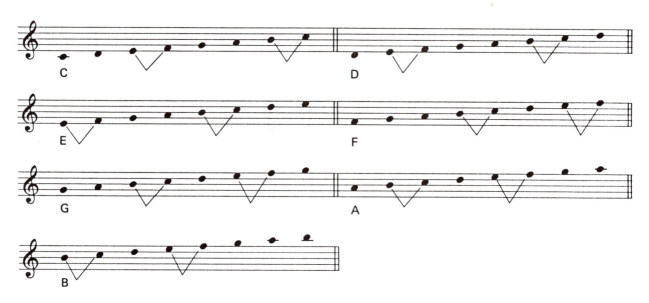

Note: Become familiar with the sounds of the intervals that occur between the tonic and the other scale degrees. Play and sing as in the example given below. Apply this procedure when playing all scales.

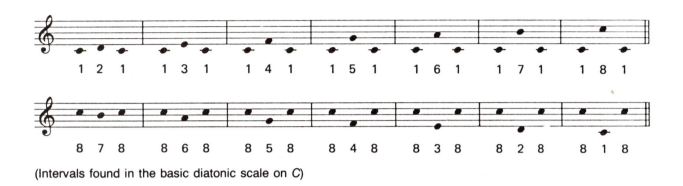

(Intervals found in the basic diatonic scale on *C*)

2. Both ascending and descending chromatic scales, noting the enharmonic spellings (sharps and flats).

3. Whole-tone scales, both ascending and descending, noting the enharmonic spellings within each one.

CHAPTER 5: SCALES II: MAJOR, MINOR, AND PENTATONIC SCALES

Playing scales at the keyboard will be beneficial to you and serves to reinforce the body of knowledge acquired in this chapter. The tetrachord as a structural element of diatonic scales can fit comfortably as a finger pattern for keyboard application. The lower tetrachord can be played by the left hand (finger numbers 5, 4, 3, 2) and the upper tetrachord by the right hand (finger numbers 2, 3, 4, 5). The thumbs need not be used, and no previous keyboard experience is necessary. Begin by playing the C-major scale in tetrachords—four keys to each hand—and remember to connect the tetrachords by a whole step. Drill: Play twelve major scales, each one beginning on a different pitch. It is suggested that you do not approach each of the major scales chromatically but rather by fifths; that is, learn C major, then G major, then D major, and so on. When all of the major scales incorporating sharps have been learned, then return to C and move through the scales that employ flats (F, B♭, E♭, etc.).

$$C♭ — G♭ — D♭ — A♭ — E♭ — B♭ — F — C — G — D — A — E — B — F♯ — C♯$$

Once all of the major scales have been learned, return to each major key and approach the minor scales through the parallel structures; for example, C major, C minor (all three forms).

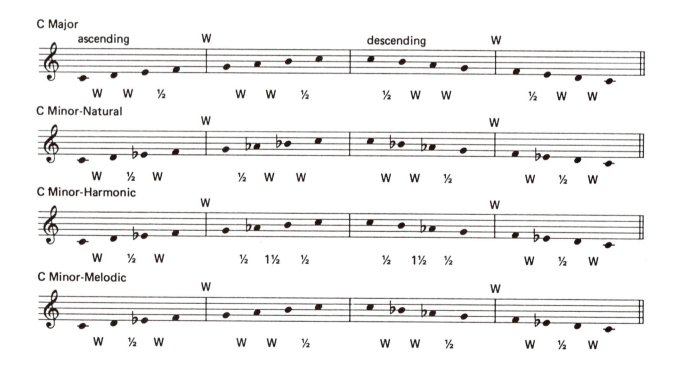

By approaching the playing of scale structures through the tetrachord, you will find that you are expressing your knowledge through your hands rather than on paper. The keyboard application of this material is quite important and useful in dealing with scale structure material.

It has been found that the playing of scale structures aids considerably in the development of aural perception and ear-training skills. *Listen carefully* while playing scales at the keyboard.

Refer to Appendix D for all major and minor scales.

CHAPTER 6: INTERVALS

1. Practice playing all types of intervals above and below each key on the keyboard. Sing the interval before and after it is played. It might be practical to concentrate on one interval at a time, such as playing perfect fifths above and below each key. Once that is mastered, choose another interval.

PROCEDURE

Choose and sing a starting pitch.

> Sing the interval.
> Play the interval.
> Sing the interval.
> Choose a new starting key and repeat the procedure.

CHART OF INTERVALS ABOVE AND BELOW C:

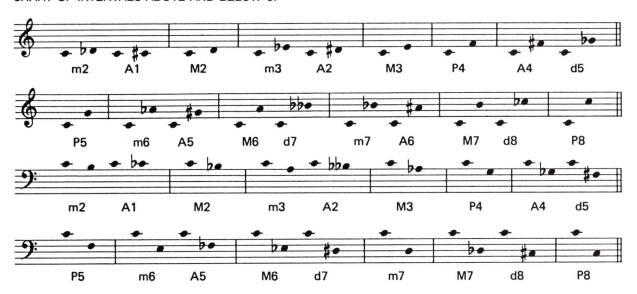

2. Begin on the note given, playing through the interval directions, and determine the final note.

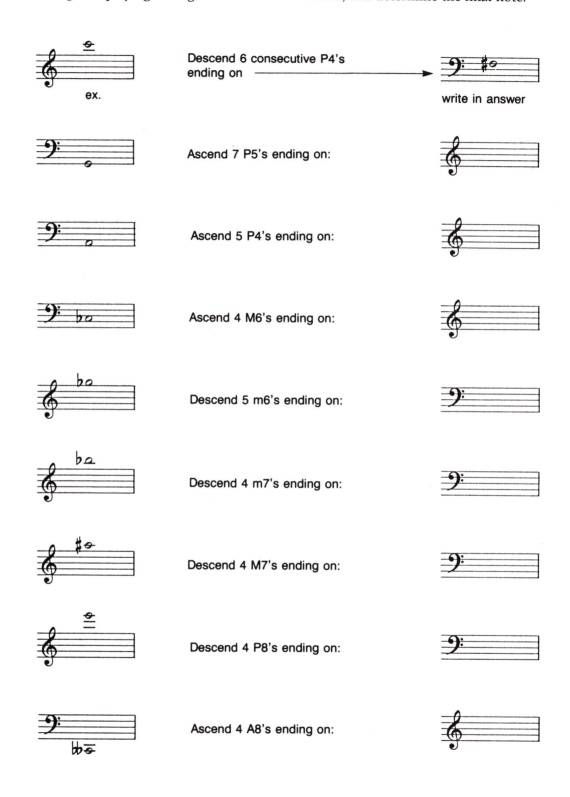

CHAPTER 9: TRIADS

Practice playing the four types of triads at the keyboard on every pitch. As the triads are played, sing the triad in arpeggiated form using numbers.

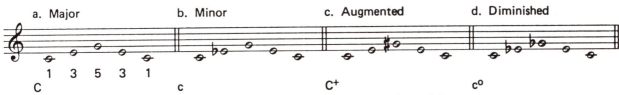

The numbers refer to right hand fingering. Left hand fingering will be 5 3 1 3 5.

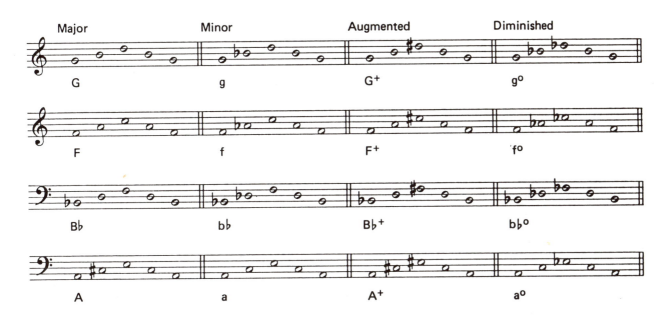

Refer to Appendix D for a complete chart of triad qualities.

CHAPTER 10: DIATONIC TRIADS

1. Practice playing the diatonic triads that occur in every major and minor key. Start on the tonic triad and continue up the scale with each diatonic scale degree serving as the root until every triad in the key has been played. *Spell and sing* each triad before and after playing.

a.

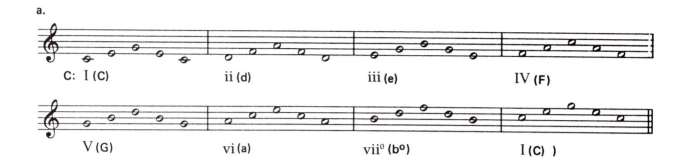

b.

2. Practice finding and playing isolated triads.

C: vi	B♭: iii	D: ii	a: III⁺
F: vii⁰	A: IV	E♭: V	E: vi
A♭: ii	B: iii	d: iv	e: ii⁰
g: VI	b: V	c: iv	f#: III⁺
f: vii⁰	c#: V	b♭: vii⁰	g#: V

3. Play the primary triads as given in every major and minor key.

   a. Use the same fingering for each key.

   b. Practice hands separately.

   c. Spell the triads as they are played.

             Major   Harmonic minor

4. Ornament the progression in this fashion:

a.

C: I   IV   V   I

b.
(Country-Western)

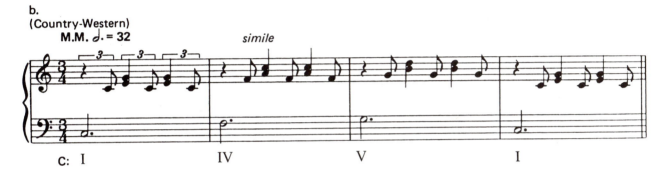

C: I   IV   V   I

These drills are intended to facilitate the comprehension of primary-triad concepts. The techniques of part writing and voice leading do not fall within the scope of this text.

CHAPTER 11: CADENCE STRUCTURES

1. Play a C-major scale to establish the tonality, and then select one of the cadences given. Continue in c minor with the same procedure.

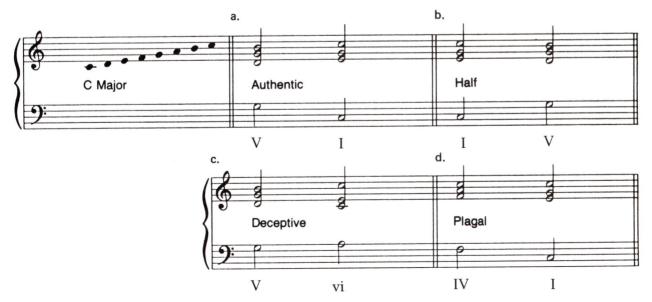

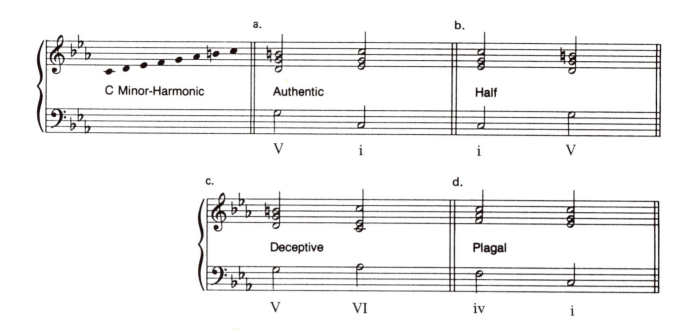

2.   In each of the following examples, a major triad is given as a V chord. Play and resolve either to tonic as an authentic cadence or to the submediant as a deceptive cadence.

		Authentic		Deceptive				Authentic		Deceptive
C: V		to I	or	vi		G: V		to I	or	vi
c: V		to i	or	VI		g: V		to i	or	VI
D: V		to I	or	vi		F: V		to I	or	vi
d: V		to i	or	VI		f: V		to i	or	VI
E: V		to I	or	vi		A: V		to I	or	vi
e: V		to i	or	VI		a: V		to i	or	VI
B: V		to I	or	vi		B♭: V		to I	or	vi
b: V		to i	or	VI		b♭: V		to i	or	VI

3. In each of the following examples a major or minor triad is given as a subdominant triad. Play and resolve as a plagal cadence.

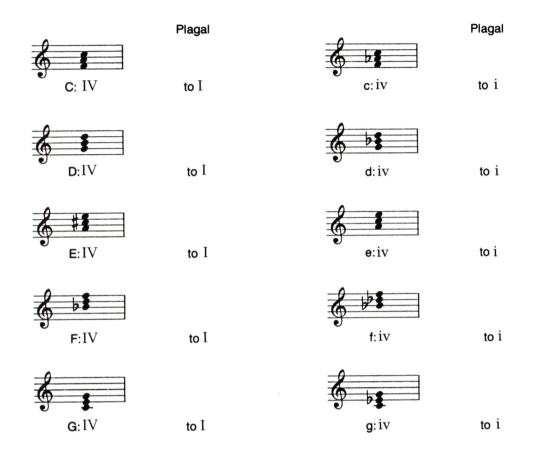

CHAPTER 12: HARMONIZATION

Practice playing these accompaniment patterns in all major and minor keys. Use these patterns to harmonize the melodies in Appendix F.

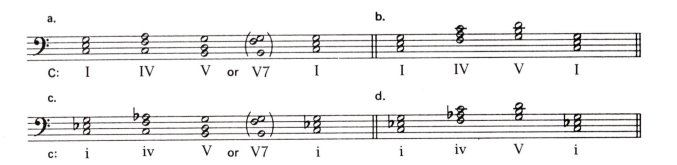

CHAPTER 13: FORM IN MUSIC (MOTIVIC AND PHRASE STRUCTURES)

1. Play the original melody. "Twinkle, Twinkle, Little Star," and the manipulations given. Attempt this exercise with other familiar melodies.

Inversion

Retrograde

Retrograde Inversion

2. Improvise various manipulations of each motive example to create a four-measure phrase. To create a convincing cadence, the last measure may be free material.

Harmonic Overtone Series

- The ability to construct the overtone series on any given pitch through the eighth partial

- The understanding of frequency/pitch ratios

OVERTONE SERIES[1] AND FUNDAMENTAL

When a sound is produced, many subsidiary (composite) pitches are often produced simultaneously as part of the single sound source. The main pitch one hears
is more prominent because it has a greater amplitude than the subsidiary sounds.
The main sound perceived is called the **fundamental**, and the subsidiary pitches are
referred to as **overtones, partials,** or **harmonics.**

The lowest note in the overtone series serves as the fundamental. Example C.1
illustrates the overtone series from the fundamental of *C* through the sixteenth partial. Note that the size of the intervals contained within the series become increas-
ingly smaller as the series progresses upward.

Example C.1

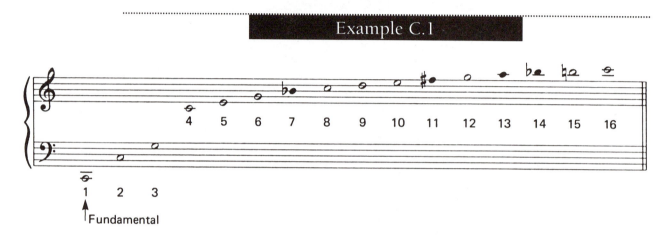

It should be noted that only the octaves above the fundamental (2, 4, 8, and 16)
correspond to pitches found in equal temperament; the mainstream Western-cul-
ture tuning system that divides the octave into twelve equal half steps. The other
pitches correspond to tunings found in just intonation: a system of tuning in which
all intervals are determined by the acoustically pure fifth and pure third. The seventh, eleventh, thirteenth, and fourteenth partials only approximate, to an even
lesser extent, equal temperament and are notated in Example C.1 with black note
heads.

OVERTONE, PARTIAL, AND HARMONIC

The terms "overtone," "partial," and "harmonic" are occasionally used interchange-
ably to describe the subsidiary tones found in the overtone series. Their exact
meanings vary slightly as described below.

Overtone: The label used to describe the subsidiary tones sounding above a given
fundamental. These overtones are numbered consecutively and *do not* include the
fundamental (Ex. C.2).

---

[1]Also called harmonic series.

Partial: The label used to describe the subsidiary tones sounding as part of the harmonic overtone series. This term *includes* the fundamental in its numbering, so that partial 1 = fundamental, partial 2 = first overtone, and so on (Ex. C.2).

Harmonic: A more general term employed for reference to any subsidiary sound such as an isolated frequency in the series. It can be more accurately used as a modifier, such as "harmonic" partial or "harmonic" overtone. More precisely, overtones may be labeled as harmonic if they have a symmetrical mathematical ratio with one another. If not, they are labeled *nonharmonic* (for example, the asymmetric [nonharmonic] timbre of bells). The term is often used in conjunction with stringed instruments to describe frequencies of a lighter quality produced by lightly touching a string.

Example C.2

Numbering of Series for Partials and Overtones

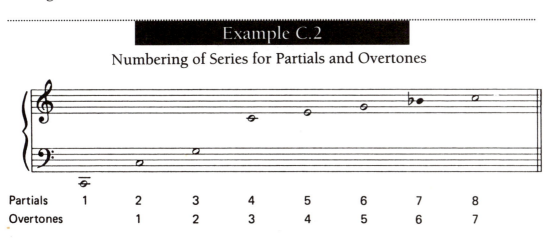

Partials	1	2	3	4	5	6	7	8
Overtones		1	2	3	4	5	6	7

Example C.3 illustrates the intervals that occur in the overtone series through the eighth partial.

Example C.3

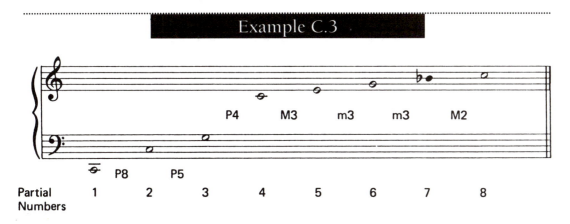

Partial Numbers	1	2	3	4	5	6	7	8

CONSTRUCTING THE SERIES

When constructing the series, the following steps facilitate writing the series.

    1.   Write the second, fourth, and eighth partials. Each partial will be a P8 above the previous partial (2:1 ratios).

Example C.4

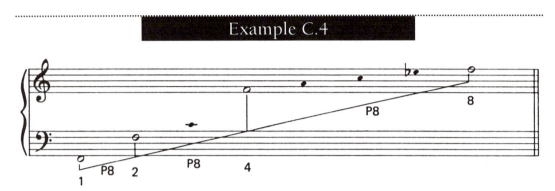

    2.   Write the interval of a perfect fifth (third partial) above the second partial (3:2 ratio). The sixth partial will be a perfect octave above the third partial (2:1 ratio).

Example C.5

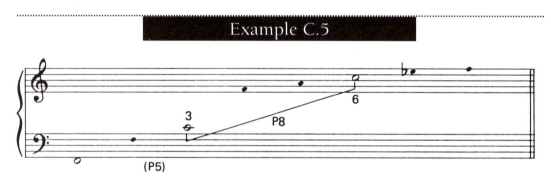

    3.   Only two partials remain to be written: the fifth partial, which is a major third above the fourth (5:4 ratio), and the seventh partial, which is a major second below the eighth (8:7 ratio).

Example C.6

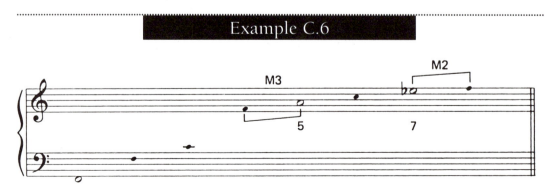

The ratios of intervals found in the overtone series (if the intervals are numbered as partials) can be useful in determining the frequency of an interval if the frequency of one of the pitches is known.[2] For example:

1. Two notes comprising a perfect octave have a 2:1 frequency ratio since the frequency doubles with each ascending octave.
2. Two notes comprising a perfect fifth have a 3:2 frequency ratio. This means that the upper note of a perfect fifth will be vibrating (relatively) three times a second while the lower note will be vibrating twice a second (frequency of lower pitch x 3 ÷ 2 = frequency of higher pitch).

The overtone series provides information concerning the ratios of intervals as well as a system for determining the frequency of intervals. In addition, the series provides a capsulized, historically chronological account of harmony from medieval organum (singing or playing a melody doubled in octaves, fifths, and fourths), through the tonal use of triads and more extended tertian structures, to the microtonal innovations of twentieth-century composers. For many musicians, the series has served as the scientific basis for explaining frequencies, tuning systems, harmony, and spacing of chords or for the creative evolution of new systems of melodic and harmonic procedures.

Drill sheets and blank staff paper follow this appendix, which may be used as an optional chapter.

---

[2]The frequency of various pitches in equal temperament are as follows: a^1 has a frequency of 440 vibrations per second (VPS); "middle" C a frequency of 261 VPS; the highest note on the piano keyboard (c^5) has a frequency of 4.176 VPS; and the lowest note on the piano keyboard (A^3) has a frequency of 27.5 VPS.

OVERTONE SERIES DRILLS AND EXERCISES

1. Construct the overtone series through the eighth partial on each fundamental given.

2. Complete the following:

   a. The interval from the first to the second partial is a _____ (interval).

   b. The interval from the third to the fourth partial is a _____.

   c. The interval from the second to the third partial is a _____.

   d. The interval from the fourth to the fifth partial is a _____.

   e. The interval from the fourth to the sixth partial is a _____.

   f. The interval from the fifth to the sixth partial is a _____.

   g. The interval from the second to the fourth partial is a _____.

   h. The interval from the third to the fifth partial is a _____.

   i. The interval from the fifth partial to the seventh overtone is a _____.

   j. The interval from the fourth partial to the second overtone is a _____.

   k. The interval from the sixth partial to the fifth overtone is a _____.

3. Complete the following:

   a. The frequency ratio of a perfect octave is _____:_____.

   b. The frequency ratio of a perfect fifth is _____:_____.

   c. The frequency ratio of a perfect fourth is _____:_____.

   d. The frequency ratio of a major third is _____:_____.

4. Practice playing the overtone series through the eighth partial on several low pitches (below small *c*) on the keyboard. The series with *C* as the fundamental is given.

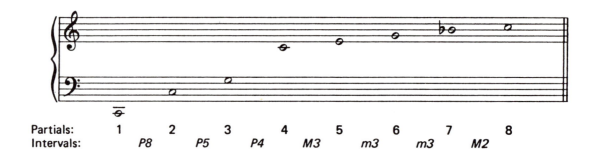

Partials: 1   2   3   4   5   6   7   8
Intervals: P8   P5   P4   M3   m3   m3   M2

5. Overtone experiment

    a. On the piano keyboard silently depress and hold in place any lower pitch (below small *c*).

    b. Predetermine the first eight partials of the series, considering the chosen pitch as the fundamental.

    c. Strike and quickly release the piano keys corresponding to the individual partials in the series.

    Result: This will cause a sympathetic vibration of that particular partial on the fundamental string depressed, and the frequency of that partial will become audible and sustain.

Reference Charts

CHART OF MAJOR SCALES

Play, spell and sing each scale.

CHART OF MINOR SCALES

Play, spell and sing each scale.

a (natural)   a (harmonic)

a (melodic)

e (natural)   e (harmonic)

e (melodic)

b (natural)   b (harmonic)

b (melodic)

f♯ (natural)   f♯ (harmonic)

f♯ (melodic)

c♯ (natural)   c♯ (harmonic)

c♯ (melodic)

g♯ (natural)   g♯ (harmonic)

Chart of minor scales (cont.).

g♯ (melodic)

d♯ (natural)　　　　　d♯ (harmonic)

d♯ (melodic)

a♯ (natural)　　　　　a♯ (harmonic)

a♯ (melodic)

d (natural)　　　　　d (harmonic)

d (melodic)

g (natural)　　　　　g (harmonic)

g (melodic)

c (natural)　　　　　c (harmonic)

c (melodic)

Chart of minor scales (cont.).

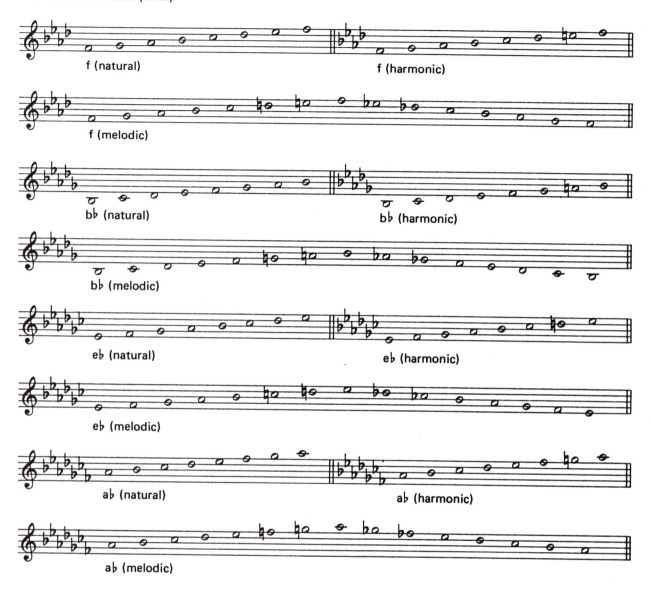

CHART OF MAJOR AND MINOR KEY SIGNATURES

C major
a minor

G major
e minor

D major
b minor

A major
f# minor

E major
c# minor

B major
g# minor

F# major
d# minor

C# major
a# minor

F major
d minor

Bb major
g minor

Eb major
c minor

Ab major
f minor

Db major
bb minor

Gb major
eb minor

Cb major
ab minor

CHART OF MAJOR, MINOR, AUGMENTED, AND DIMINISHED TRIADS

Play, spell and sing each triad.

GUITAR CHORD FINGERINGS

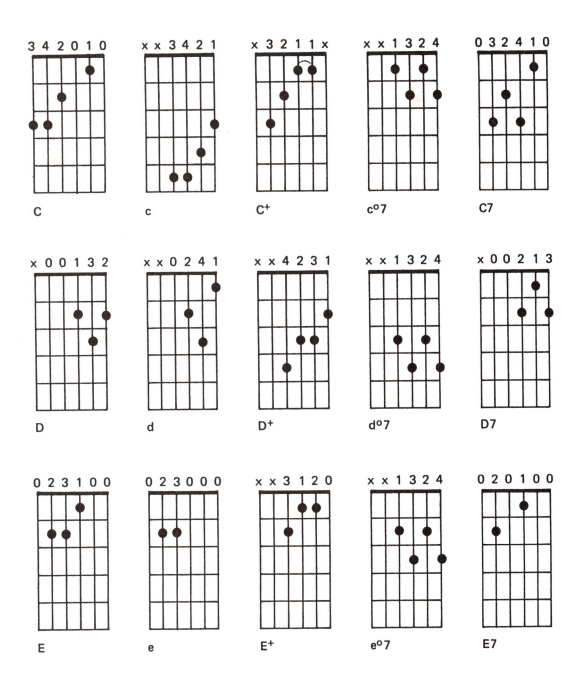

Fingering Chart Symbols:

0 – open string
X – string not played
1 – left index finger
2 – left middle finger

3 – left ring finger
4 – left little finger
⌢ – Barre, finger across
two or more strings

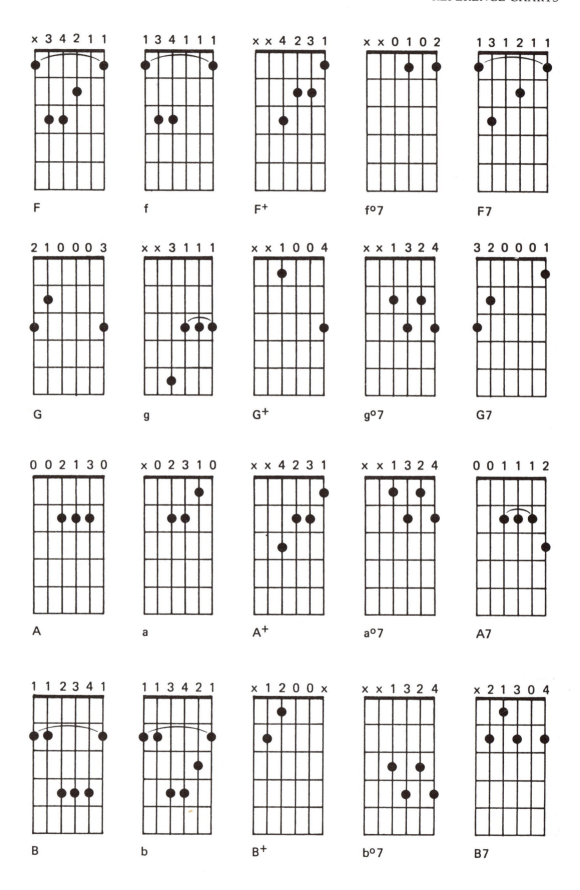

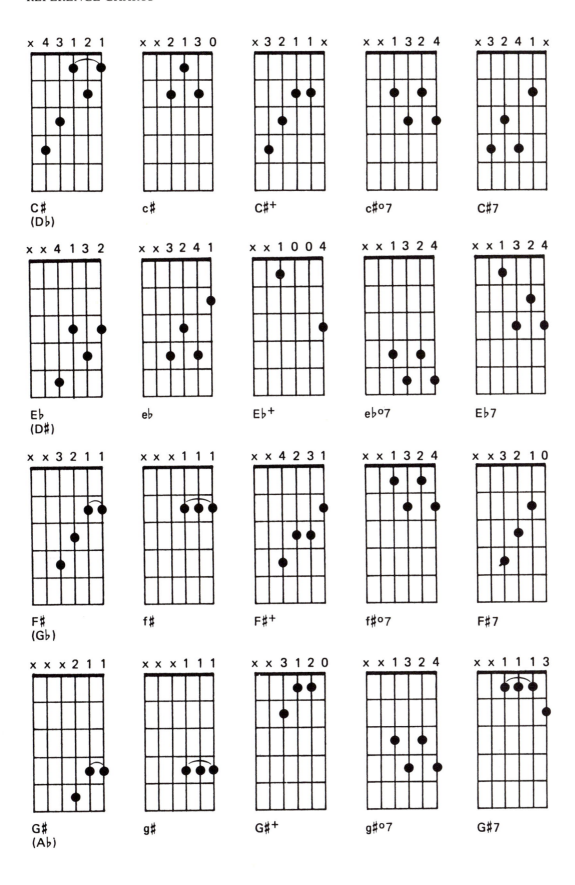

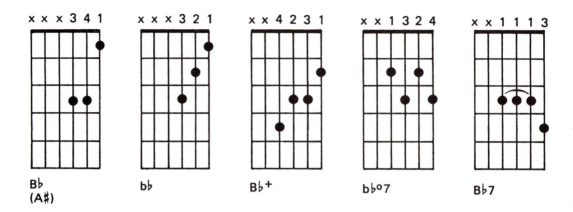

Bb
(A#)   bb   Bb+   bb°7   Bb7

Modal Scale Structures

The seven basic diatonic scales (presented in chapter 4) served as the basis for the music of the Medieval (ca. 600–1450) and Renaissance (ca. 1450–1600) periods. Tonality, as we know it today, and for all practical purposes, emerged early in the Baroque period (ca. 1600–1750) and replaced the earlier modal concepts. Each of the basic diatonic scales represents one of the modal scales. They are as follows.

1. ionian: the basic scale from *C* to *C* (half steps between 3 and 4 and between 7 and 8)
2. dorian: the basic scale from *D* to *D* (half steps between 2 and 3 and between 6 and 7)
3. phrygian: the basic scale from *E* to *E* (half steps between 1 and 2 and between 5 and 6)
4. lydian: the basic scale from *F* to *F* (half steps between 4 and 5 and between 7 and 8)
5. mixolydian: the basic scale from *G* to *G* (half steps between 3 and 4 and between 6 and 7)
6. aeolian: the basic scale from *A* to *A* (half steps between 2 and 3 and between 5 and 6)
7. locrian: the basic scale from *B* to *B* (half steps between 1 and 2 and between 4 and 5)

Note that each modal scale contains two half steps and five whole steps. Only the dorian, phrygian, lydian, and mixolydian (and their plagal forms—hypodorian, hypophrygian, etc.) were recognized modal scales of the medieval period. The plagal forms were simply a means by which the range of the scale could be shifted down a perfect fourth. The ionian (major) and aeolian (minor) modes were categorized and added during the sixteenth century. The locrian mode was merely a theoretical mode, constructed for the purpose of completing the series.

Memorization of the position of the half steps for each of the modal scales is not necessary if you can visualize their keyboard positions and then determine where the half steps occur (NOHS). If this is not possible, memorization might be necessary. The keyboard visualization skill is well worth the effort because it is a skill applicable to almost all areas covered in this text and can aid in unifying the various elements of music theory.

The following keyboard diagrams illustrate the varying positions of the half steps within the modal scales.

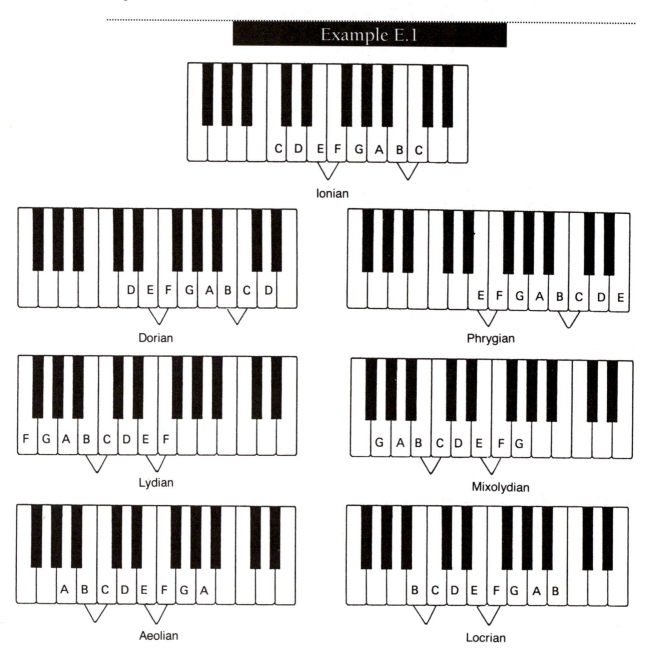

Any modal scale can be written beginning on any given pitch as long as the designated whole- and half-step configuration is maintained. This can be achieved by altering certain pitches through the use of chromatic signs. In doing this you should adhere to the following guidelines:

1. Write the basic scale beginning on a given pitch (the beginning pitch could be altered with a chromatic sign).
2. Determine the position of the half steps for the given mode.
3. Number the scale degrees.
4. Begin at the first scale degree and adjust all subsequent notes (if necessary) to conform to the whole- and half-step configuration of the scale.
5. Continue in this manner until the last note (octave repetition) is reached.

Example E.2

Procedure for Writing a Phrygian Scale Beginning on the Pitch *F*

STEP 1: WRITE BASIC SCALE

STEP 2: DETERMINE POSITION OF ½ STEPS

Phrygian = ½ – 1 – 1 – 1 – ½ – 1 – 1

STEP 3: NUMBER SCALE DEGREES

    1   2   3   4   5   6   7   8

STEPS 4 & 5: APPLY APPROPRIATE CHROMATIC SIGNS

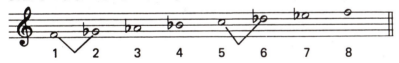

    1   2   3   4   5   6   7   8

TRANSPOSITION OF MODES

By following the steps given in Example E.2, the correct form and spelling of the scale is virtually ensured. This procedure is called transposition: the technique of rewriting or performing music beginning at a different pitch level. Therefore, any modal scale is capable of beginning on any given pitch. Throughout the transposition process, the integrity of the whole- and half-step configuration must be maintained.

MAJOR AND MINOR MODES

Modal scales may be categorized as basically major or minor by comparing their similarities with major and minor (natural form) scales. Major modes have a tonic triad that is major in quality, and minor modes have a minor tonic triad. Major and minor scales can be altered to form other modal scales. To do this requires the raising or lowering of one of the scale degrees a chromatic half step. This altered pitch represents the characteristic scale degree for the mode.

Major Modes

ionian	same as major
lydian	like major with a raised fourth scale degree
mixolydian	like major with a lowered seventh scale degree

Minor Modes

aeolian	same as minor (natural form)
dorian	like minor with a raised sixth scale degree
phrygian	like minor with a lowered second scale degree

The locrian mode may be thought of as being similar to minor with lowered second and lowered fifth scale degrees.

MODAL TETRACHORDS

Four different tetrachords are found in the seven modal scales: (1) W–W–H; (2) W–H–W; (3) H–W–W; and (4) W–W–W. The lower and upper tetrachords (first four notes and upper four notes) for each mode are:

Lower Tetrachord

W – W – H	ionian and mixolydian
W – H – W	dorian and aeolian
H – W – W	phrygian and locrian
W – W – W	lydian

Upper Tetrachord

W – W – H	ionian and lydian
W – H – W	mixolydian and dorian
H – W – W	phrygian and aeolian
W – W – W	locrian

Note that in modal scales, connection of tetrachords may be by either a whole or half step.

TRANSPOSITION OF MODES USING MAJOR KEY SIGNATURES

In addition to transposing modal scales by employing the proper whole- and half-step arrangement for each mode, you may also transpose and identify modal keys and scales by using your knowledge of (1) major key signatures; (2) the intervals that occur in major scales between the tonic and the remaining ascending scale degrees; and (3) the intervallic relationship of the tonics of the untransposed modes (basic diatonic scales) to the tonic scale degree in the C-major scale. Example E.3 shows the intervallic relationships of the untransposed modes to the tonic in the C-major scale. Note that in this example, all of the modes have the same key signature, C major (no sharps or flats).

Example E.3

Intervallic Relationship of the Basic Modes to the Tonic Scale Degree in C Major

Ionian	Dorian	Phrygian	Lydian	Mixolydian	Aeolian	Locrian
same as major	M2 above tonic	M3 above tonic	P4 above tonic	P5 above tonic	M6 above tonic	M7 above tonic

Example E.3 should help to clarify the following:

1. The transposed dorian mode will employ the key signature of the major key that is a major second below the tonic of the transposed mode. Think of a transposed dorian scale as a major scale beginning and ending on the supertonic scale degree.
2. The transposed phrygian mode will employ the key signature of the major key that is a major third below the tonic of the transposed mode. Think of the transposed phrygian scale as a major scale beginning and ending on the mediant scale degree.
3. The remaining modes may be transposed by following the same procedure while using the proper intervallic relationship: (a) lydian mode, use the major key signature that is a perfect fourth below the tonic of the transposed mode; (b) mixolydian mode, a perfect fifth below; (c) aeolian mode, a major sixth below; and (d) locrian mode, a major seventh below.

In transposing the aeolian and locrian modes, you may choose to use the inversion of the proper interval. That is, you may ascend a minor third (the inversion of a major sixth) to find the key signature for the aeolian mode, a minor second (the inversion of a major seventh) to find the key signature for the locrian mode.

To summarize: the basic dorian (*D* to *D*) scale can be thought of as a *C*-major scale beginning and ending on the second (supertonic) scale degree; phrygian (*E* to *E*) as a *C*-major scale beginning and ending on the third (mediant) scale degree, and so on. In order to facilitate this skill, relate each of the basic modal scales to a scale-degree number in *C* major:

dorian	= second scale degree in *C* major
phrygian	= third scale degree in *C* major
lydian	= fourth scale degree in *C* major
mixolydian	= fifth scale degree in *C* major
aeolian	= sixth scale degree in *C* major
locrian	= seventh scale degree in *C* major

Once this is understood, the basic analogy is as follows:

D dorian is to *C* major as *E* dorian is to *D* major.
Dorian on *D* is to *C* major (beginning and ending on the second scale degree) as the dorian on *E* is to *D* major (beginning and ending on the second scale degree), employing the two sharps (*F*♯ and *C*♯) that are needed for *D* major.

Example E.4 illustrates transposed modes that would employ the key signature of *E*♭ major.

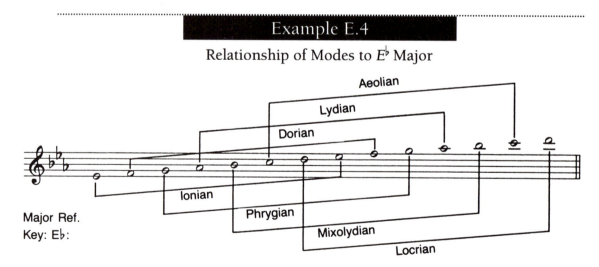

Example E.4
Relationship of Modes to *E*♭ Major

Procedures for transposing modal scales using key signatures:

- Ionian: use the same key signature as major.
- Dorian: descend a major second from the tonic of the transposed mode to find the (major) key signature.
- Phrygian: descend a major third to find the key signature.
- Lydian: descend a perfect fourth to find the key signature.
- Mixolydian: descend a perfect fifth to find the key signature.
- Aeolian: descend a major sixth (or ascend a minor third) to find the key signature.
- Locrian: descend a major seventh (or ascend a minor second) to find the key signature.

The procedure for identifying a transposed mode (when the key signature and tonic are given) is:

1. Determine the major key represented by the key signature (or examine the number of flats or sharps appearing in the music).
2. Determine the ascending interval from the tonic of the major reference key represented to the tonic of the transposed mode (the note that is given). Refer to Example E.3 for the chart of intervallic relationships.
3. Name the mode that has the determined intervallic relationship from the tonic of the major reference key to the tonic of the transposed mode.

Example E.5

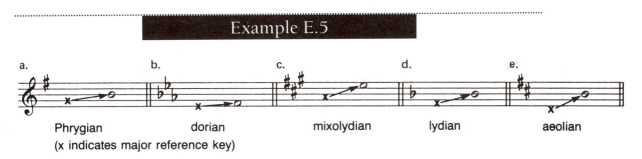

a.   b.   c.   d.   e.

Phrygian   dorian   mixolydian   lydian   aeolian

(x indicates major reference key)

In Example E.5a, the key signature would represent the key of *G* major. The interval from *G* (reference key) ascending to *B* (tonic of the transposed mode) is a major third. Therefore, the mode beginning on *B* and utilizing the key signature of one sharp would be phrygian.

In Example E.5b, the key signature would represent the key of *E♭* major. The interval from *E♭* (reference key) ascending to *F* (tonic of the transposed mode) is a major second. Therefore, the mode beginning on *F* and utilizing the key signature of three flats would be dorian.

In Example E.5c, the key signature would represent the key of *A* major. The interval from *A* (reference key) ascending to *E* (tonic of the transposed mode) is a perfect fifth. Therefore, the mode would be mixolydian.

In Example E.5d, the interval from the major reference key (*F*) to the tonic of the transposed mode (*B♭*) is a perfect fourth, which would indicate a transposed lydian mode. In Example E.5e, the interval from the major reference key (*D*) to the tonic of the transposed mode (*B*) is a major sixth, which would indicate a transposed aeolian mode.

In determining the intervallic relationship between the tonic of the major reference key and the tonic of the transposed mode, always choose the ascending interval (from the tonic of the major reference key up to the tonic of the mode given).

In many modal compositions, publishers and composers tend to use the major or minor key signature most closely associated with the tonic of the transposed mode and then systematically add the chromatic signs that are needed to create the desired mode. Because of this, you should examine the music carefully and not rely solely on the key signature and tonic to determine the mode being used. Also, keep in mind that several different modal keys could appear within the same composition.

To determine the key signature of a transposed mode when the name and tonic (keynote) of the mode are known factors, descend from the tonic of the transposed mode to the major reference key using the interval appropriate to the given mode (Ex. E.6).

Example E.6

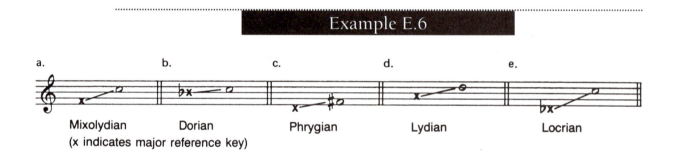

Mixolydian   Dorian   Phrygian   Lydian   Locrian
(x indicates major reference key)

The correct key signatures for Example E.6 would be: (a) one flat; (b) two flats; (c) two sharps; (d) three sharps; and (e) five flats.

To determine the tonic (keynote) of a transposed mode when the name of the mode and key signature are known factors, ascend to the tonic of the transposed mode from the tonic of the major reference key using the interval appropriate to the given mode (Ex. E.7).

Example E.7

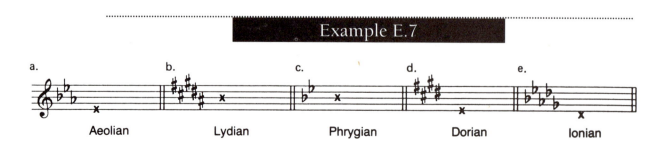

Aeolian   Lydian   Phrygian   Dorian   Ionian

The correct tonics (keynotes) for Example E.7 would be: (a) *C*; (b) *E*; (c) *D*; (d) *F*♯; and (e) *D*♭.

All modal scales contain two half steps and five whole steps. Changing the order of these intervals can greatly alter the aural effect of a melody, as illustrated in the following example. Play or sing as written, then change the mode by using the key signatures given below the example.

Example E.8

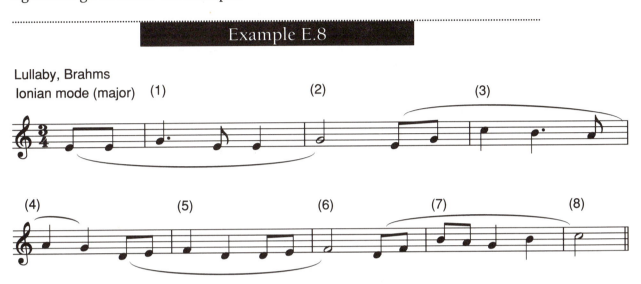

Lullaby, Brahms
Ionian mode (major)

(With apologies to Brahms)

lydian	play with a key signature of one sharp (*F*♯)
mixolydian	play with a key signature of one flat (*B*♭)
dorian	play with a key signature of two flats (*B*♭, *E*♭).
aeolian	play with a key signature of three flats (*B*♭, *E*♭, *A*♭)
phrygian	play with a key signature of four flats (*B*♭, *E*♭, *A*♭, *D*♭)
locrian	play with a key signature of five flats (*B*♭, *E*♭, *A*♭, *D*♭, *G*♭)

APPENDIX E DRILLS AND EXERCISES

1. Write the modal scales indicated on the pitches given. Insert chromatic signs to create the correct whole- and half-step sequence.

a. Dorian

b. Phrygian

c. Lydian

d. Mixolydian

e. Aeolian

f. Locrian

g. Dorian

h. Phrygian

i. Lydian

j. Mixolydian

2. Identify each modal scale given.

a. _____

b. _____

c. _____

3. Indicate the mode(s) that would have the tetrachord given as the lower or upper tetrachord.

    a. W - H - W   (ex.)   lower _Dorian_____   and   _Aeolian_____
                              upper _Mixolydian_____   and   _Dorian_____

    b. W - W - H   lower _____   and   _____
                             upper _____   and   _____

    c. W - W - W   lower _____
                             upper _____

    d. H - W - W   lower _____   and   _____
                             upper _____   and   _____

4. Determine the name of each mode. The major reference key signature and beginning pitch (tonic) of each mode are given.

        ex. _____   _____   _____   _____

        _____   _____   _____   _____

        _____   _____   _____   _____

5. Determine the key signature for each mode. The name and tonic of each mode are given.

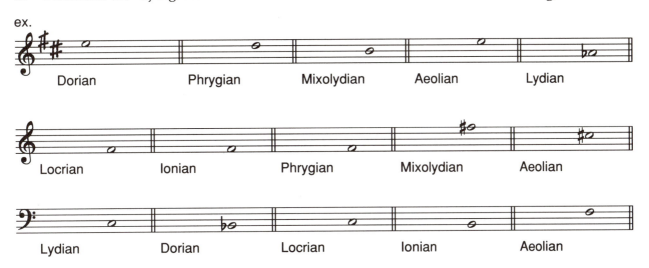

6. Determine the tonic for each mode. The major reference key signatures and modal names are given.

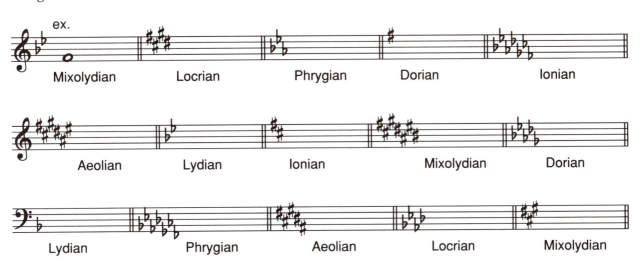

MODAL SCALES REVIEW (SELF-TEST: APPENDIX E)

1. Complete the following:
    a. Half steps in the phrygian mode are found between _____ and _____ and between _____ and _____ (scale degree numbers).
    b. Half steps in the mixolydian mode are found between _____ and _____ and between _____ and _____.

    c.   Half steps in the aeolian mode are found between _____ and _____ and between _____ and _____.

    d.   Half steps in the dorian mode are found between _____ and _____ and between _____ and _____.

    e.   Half steps in the lydian mode are found between _____ and _____ and between _____ and _____.

2.   The only two modes in which tetrachords are connected by a half step are the _____ and _____ modes.

3.   Each modal scale contains two half steps and five whole steps. True _____ False _____

4.   The major scale is the same as the _____ mode.

5.   The minor scale (natural form) is the same as the _____ mode.

6.   Given the key signature of two sharps, name the modes beginning on the tonics given.

    $F^\sharp$ _____   E _____ $C^\sharp$ _____

    A _____   G _____   B _____

7.   Complete the following:

    a.   The lydian scale beginning on A has a key signature of _____ (number) _____ (sharps or flats).

    b.   The dorian scale beginning on F has a key signature of _____ _____.

    c.   The locrian scale beginning on $G^\sharp$ has a key signature of _____ _____.

    d.   The phrygian scale beginning on D has a key signature of _____ _____.

    e.   The mixolydian scale beginning on C has a key signature of _____ _____.

    f.   The aeolian scale beginning on B has a key signature of _____ _____.

8.   As compared to major and minor (natural form) scales, complete the following:

    a.   The distinctly characteristic scale degree of the mixolydian mode is the _____ (raised or lowered) _____ (scale degree number).

    b.   The distinctly characteristic scale degree of the lydian mode is the _____ _____ scale degree.

    c.   The distinctly characteristic scale degree of the dorian mode is the _____ _____ scale degree.

    d.   The distinctly characteristic scale degree of the phrygian mode is the _____ _____ scale degree.

Melodic Literature from around the World

FOR HARMONIC, MOTIVIC, AND FORM ANALYSIS AND KEYBOARD PRACTICE

THE WATER IS WIDE   Traditional American

RED RIVER VALLEY   Cowboy

ROCK OF AGES   **Hebrew**

French

Allegretto

AMERICA, THE BEAUTIFUL

Symphony No. 40 in G minor, K. 550

Mozart

Allegro

ARIRANG

Korean

ON TOP OF OLD SMOKY

American Folk

Etude **Allegro**   Haydn

Allegretto   Dutch

Allegro   Polish

March

British

Moderato

Danish

WE GATHER TOGETHER

Traditional Dutch

Piano Sonata in D major, K. 576

Mozart

Andante

Israeli

Allegretto

British

Sonatina in G Major

Beethoven

French Suite No. 5, Gavotte   Bach

Mazurka, Op.7, No.1   Chopin

Andante and Variations, Op.46, for Two Pianos

Schumann

JOY TO THE WORLD

Traditional Carol

Andante

German

Songs Without Words, Op.53, No.2

Mendelssohn

Allegro non troppo

Tyrolese

Briskly

Allegro

Poland

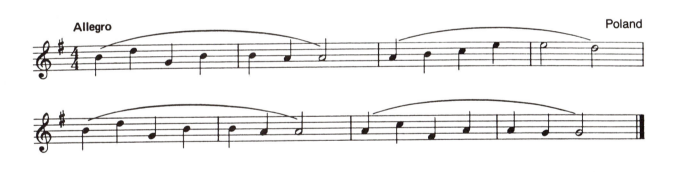

THE ASH GROVE

Welsh

Corrente, for Two Violins and Continuo

Vivaldi

LINCOLNSHIRE POACHER

English

Slowly

British

ALOHA OE

Hawaiian

BATTLE HYMN OF THE REPUBLIC

American

MAÑANA   Spanish

LA CALLE ANCHA   Puerto Rican

DUERMETE, NIÑO LINDO

Spanish

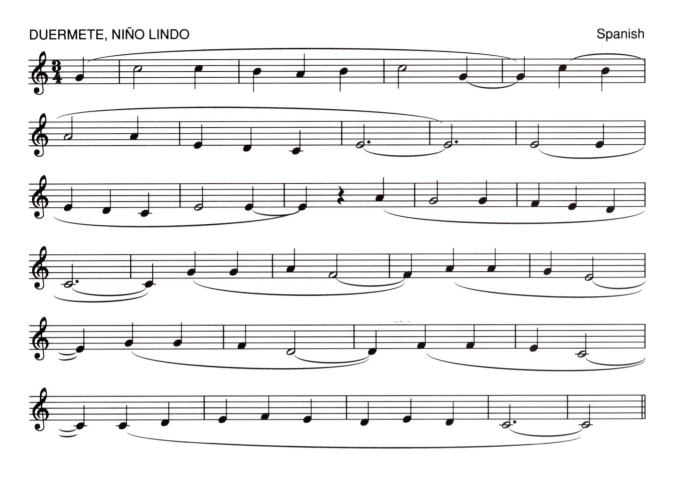

EL ZAPATERO

Spanish

MI CHACRA   Argentina

SAKURA   Japanese

FOLK SONG   Ghana

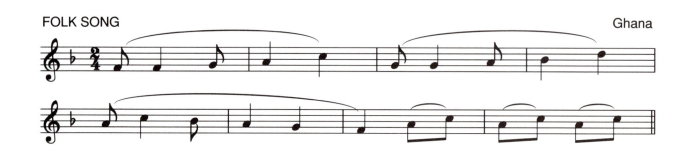

INDIAN MELODY

Navajo

FOLK SONG

Chinese

ARE YOU SLEEPING
Traditional Round

OH, HOW LOVELY IS THE EVENING
German Round

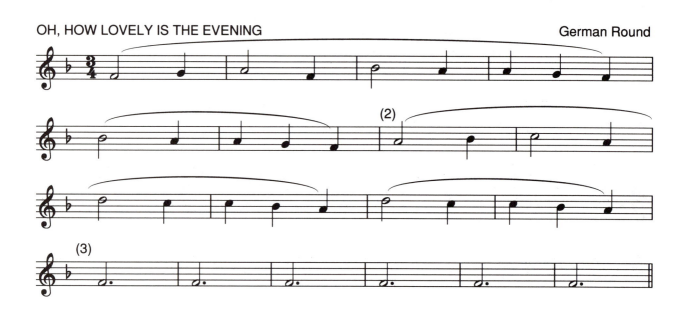

SULIRAM
Indonesian Folk Song

FOLKSONG

Vietnamese

HULA CHANT

Hawaiian

Index